ACTIVITIES HANDBOOK

FOR THE TEACHING OF PSYCHOLOGY

VOLUME 1

LUDY T. BENJAMIN, JR.
KATHLEEN D. LOWMAN

EDITORS

AMERICAN PSYCHOLOGICAL ASSOCIATION
WASHINGTON, D.C.

Library of Congress Cataloging in Publication Data

Main entry under title:
Activities handbook for the teaching of psychology.
Volume 1

  Bibliography: p.
  1. Psychology—Study and teaching. 2. Psychology—
Problems, exercises, etc. I. Benjamin, Ludy T., Jr.,
1945–   II. Lowman, Kathleen D., 1948–
BF78.A28   150'.7   81-1648
AACR2
ISBN 0-912704-34-9   (acid-free paper)

Twelfth printing January 1996

Published by the American Psychological Association, Inc.
750 First Street, NE, Washington, DC 20002
Copyright © 1981 by the American Psychological Association.

Printed in the United States of America.

CONTENTS

427923

A NOTE TO INSTRUCTORS

The idea for an *Activities Handbook for the Teaching of Psychology* originated with the Committee on Psychology in the Secondary Schools of the American Psychological Association (APA). It grew out of a need for new classroom ideas and activities perceived by teachers of psychology. Providing such classroom activities and exercises has long been a service of the Association, first emerging with the publication of a newsletter entitled *Periodically* (now, *High School Psychology Teacher*). It is this newsletter's regular and very popular column of classroom activities and demonstrations that provided the impetus and served as a model for this *Handbook*. Approximately half of the activities included here first appeared either in *Periodically* or *High School Psychology Teacher;* they have been revised and edited into a standard format for this volume. Also, many of these previously published activities have been extended to include more detail and additional ideas enhancing the scope of the activity.

This book was originally conceived as one for the high school teacher only; however, it quickly became clear that most of the activities would be equally appropriate for the college and university introductory psychology course as well because most of the activities were contributed by college and university instructors. Those activities typically represented the most effective instructional demonstrations and would work in the psychology classroom regardless of level.

In selecting new activities and in revising those published previously, we have been especially sensitive to compiling a diverse collection of activities, demonstrations, and experiments appropriate to all introductory-level psychology courses. While a few of the 88 activities in this book require specialized laboratory equipment, most are designed with no such requirement, or the activity describes

several procedures, some with apparatus and some without. In some cases equipment construction procedures are supplied where the apparatus required is uncomplicated and inexpensive.

In all instances, instructors will have to decide whether a particular activity is appropriate for their classes. The format selected for the presentation of these activities is intended to facilitate rapid decisions about their usefulness. The "Concept" section is typically a brief paragraph that describes the principle, phenomenon, or idea that is to be illustrated by the activity. The "Instructions" section offers a detailed description of the conduct of the activity, including (where necessary) information on the construction of materials such as questionnaires or apparatus, examples of stimulus materials, sample data-collection sheets, and verbatim instructions for subjects and/or students in the class.

The "Discussion" section of each activity describes the expected outcome of the exercise and often provides information explaining that outcome and other potential results. In addition, this section usually provides some sample questions and topics for class discussion following completion of the activity.

It is our intent that the information contained in each activity be sufficient for the conduct of that activity. That is, in most if not all cases, an instructor should be able to use the activity without having to go to other sources for additional material. However, some instructors may feel that some of the activities offer more information than they need, especially when the activity topic falls within their psychological specialty. Others, however, may feel they want additional material, and for these individuals relevant references are provided in each activity in the final section entitled "Suggested Background Readings."

When we designed the book, we decided

to include several appendixes which instructors should find useful. Appendix A, for example, is intended to provide a quick reminder on basic statistical methods for teachers wishing to include data collection in some activities. We recognize that many instructors will have ready access to a statistics textbook for such information. This appendix, however, is intended as a quick and easy-to-use reference. Note that while the use of statistics is specifically suggested in only a few individual exercises, many of these activities also lend themselves to simple data collection and descriptive statistical procedures. Again, the book is designed so that instructors can incorporate what best suits their classes.

Appendix B is intended to aid those teachers who wish to build simple apparatus for classroom demonstrations and experiments. A variety of equipment is represented in this annotated bibliography. Projects range from setting up an entire high school psychology laboratory to constructing slide transparencies or observation windows.

Appendix C is an annotated bibliography of additional activities and demonstrations for classroom use. These activities are categorized according to the chapters in this book.

Appendix D is a selected bibliography of ethical principles and guidelines for the teaching of psychology. Some of these guidelines are intended for secondary-school psychology teachers, while others are more appropriate for college instructors. All of the guidelines have been adopted by the American Psychological Association's governing body, the Council of Representatives, and copies of all guidelines may be obtained from the APA. Please note specific offices from which to request these guidelines.

This book is a compilation of activities from many teachers, and we are indebted to these persons for their ideas and contributions. The *Activities Handbook* would not have been possible without their efforts. The names and addresses of contributors are listed at the back of the book. In several instances we were not able to locate the authors of articles; as a result, their addresses have not been included in the list of contributors. These omissions are deeply regretted.

A statement regarding authorship is warranted here. It is the nature of teaching activities and classroom exercises that they are passed from teacher to teacher and friend to friend. In this sharing process, the source of original materials is often lost or forgotten. If the material was never printed, the creator of the activity is often never known. We have made every effort to locate the original authors and copyright owners, and we hope that appropriate credit has been cited for each activity. However, in the event that an activity has been published previously and not appropriately cited, we ask that you call this to our attention. We apologize for any oversights of this kind.

We are grateful to Betty M. Shingleton of Hollins College, who patiently tracked down and annotated many of the bibliographic entries in Appendixes B and C, and to Rosemary T. Beiermann of APA's Educational Affairs Office, who turned a scribbled sheaf of papers into typed copy.

Finally, a very special thank-you goes to Charles M. Stoup of Texas A&M University for writing Appendix A, "Basic Statistical Methods." We especially appreciate his successful efforts in providing our readers with this often needed and easy-to-follow guide to the use of statistical methods.

We, and the American Psychological Association as publisher, are pleased to provide this *Activities Handbook* as a service to teachers of the fundamentals of psychology. We hope that through the use of these activities, students of psychology will better understand the rationale for the scientific study of behavior and more fully appreciate both its immense promise and its limitations.

Ludy T. Benjamin, Jr.
Kathleen D. Lowman
Educational Affairs Office
American Psychological Association

CHAPTER I
METHODOLOGY

The activities in this chapter cover the experimental method and systematic observation as strategies in behavioral science. Nine of the 11 activities are designed for in-class use.

Two activities deal specifically with observational methods: Activity 1 focuses on the problems of interobserver agreement using a standardized experience for all observers, and Activity 2 demonstrates the accuracy of observation. Similarly, Activities 3 and 4 illustrate investigations employing the experimental method; both emphasize appropriate control procedures.

Activity 5 is designed to provide examples of sampling procedures and the nature of probability. Hypothesis formation and testing are stressed in Activities 6 and 7, which also illustrate components of the experimental method.

The final four activities in this chapter emphasize factors that can lead to erroneous conclusions in observation and experimentation. Activity 8 deals with the issues of randomization, particularly the random assignment of subjects to differing conditions. Activity 9 demonstrates the relationship of experimenter expectancy and subject performance. Activity 10 allows students to experience errors in measurement, and Activity 11 illustrates a large number of factors that, left uncontrolled, can bias experimental results.

1

OBSERVATION:
A STANDARDIZED EXPERIENCE
Nancy Felipe Russo

Concept

Observation is a primary technique of psychological investigation. Watching television is a major pastime of students. Why not put the two together as a learning experience? One caution: All students may not have access to a television.

Many kinds of behaviors can be studied through direct observation—learning activities in the classroom, student behavior in cafeterias, parent–child interaction in the home, and so forth. Observing television, however, has some special benefit. By having students observe programming for a specific time period on a designated channel, you can expose them to a standardized experience. That standardized experience can be used to demonstrate how differently students perceive the same experience and also to illustrate the difficulty and importance of developing agreed-on observational strategies.

Instructions

You could begin by asking students to observe all of the commercials on Channel X one evening between 7:00 and 7:30 p.m., having them note the product that is being advertised and the social motivation to which the advertiser is appealing. Give students some examples of types of motivation—desires for material wealth, status needs, conformity needs, attractiveness to the opposite sex—but be somewhat vague. At the next class session, have students report on their observations. List the commercials on the chalkboard; beside each one write the motivations identified by the students and the number of students who noted each motivation. Determine how much consensus there is and how much disagreement. Where there is a disagreement, ask why. It will likely be the result of your vague examples. The next step is to select and define categories of motivation.

There are a number of ways to categorize motivation. A classic one is H. A. Murray's (1938) list of 28 fundamental social motives, which can be found in many introductory texts. Give students some practice in using the coding categories by presenting some examples from magazine ads. Be sure to tell students that a commercial may appeal to more than one motivation. Then have them repeat their commercial watching (same time and channel) and compare the results with those of the previous session.

Discussion

Ask students why they classified commercials the way they did, and analyze their answers with respect to such influences as response set, selective attention to different aspects of the commercial, and student characteristics (e.g., sex and age).

Not all of the 28 motives will be appealed to in television commercials. If there is substantial agreement on the use or nonuse of certain categories, the activity can be carried further. Using a subset of the most agreed-on commercials, students can study relationships among product, intended consumer, and category of motivation. For example, do advertisers appeal to aggressiveness more in commercials on products for men than in commercials on products for women? Are certain categories of motivation consistently used with certain age groups—for example, acquisition motives with adults, affiliation motives with adolescents?

Suggested Background Readings

Bickman, L. Observational methods. In C. Selltiz, L. S. Wrightsman, & S. W. Cook, *Research methods in social relations* (3rd ed.). New York: Holt, Rinehart & Winston, 1976.

Hutt, S. J., & Hutt, C. *Direct observation & measurement of behavior.* Springfield, Ill.: Charles C Thomas, 1970.

Levin, M. *Understanding psychological research.* New York: Wiley, 1979. (chap. 11)

Murray, H. A. *Explorations in personality.* New York: Oxford University Press, 1938.

Webb, E. J., Campbell, D. T., Schwartz, R. D., & Sechrest, L. *Unobtrusive measures: Nonreactive research in the social sciences.* Chicago: Rand McNally, 1966. (chaps. 5, 6)

2

ACCURACY OF OBSERVATION
Paul J. Woods

Concept

This activity provides an intriguing introduction to discussions of the accuracy and reliability of humans as observers of behavioral events and environmental characteristics.

Materials Needed

A portable tape recorder, some imagination, and decent weather.

Instructions

Introduce the activity to the students simply by explaining that you are going to test their powers of observation—their skill as observers. Tell them that you are going to ask a colleague of yours (or a particular member of the class) to lead the class on a 15- or 20-minute journey around the school grounds. Inform the students that nothing unusual has been planned, and instruct them simply to observe the normal activities and circumstances in which they find themselves. They can be told that following the walk, you will be asking them some questions about their observations.

As your colleague or class member is leading the class on the journey around the campus, follow a short distance behind—close enough to be able to observe the class and its environment but sufficiently removed to be able to speak quietly into a portable tape recorder without being heard by the class. As the walk proceeds, record approximately 50–60 questions on the tape, spontaneously drawn from your own observations of events and objects. (You may wish to prearrange the route to be followed and walk it through once by yourself to practice the questioning routine.) Each question you record should be followed immediately by the answer. Questions should be completely factual and objectively confirmable. Following are some examples:

"How many planes flew overhead as we reached the playing field?"

"In what activity was the first group of students encountered by the class engaged?"

"Where was the class when the nearby truck backfired?"

"What color was the car that passed the class at the entrance to the parking lot?"

Avoid questions with answers that are a matter of opinion ("Was it a nice day?" "Did it seem warm?").

Upon returning to the classroom, play each recorded question in turn and stop the recorder before the correct answer is played. Have students write their answers down on paper, and then play back the correct answer. On the chalkboard, keep a record of the number of right and wrong answers to each question.

Discussion

The broad variation in student responses should provide gist for a discussion of (a) the reliability of human observations, (b) the "truth" of courtroom testimony, (c) the benefits of structuring the collection of observations (perhaps by specifying beforehand what information is to be sought), and (d) the value and necessity of independent replication and confirmation of answers. Comparing the accuracy of the teacher's answers with that of the students' answers should provide compelling demonstration of the value of specifying the information to be sought before it is collected.

Suggested Background Readings

Bickman, L. Observational methods. In C. Selltiz, L. S. Wrightsman, & S. W. Cook, *Research methods in social relations* (3rd ed.). New York: Holt, Rinehart & Winston, 1976.

Hutt, S. J. & Hutt, C. *Direct observation and measurement of behavior.* Springfield, Ill.: Charles C Thomas, 1970.

Levin, M. *Understanding psychological research.* New York: Wiley, 1979. (chap. 11)

Webb, E. J., Campbell, D. T., Schwartz, R. D., & Sechrest, L. *Unobtrusive measures: Nonreactive research in the social sciences.* Chicago: Rand McNally, 1966. (chaps. 5, 6)

ACTIVITY
3

DEMONSTRATING EXPERIMENTAL DESIGN LOGIC

Concept

As part of the scientific enterprise, psychologists seek the answers to empirical questions about behavior. The strategy of investigation they use is, of course, the experimental method—a technique in which they manipulate certain variables to discover what effect that manipulation has (if any) on other variables. The experimental method is a relatively simple and straightforward design that dictates the conditions necessary to demonstrate cause-and-effect relationships. However, when applied to behavioral questions, the design usually becomes amazingly complex, owing to the sheer complexity of behavior. This exercise is intended to stimulate thinking about the number and nature of variables that must be considered in doing behavioral research. It also focuses on the control of relevant variables as a necessary condition for interpreting such research.

Materials Needed

A printed list of 15 unrelated, single-syllable nouns and a clock or watch.

Instructions

Propose a behavioral hypothesis (or have the class do so) and ask the class to help design an experiment to test the hypothesis. An example is, "Chocolate-covered peanuts enhance memory." This exercise will lead to the necessity for operational definitions, control procedures, and inferential statistics.

1. Construct a formal hypothesis using operational definitions. Concepts such as learning, memory, emotions, motives, thinking, perception, etc., are all unobservable. We cannot see memory directly but must assess it indirectly in order to measure it. In the example, "Chocolate-covered peanuts enhance memory" can be formalized by writing it as "Chocolate-covered peanuts improve recall scores from a list of unrelated nouns." Recall scores *are* observable and measureable.

2. Manipulate the independent variable—in this case, the presence or absence of chocolate-covered peanuts, or the number of chocolate-covered peanuts—while controlling all other relevant variables. A control group (or groups) is usually used for this purpose. The categories of relevant variables are as follows:

(a) *Subject-relevant variables* are usually the product of long-term history, maturation, or genetic inheritance (e.g., age, educational level, IQ, sex, number of siblings, aptitudes, parents' income). These variables cannot be *directly* manipulated but are indirectly varied through selection and group assignment. *Matching* and *randomizing* are the usual controls for subjects' assignment to groups so that no group is "loaded"

Adapted from *Psychology and Life,* 8th Edition by Floyd L. Ruch and Philip G. Zimbardo. Copyright © 1971, 1967 by Scott, Foresman and Company. Reprinted by permission.

with more of a particular variable than other groups. For the present example, you might have two groups, one that eats chocolate-covered peanuts and another that doesn't. The groups can be matched for sex (so that they each have equal numbers of males and females), and the other variables can be controlled through randomization of assignment.

(b) *Situation-relevant variables* (test conditions, experimenter behavior, timing, etc.) are usually controlled by *matching conditions* for the groups so that everything, with the exception of the independent variable, is identical for the two groups. In this example, the list of nouns, the amount of time given to study them (1 minute), the amount of time for free-recall (1 minute), and the instructions should be identical for both groups. The only difference should be the chocolate-covered peanuts.

3. Observe the outcome, that is, measure the dependent variable. In this case, compute the mean number of words correctly recalled by each group.

4. Decide how much confidence you can place in the findings—that is, what inferences you can make about the rest of the population. In this case, employ a statistical test (Student's *t* test) comparing the mean number of correctly recalled words for both groups.

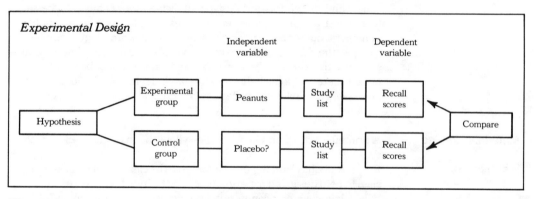

Experimental Design

Discussion

The major emphasis of the discussion should be on the *logical* role of the two groups in reaching a decision regarding the hypothesis. Explain that the experimental and control groups were both selected from the same population and then randomly assigned to the two conditions. Even if subjects were matched on a relevant variable (i.e., pairs of subjects with the same sex or educational level are matched), assignment to conditions is random. There should be no systematic differences between the groups. The control group represents the population as it now exists (and so must be selected to be representative). The experimental group represents the population *as it would be* if subjected to the independent variable (so it must also be representative). The elements of the experimental design are primarily used to assure that everything about the two groups, including selection and testing procedures, is as identical as possible, with the *sole exception of the independent variable*. Then, if the dependent variable shows differences, they must be attributed to the independent variable and not to some other difference between the groups.

A discussion of inferential statistical reasoning is also useful at this time, since the comparisons being made are fairly clear and the need for generalization is obvious. Basically, even if the peanuts had *no* effect on the recall scores, the final scores would be expected to differ somewhat from the control-group scores. The question is, how different must the two groups' scores be before that difference can be attributed to the independent variable and not to "chance" factors. Inferential statistics specifies the amount of difference between the groups necessary to be confident (with a known margin of error) that the difference is due to the independent variable.

You might also point out the need for a "placebo" control—that is, to have the control group ingest something that looks, tastes, and smells like chocolate-covered peanuts but is not. Good luck in finding a suitable placebo!

Suggested Background Readings

Kasschau, R. A. *Psychology: Exploring behavior*. Englewood Cliffs, N.J.: Prentice-Hall, 1980. (chap. 17)

Martin, D. W. *Doing psychology experiments*. Monterey, Calif.: Brooks/Cole, 1977.

Mostellar, F., Kruskal, W. H., Link, R. F., Peters, R. S., & Rising, G. R. *Statistics by example*. Reading, Mass.: Addison-Wesley, 1973.

Wood, G. *Fundamentals of psychological research* (2nd ed.). Boston, Mass.: Little, Brown, 1977.

ACTIVITY
4

EXPERIMENTAL DESIGN: VARYING HEART RATE
Samuel Cameron, Jack Christiano, and Bernard Mausner

Concept

This activity illustrates the experimental method, the difference between an independent and a dependent variable, and the concept of control in experimentation. It also demonstrates that a measure of physiological arousal—pulse rate—can be affected by both thought processes and physical activity.

Materials Needed

You will need a handout, one per experimenter, that contains a short news story describing an act of violence—for example, a shooting. Select the story from an old or out-of-town paper so that the story will be novel and the persons involved will have no connection with the families or friends of your students. Each experimenter will also need a watch with a sweep second hand.

Instructions

Describe the following experiment to students and explain its purpose. Randomly designate students as experimenters or subjects. Teach the experimenters the correct method of taking a pulse. (If you do not know the correct method, ask school health personnel.) To save time, have the experimenters count pulse beats over a 15-second interval and multiply that rate by four. Then equip each experimenter with a watch and a handout, and randomly pair him or her with a subject.

The experimenter's first task is to take the subject's pulse while the subject is at rest and comfortably seated. The pulse should be taken twice, with about 1 minute intervening between readings, and the rates should be recorded. Then the subject should read the handout aloud. Immediately after the reading, the experimenter should again take the subject's pulse and record the rate. The subject should then rest comfortably for 3 minutes, after which the experimenter should take the pulse twice again, with 1 minute intervening between readings. These rates should also be recorded. Finally, the experimenter should have the subject run in place for 30 seconds and should then take the subject's pulse and record the rate one last time.

On the chalkboard, collect the data for each subject under each condition: at rest #1, at rest #2, immediately after reading, 3 minutes after reading, 4 minutes after reading, and immediately after running. Total the rates under each condition and calculate the means.

Discussion

Focus on the following questions: What was the dependent variable? What were the independent variables? What other variables might have influenced the dependent variable? What was the purpose of the method of selecting experimenters and subjects? Are there any improvements that could be made in this method?

Students may point out that many other variables—psychological, physiological, and social—could have affected the dependent variable.

Since the experiment was designed with that possibility in mind, students should be encouraged to pursue this line of reasoning.

Suggested Background Readings

Kasschau, R. A. *Psychology: Exploring behavior.* Englewood Cliffs, N.J.: Prentice-Hall, 1980. (chap. 17)

Martin, D. W. *Doing psychology experiments.* Monterey, Calif.: Brooks/Cole, 1977.

Mostellar, F., Kruskal, W. H., Link, R. F., Peters, R. S., & Rising, G. R. *Statistics by example.* Reading, Mass.: Addison-Wesley, 1973.

Wood, G. *Fundamentals of psychological research* (2nd ed.). Boston, Mass.: Little, Brown, 1977.

ACTIVITY
5

SAMPLING AND PROBABILITY
Louis Snellgrove

Concept

An understanding of sampling issues and the nature of probability is critical to an understanding of research, whether one uses the experimental method, survey techniques and opinion polling, or naturalistic observation. The exercises described in this activity illustrate sampling procedures and the relation of sample characteristics to population characteristics, as well as some elementary facts about probability.

Materials Needed

Painted BBs (500 of them)—or one can substitute other small objects marketed in different colors, such as sequins, buttons, or beads.

Instructions

Place 500 BBs—100 each of red, blue, green, yellow, and natural—in a container that will comfortably accommodate them, and shake it vigorously.

To demonstrate sampling, first ask a blindfolded student to draw, one by one, a one-fifth sample of the total; record the percentages by color on the chalkboard. Have the same student repeat the procedure four more times, returning the BBs to the container after each one-fifth sampling is completed. Then ask three other students, in succession, to draw one-fourth, one-third, and one-half samples, respectively, five times each. Again record percentages by color.

To demonstrate probability, place varied numbers of differently colored BBs in the container. Record on the chalkboard the probabilities of drawing each color on the first trial, as a function of frequency over population. An example follows:

Frequency	Probability of drawing on first trial
10 red	20% (10/50)
5 yellow	10% (5/50)
15 green	30% (15/50)
10 blue	20% (10/50)
10 natural	20% (10/50)
$N = 50$	

Next have a blindfolded student draw 10 BBs at random, returning the drawn BB to the container each time. Record each selection and check it against the probabilities noted above. Repeat the procedure with different total populations and different percentages of colors.

Discussion

Focus on the following questions: Under which conditions did the sample come closest to the value of the population? Why do we sample a population rather than poll it in its entirety?

How is sampling similar to a teacher preparing a test?

If you survey TV audiences by telephone during the day, what biases are you introducing? What is bias in a sample?

What would happen to the probabilities of drawing particular colors if the BB were not returned to the container after each drawing?

What is the probability of drawing the four of hearts from a deck of cards? Of drawing a four? Of drawing a heart? Of drawing the four of hearts on three consecutive tries without returning the drawn card to the deck?

Suggested Background Readings

Borkowski, J. G., & Anderson, D. C. *Experimental psychology: Tactics of behavioral research.* Glenview, Ill.: Scott, Foresman, 1977. (chap. 3)

Chein, I. An introduction to sampling. In C. Selltiz, L. S. Wrightsman, & S. W. Cook, *Research methods in social relations* (3rd ed.). New York: Holt, Rinehart & Winston, 1976.

Lewin, M. *Understanding psychological research.* New York: Wiley, 1979. (chap. 7)

Wood, G. *Fundamentals of psychological research* (2nd ed.). Boston: Little, Brown, 1977. (chap. 3)

ACTIVITY

6

HYPOTHESIS TESTING

Concept

This exercise illustrates some of the procedures of the experimental method. The development of a hypothesis, the design of an experiment to test it, and the creation of new hypotheses are all part of this learning experience. The exercise requires at least two persons, an experimenter and a subject.

Instructions

The first step is to develop the hypothesis. Use this one as an example: "If the loudness of an auditory stimulus increases, the reaction time to that stimulus decreases." The independent variable is level of loudness of the auditory stimulus. The dependent variable is reaction time. The second step is to devise a means to manipulate and measure the variables. In this case, manipulating the independent variable is simple: The experimenter can whisper, speak normally, or shout "now." If you have a yardstick and a doorjamb or a pillar, the dependent variable, reaction time, can be readily measured. Have the subject stand in a doorway with the palm of his or her hand on the doorjamb, fingers curved around the doorjamb's side, but not touching the doorjamb. Have the experimenter hold the yardstick flat against the doorjamb, perpendicular to the subject's fingers and positioned so that the beginning edge is under the subject's middle finger. At random intervals have the experimenter whisper, speak normally, or shout "now," simultaneously releasing the yardstick so it slides down the doorjamb. The subject's task is to stop the yardstick as it falls, without moving the palm of his or her hand from the doorjamb. Because the yardstick slides at the rate of approximately 32.2 feet/second (or g), the distance that it falls can be translated into reaction time by using the table below.

Table for Translating Distance Into Reaction Time

Inches	Seconds	Inches	Seconds
1	.072	10	.227
2	.102	11	.238
3	.125	12	.250
4	.144	16	.288
5	.161	18	.305
6	.176	20	.322
7	.190	24	.352
8	.203	30	.394
9	.216	36	.432

Formula:
$$d = \frac{1}{2} g t^2$$
$$t \text{ (in secs)} = \sqrt{d} \text{ (in inches)} \div 13.9$$

Discussion

Ask the class to develop other hypotheses about what affects reaction time. Combinations of variables can be looked at to assess the effects of the signal's complexity and/or meaning on reaction time. For example, suppose the subject is supposed to react if the word "now" is used but not if the word "go" is used. Will it make a difference if the subject must process the meaning of the stimulus word? Suppose that three words—"now," "go," and "begin"—are used. Will reaction time be even longer? Suppose that instead of the word "go," the word "stop" is used. Does that make a difference? If the subject has to tell the difference between "go" and "snow," will that affect reaction time? Besides illustrating experimental design, this exercise can be used for discussing information processing in the brain and the interaction between sensory, cognitive, and motor activities. These are but a few suggestions. As you can see, after beginning to look at what affects a dependent variable, alternative hypotheses are easy to develop.

The next step is to ask the class if their hypotheses are related. Then talk about the importance of theory building. You can ask what the difference is between saying "Let's see what effect this will have" and "Let's see how we can build a theory that will help us predict what effect to expect from a particular manipulation." Then you can talk about the difference between making predictions based on theoretical models and just thinking up possible influences with no basis other than "intuition."

Suggested Background Readings

Arnoult, M. D. *Fundamentals of scientific method in psychology* (2nd ed.). Dubuque, Iowa: William C. Brown, 1976.

Borkowski, J. G., & Anderson, D. C. *Experimental psychology: Tactics of behavioral research.* Glenview, Ill.: Scott, Foresman, 1977.

Sheridan, C. L. *Fundamentals of experimental psychology.* New York: Holt, Rinehart & Winston, 1971.

7

HYPOTHESIS TESTING— TO "COIN" A TERM
William J. Hunter

Concept

The scientific method involves the logical deduction of hypotheses that are then tested by systematic observation.

Instructions

Encourage students to speculate about the number of pennies (or nickels) minted each year. Ask whether the number minted is the same every year. Have students discuss briefly how they might find out if the same number of pennies was minted in any given four-year span (choose four recent years as an example). Solutions generally involve (a) contacting a local coin dealer or (b) checking records (in a library, perhaps). Claim that you have a "theory" that different numbers of pennies were minted in the years you gave as examples. State that you have tried to find out if this is true but that you have been told this information is "classified" so you want to conduct an experiment to find out if you are right.

Ask students to take out all of the pennies in their pockets or purses and place them on their desks. Have them count and report the number of pennies they have. Write the total on the board and say, "Okay, if I'm wrong and the government really *did* mint the same number of pennies in 19___, how many pennies out of this total *should be* 19___ pennies?"

Continue until the class has estimated that 25% of the total should be the answer for any given year. Get a student to explain why this *ought* to be the case. Encourage any student who can see that it would be foolish to expect an *exact* 25% in each of the four study years. If no student makes this argument, introduce it and try to have students justify it.

When this reasoning seems clear to the class, ask them to count the number of pennies they have in each of the four years under study. Record the totals for each year on the board. Ask whether this is "approximately a 25% distribution for each year." Depending on the class and your exact purpose, you may wish to go on and identify 25% of the total number of coins as "the frequency we expected to find (f_e)" and the actual numbers reported for each year as "the frequencies we have observed (f_o)". You may then want to demonstrate chi-square as

$$\chi^2 = \sum \frac{(f_o - f_e)^2}{f_e}.$$

Again, depending on your purpose (for example, if you were introducing the concept of significance testing), you might want to show that this value was (or was not) too large to be a coincidence (exceeds a tabled "standard") and therefore disproves (or fails to disprove) the belief or guess that equal numbers were minted. (See Appendix A for chi-square computation.)

Discussion

Whether or not you pursue the statistical ending to this demonstration, you should help the students achieve closure by going back over the whole process and identifying the components of scientific investigation. For example, you might point out the following:

the population	all pennies minted in the year under study
the sample	pennies in this classroom
the method of sampling	convenience
the theory	unequal annual minting
the hypothesis	"different numbers of coins will be present in the sample for the years specified"
the null hypothesis	25% in each year

Of course, much more can be learned from this experience, but you must decide which points to emphasize. I have found this little study to be useful in many ways, so I try to introduce it early and then refer back to it occasionally. I believe there are advantages in the fact that the demonstration does not use psychological content. For one, it should help to show that the scientific method is a general approach to problem solving. It should also help students to see the role of science in psychology. Most important, it keeps students focused on the *method*, rather than on the research question or content.

Suggested Background Readings

Emerson, J. D. Introductory statistics: A contemporary approach. *Mathematics Teacher*, 1977, *70*, 258–261.

Noether, G. E. The nonparametric approach in elementary statistics. *Mathematics Teacher*, 1974, *67*, 123–126.

Selltiz, C., Wrightsman, L. S., & Cook, S. W. *Research methods in social relations* (3rd ed.). New York: Holt, Rinehart & Winston, 1976. (pp 15–48)

Wood, G. *Fundamentals of psychological research* (2nd ed.). Boston: Little, Brown, 1977. (chap. 3)

8

RANDOMIZATION
David J. Stang

Concept

The word *random* and its variations occur frequently in psychological literature and discourse because of the importance of randomization in scientific research design. This exercise illustrates the purpose of one aspect of randomization in experimentation—random assignment of subjects to conditions.

In a simple experiment, a researcher wants to study the effects of one variable at a time and doesn't want the effects of that variable to be confused with the effects of another variable. Such confusion—or "confounding"—makes interpretation of results difficult or impossible. One way to avoid confounding is random assignment, a procedure by which subjects are placed into conditions on the basis of chance, each subject having an equal chance of being in any condition. Random assignment assures that on the average, the people in one condition will be very similar to the people in another condition. There are many ways that random assignment can take place: Numbers can be drawn from a hat or taken from a table of random numbers, or a coin can be tossed. Whatever method is used, there must be no systematic basis for putting a person into one condition over another. The following activity demonstrates the purpose of randomization. It uses a "one-potato-two-potato" technique of haphazard assignment.

Instructions

Begin at the front of the room in one corner and, going across the rows, have students count off in sixes (or higher—as high as the number of conditions you want). Write the numbers 1–6 on the chalkboard horizontally, and under each number write the exact height in inches of all of the students with that number. Then find the mean height of the students in each condition. Now combine students with Numbers 1, 3, or 5 into one group and calculate a mean height for it. Do likewise for students with Numbers 2, 4, and 6. You should discover that the means from the two large conditions—(1+3+5) and (2+4+6)—are very close and that the means from the six small conditions are farther apart. Two conclusions may be drawn: Random assignment creates very similar groups; and the more people assigned to a condition, the more similar the conditions.

If time allows, examine the six small conditions and the two large conditions for the prevalence of some other variable—for instance, the number of males and females in each group. You should reach the same conclusions you reached in looking at mean heights.

Next illustrate what can happen without random assignment. Assign males to one condition and females to another, and calculate mean heights for each group. The difference between conditions should be larger than those calculated from randomly created conditions.

Discussion

Discuss with the class how such confounding of sex with condition would make it difficult to interpret a study such as the following: You hypothesized that Sure-Grow Sugar Cookies would make people grow taller. You put 20 seventh-grade boys, each 5 feet tall, in one condition, and 20 seventh-grade girls, each 5 feet tall, in another condition. You fed the sugar cookies to the boys every afternoon for 3 years; the girls got ordinary ginger cookies. After 3 years, you measured the heights of all subjects and found that the subjects who were fed the Sure-Grow Sugar Cookies were considerably taller.

Are there times when an experimenter would not want to randomly assign subjects? What other roles should randomization play in experimentation?

Suggested Background Readings

Borkowski, J. G., & Anderson, D. C. *Experimental psychology: Tactics of behavioral research.* Glenview, Ill.: Scott, Foresman, 1977. (chap. 3)

Wood, G. *Fundamentals of psychological research* (2nd ed.). Boston: Little, Brown, 1977. (chap. 3)

9

EXPERIMENTER EXPECTANCY
Carolyn Stierhem

Concept

One source of bias in experimentation concerns the expectations of the experimenter about subject performance. Sound research is designed to minimize (or, if possible, to eliminate) this kind of bias, typically through the use of "blind" or "double blind" procedures. This exercise is designed to illustrate how experimenter expectations can influence performance outcome.

Instructions

Select three students to function as experimenters. Divide the rest of the class into three groups of subjects, with at least 10 subjects per group.

Brief each experimenter individually. Tell all three that the task will be for each of their 10 subjects to guess, on each of 10 trials, which of two numbers—0 or 1—the experimenter is thinking of. Give each experimenter a random sequence of 0s and 1s. (Sequences may be taken from a table of random numbers by substituting 0 for even numbers and 1 for odd numbers.) Ask each experimenter to keep a record for each subject, noting whether the 10 successive guesses are correct or not. Caution each experimenter not to discuss his or her instructions with anyone else. In addition, tell

○ Experimenter A to concentrate hard on the number at hand and to expect a high degree of accuracy from the subjects because some people have the uncanny ability to perform well at this kind of task;

○ Experimenter B not to expect a high degree of accuracy because subjects' guessing of the right number is purely a matter of chance;

○ Experimenter C nothing more. This experimenter and group will be your controls.

When you have finished with the instructions, give each experimenter a separate quiet area where he or she can conduct the experiment. Have subjects go one at a time to their respective experimenters until all have had 10 trials each. Then have experimenters calculate the percentage of accurate guesses made by each subject and an average percentage for the group. Compare the average performances across groups. The control group's performance should yield a normal distribution, Experimenter B's group should yield a negatively skewed distribution, and Experimenter A's group should yield a positively skewed distribution.

The number of trials per subject and the number of subjects under each experimental condition should be at least 10 to get a normal distribution in the control group's performance. The probability of a normal distribution in the control group can be increased by increasing the number of trials per subject and/or the number of subjects, provided that the numbers are kept constant across groups. If there are fewer than 33 students in your class, use only two experimenters and two groups of

10 subjects each, eliminating the experimenter who is instructed not to expect a high degree of accurate guesses.

Discussion

If there were differences between groups, what factors might have caused them? What cues might have been present? If there were no differences, how do you account for the similarities? What procedures can be used to control for this kind of experimental bias? How might expectancy affect an instructor's evaluation of student performance?

Suggested Background Readings

Rosenthal, R. On the social psychology of the psychological experiment: The experimenter's hypothesis as unintended determinant of experimental results. *American Scientist,* 1963, *51,* 268–283.

Rosenthal, R. Covert communication in the psychological experiment. *Psychological Bulletin,* 1967, *67,* 356–367.

Rosenthal, R. Teacher expectation and pupil learning. In N. V. Overly (Ed.), *The unstudied curriculum: Its impact on children.* Washington, D.C.: Association for Supervision and Curriculum Development, 1970.

Sheridan, C. L. *Fundamentals of experimental psychology.* New York: Holt, Rinehart & Winston, 1971. (chap. 1)

10

TO ERR IS HUMAN, ESPECIALLY IN MEASUREMENT
William J. Hunter

Concept

The basis of traditional measurement theory and of both theoretical and operational definitions of reliability is the assumption that any observation (0) consists of two components, true or accurate measurement (T) and error (E). The formula $0 = T + E$ symbolically represents this assumption. Students, whose experience with measurement has often been limited to physical measurements, sometimes have difficulty understanding what measurement error is. This demonstration should not only reveal what error is but also illustrate how error operates.

Materials Needed

True–false answer sheets (10 items) in a quantity sufficient for size of class, but not fewer than 20; transparencies (to be described); and an overhead projector.

Instructions

Distribute answer sheets to the class and explain that they are about to take the *Extra-Sensory Aptitude Test* (ESAT). Explain briefly that it is a test of extrasensory perception: "You will have to give answers, true or false, to each of the 10 questions I will think of. Ready? OK. Number 1 (pause), is that true or false? Number 2 (pause), etc." During each pause, the instructor should strain to concentrate on the "question" he or she is trying to communicate. Offering to repeat a question or claiming, "I'm sorry, *that's* Question 6, this is Question 5," will help to break the monotony. One can also claim to do Questions 7–10 in rapid succession using "speedthink" in order to save time. (For small classes, $N < 20$, have each student complete two "independent" tests, one taken left-handed and one right-handed.)

When everyone is finished, ask them to mark their own papers following the scoring key provided on the overhead (a random assortment of 10 true/false responses). The "score" should be the number correct minus the number wrong. Ask the class to predict what the class average will be and to explain their predictions; then summarize the class results in a frequency chart on the overhead projector and compute the class mean. It should be very close to zero.

Discussion

At this point, you may end the lesson with a discussion of measurement error (or a lecture), using this test as an example of a test that is "pure error." Ask students to identify sources of error in classroom tests and standardized tests. Identify sources of error in individualized psychological tests. It is advisable to extend the discussion/lecture to include errors in physical measurement as well, so that students do not conclude that this is a "problem" for psychology alone.

For a good class (or if you are daring), however, you may want to carry the demonstration a little further. Select those students who "have poor ESP skills"—for example, those with scores of −4 or less. Compute the average for this group and put it on the board. Now give them "treatment" designed to improve their performance. A good treatment is to have them cover the eye that is opposite their handedness "in order to eliminate distractions to the right hemisphere which we know to be the seat of ESP functioning." Give the remedial group a posttest and compute the average—it should be near zero, showing substantial improvement over the pretest average for this group. The treatment will seem to have been very effective, but what will in fact have been demonstrated is regression toward the mean. Few classes are likely to benefit from an explanation of this statistical artifact as a threat to the internal validity of a research design, but all could benefit from this exercise as a demonstration of the deceptive (even self-deceptive) use of research and statistics.

If the demonstration is extended like this, it is still appropriate to end with a discussion or lecture, adding the above points to the content. Be sure, too, that students are properly debriefed about ESP (some may find this a very convincing demonstration unless specifically told that it is a trick or hoax) and correct any allusions to knowledge of ESP as a right-hemisphere function.

Suggested Background Readings

Hunter, W. J., & Howitz, S. Regression? That's mean! *CEDR Quarterly,* 1977, *10,* 18–19.

Hunter, W. J. Where do errors regress to? *CEDR Quarterly,* 1979, *12,* 20–21.

Nunnally, J. C. *Psychometric theory* (2nd ed.). New York: McGraw-Hill, 1978.

ACTIVITY
II

FINDING MEANING IN THE METHOD
Philip G. Zimbardo

Concept

The "experiment" is the most powerful analytical tool used in science. Cause–effect relationships can be established only through the use of well-controlled experiments. Psychologists employ this tool in the investigation of virtually all aspects of behavior, including perception, learning, memory, cognition, motivation, physiological processes, sensory processes, social behavior, development, and therapeutic procedures. While the specific details of the methodology vary within each of these areas of investigation, the *logic* of experimentation is essentially the same.

The following classroom demonstration and discussion should help to elucidate the need for, and logic of, experimental methods in the study of behavior.

Materials Needed

Reaction-time device constructed from light cardboard (see template on next page).

Instructions

1. Propose a hypothesis: "Males react faster than females" (if you are male), or "females react faster than males" (if you are female). This will usually elicit protests from the hypothesized "slower" sex.

2. Define reaction time—the time interval between stimulus presentation and a subject's reaction.

3. *Select* a student of the sex hypothesized as *slower.* Ask the student to come to the front of the room and *stand* with his or her hand about *even with* the tip of the meter, with the thumb and forefinger about two inches apart. Then, *without explanation or warning,* drop the meter between the subject's fingers. The subject will probably catch it. Record the reading, measuring from the top of the thumb. Reaction time is measured in centimeters here rather than seconds. Give only the one trial.

4. Then ask for a *volunteer* of the opposite sex. Have this student come to the front of the room, *sit down, relax,* and tell you his or her *preferred* hand. Then *define the task*—to stop the meter as soon as possible when it is dropped. Hold the meter so that the point is *two inches above* the student's fingers (instead of even with them). Give the subject *two practice trials* and a verbal *warning signal* of "ready." Then

From *Instructor's Resource Book* to accompany *Psychology and Life,* Tenth Edition by Philip G. Zimbardo. Copyright © by Philip G. Zimbardo. Reprinted by permission of Scott, Foresman and Company.

The reaction time meter is from *Working with Psychology,* A Student's Resource Book to accompany *Psychology and Life,* 8th Edition by Philip G. Zimbardo and Ronald Ray Schmeck. Copyright © 1971, 1967 by Scott, Foresman and Company. Reprinted by permission of Scott, Foresman and Company.

give *two* test trials and record only the *fastest* one. Then announce the "obvious conclusion" that the hypothesis has been confirmed.

5. At this point the losing sex will protest, pointing out some of the biases you introduced. List them: (a) the first student was selected, the other volunteered; (b) the first student had to use cognitive processes (since the task wasn't explained before the trial), the second student used simple reaction time; (c) the first student started with the point at fingertip level, the second started with it two inches above the fingertips (leads to a discussion of the accuracy of measurement); (d) the first student had no "ready" signal, the second did; (e) the first student was standing, the second was sitting; (f) the first student had no practice, the second had practice trials.

6. Now pretend to run an unbiased test following the class suggestions. Eliminating all of the previous biases (by essentially following the procedure for the second subject), you can still easily bias the results: (a) by having a fixed foreperiod *(warning-signal-to-stimulus-onset)* for one subject versus a widely variable one for the other; (b) by using different motivating instructions or feedback ("That wasn't very good now, was it?"); (c) by giving one a motor set (to respond—"get ready to grab it"), which is faster than a sensory set (to observe—"watch for it to drop"); (d) by letting one subject but not the other see you "prepare" to release the stimulus.

7. Using any of the above (or in combination), your hypothesis will again be "proven." Again, have the students list the biases in this test. This may be repeated, using more subtle differences each time.

Discussion

The discussion should lead to the notion of relevant-vs-irrelevant variables in an experimental situation. Relevant variables are those likely to affect the dependent measure (reaction time), such as those used to bias this experiment. Irrelevant variables are those unlikely to affect the results, such as, in this case, barometric pressure, hair color, socioeconomic level, etc. This should lead to a discussion of the need for experimental control procedures in order to

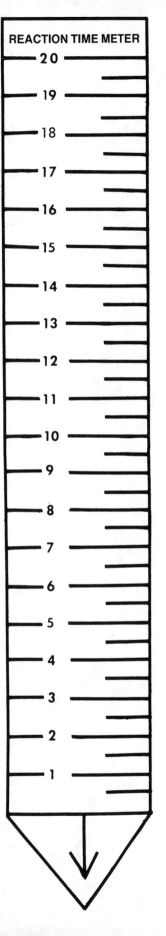

REACTION TIME METER

20
19
18
17
16
15
14
13
12
11
10
9
8
7
6
5
4
3
2
1

identify and control relevant variables so that both experimental conditions are the same in *every regard except* the independent variable. Then, any differences in results can be attributed to the independent variable.

Suggested Background Readings

Agnew, N. M. & Pyke, S. W. *The science game: An introduction to research in the behavioral sciences* (2nd edition). Englewood Cliffs, N.J.: Prentice-Hall, 1978.

Arnoult, M. D. *Fundamentals of scientific method in psychology* (2nd edition). Dubuque, Iowa: William C. Brown, 1976.

Martin, D. W. *Doing psychology experiments.* Monterey, Calif.: Brooks/Cole, 1977.

Townsend, John C. *Introduction to experimental method.* New York: McGraw-Hill, 1953.

CHAPTER II
SENSORY PROCESSES
AND PERCEPTION

The 11 activities in this chapter, all of which are designed for in-class use, cover a range of sensory and perceptual phenomena. These exercises focus on individual sensory systems, as well as on the interaction of two or more of these systems.

The first three activities deal with taste, smell, and tactile perception. Activity 12, a study of taste preferences, looks at the influence of smell and sight. Activity 13 measures cutaneous sensitivity by means of the classic two-point threshold technique. Seven basic smells are studied in Activity 14, which relates to the stereochemical theory of odor.

The next four activities illustrate various visual phenomena: Activity 15 deals with blue-blindness or tritanopia, Activity 16 is about the process of accommodation, Activity 17 uses the Pulfrich pendulum effect to discuss information transmission from the eye, and Activity 18 concerns the retinal blind spot.

Two activities demonstrate interactions with the visual system. Activity 19 uses the size-weight illusion to study the relationship between vision and touch. Activity 20 investigates the role played by vision in the maintenance of a person's equilibrium.

Activity 21 shows the effects of delayed auditory feedback on speech, and Activity 22 illustrates the nature of perceptual adaptation to displaced vision.

TASTE PREFERENCES:
INFLUENCE OF SMELL AND SIGHT
Bernadette Fantino

Concept

This activity illustrates how cues can combine in complex ways to produce sensory experiences usually taken for granted, such as taste. Why do we develop preferences for certain foods? The following demonstrations show that more than just taste is involved.

Instructions

To show how food preference results from a combination of taste and smell, obtain four identical containers. Put bite-sized cubes of each of the following foods into separate containers: potato, apple, pear (a hard one), and onion. Ask for "taste study" volunteers and have them leave the room. Identify the foods for the class. Bring the volunteers into the room, one at a time, blindfolded and with their nostrils closed off (e.g., use a swimmer's nose clip or the "finger-pinching method"). Instruct the subjects not to breathe through their noses at any time, including between tastings. For Trial 1, feed the chunks of pear, potato, apple, and onion to the subject in random order. Ask what is being tasted. If the subject does not name all four foods after Trial 1 (e.g., if the subject mentions only apples and potatoes), tell the subject that those foods (e.g., apples and potatoes) and a mystery food are involved and to try again. On Trial 2, if the subject doesn't guess which foods are being offered, reveal the names of the four foods and provide a final trial on the taste test. Do this for several students to illustrate individual differences. If you choose to look at sex differences, use more than one person of each sex so that sex differences are not confused with individual differences. Use the table below for recording answers.

Conditioning

The first demonstration shows that the sensation of taste can involve the nose as much as the taste buds. The next demonstration, in showing how visual cues—seemingly unrelated to taste—can influence food preference, illustrates the effects of earlier conditioning on our food

Table for Recording Answers

Trial # _____ Sample given	Subject's guess			
	Apple	Pear	Potato	Onion
Apple				
Pear				
Potato				
Onion				

preferences. Students may wish to hypothesize about other ways in which early conditioning affects these preferences.

This activity requires some advance preparation. Obtain (a) two clear glasses filled with orange juice, one with a dose of food coloring added so that the juice turns black, (b) two hard-boiled eggs, one colored bright green, (c) two pieces of toast, one covered with a smattering of different colors so it looks moldy, and (d) two glasses of milk, one colored yellow. Set up a breakfast table for two blindfolded volunteers who have not seen what they are to eat. Ask them to eat breakfast and quiz them about the taste of each food. Then remove their blindfolds and ask them to continue eating. While they're eating, have other students record the volunteers' reactions, both before and after removal of the blindfolds, as well as the audience reactions.

Discussion

In discussing this activity, focus on how we learn our food preferences. Ask students why some food producers use food coloring in their products. Discuss the influence of table-setting design on food taste, and have students offer examples of how their own preferences are affected by visual, olfactory, and taste cues. What happens to taste when you have a head cold? Why do microwave ovens have a browning cycle? Think of other ways in which vision and olfaction interact with taste.

Suggested Background Readings

Christman, R. J. *Sensory experience*. Scranton, Pa.: Intext Educational Publishers, 1971. (chap. 17)

Geldard, F. A. *The human senses* (2nd ed.). New York: Wiley, 1972. (chap. 16)

Scharf, B. (Ed.). *Experimental sensory psychology*. Glenview, Ill.: Scott, Foresman, 1975. (chap. 6)

Schiffman, H. R. *Sensation and perception: An integrated approach*. New York: Wiley, 1976. (chap. 9)

13

CUTANEOUS TWO-POINT THRESHOLDS
J. Russell Nazzaro

Concept

This activity demonstrates that different areas of the skin have varying densities of nerve endings and provides a procedure for measuring this density. The demonstration requires the use of a caliper, a two-pronged measuring instrument. Depending on how many calipers are available, the demonstration can be done by students working in trios or by the teacher and two students. The procedure involves using the caliper to determine a subject's two-point threshold. Operationally defined, the two-point threshold is the distance at which, 50% of the time, a subject feels two points of contact with the body surface as two separate points rather than one point of contact. The two body areas to be tested are the palm and the biceps, where thresholds average 2 cm and 7.1 cm, respectively.

Instructions

Introduce the demonstration by displaying a homunculus for the somesthetic area of the cortex and explaining its meaning. (A homunculus is an anatomical drawing showing the parts of the body in proportion to the amount of cortex related to each part. Many texts contain such drawings.) Then have students form trios, with one student designated as the experimenter, one as the subject, and one as the recorder.

Before starting the trials, have the experimenter practice using the caliper. The experimenter should apply uniform moderate pressure for about 1 second. Both tips of the caliper should touch the body surface simultaneously. A good procedure to follow is to approach the body surface slowly, holding the tips of the caliper slightly elevated above its base; when a distance of about 2 mm from the skin is reached, the tips can be quickly lowered, applied, and raised. The caliper should be kept close to body temperature by periodically warming it with the hands.

To start, the experimenter should blindfold the subject. Then, setting the caliper at 1 cm and *increasing* the setting 1 mm on every trial, the experimenter should apply the caliper to the subject's palm until the subject reports perceiving *two* points of contact. The setting at which this report occurs should be noted by the recorder. The experimenter should then set the caliper at 3 cm and *decrease* the setting 1 mm on every trial until the subject reports perceiving *one* point of contact. The setting at which this occurs should also be noted. The procedure should be repeated six more times according to the following pattern: decreasing, increasing, decreasing, increasing, increasing, decreasing. Each time, the recorder should note the setting at which the subject reports "two" on the increasing trials or "one" on the decreasing trials. The subject's two-point threshold can then be calculated by averaging the settings on the increasing trials at which the subject reported "two," averaging the settings on the decreasing trials at which the subject reported "one," and figuring the midpoint between the averages. The two-point threshold for the biceps can be determined in a similar manner, with the caliper set at 6 cm to start the increasing trials and 8 cm to start the decreasing trials.

Discussion

Focus discussion on the practical implications of the variations in density. The amount of cortex related to motor function in various areas can also be pointed out and discussed. Other topics raised by this activity include the nature of threshold measurement. Why did some trials use decreasing and other trials increasing steps on the caliper? If differences existed in the averages for the decreasing trials compared to the increasing trials, why might those differences have occurred? Were those differences consistent across subjects? In addition, this exercise may be extended to measuring sensitivity in other body areas.

Suggested Background Readings

Corso, J. F. *The experimental psychology of sensory behavior*. New York: Holt, Rinehart & Winston, 1967. (chaps. 4, 8)

Geldard, F. A. *The human senses* (2nd ed.). New York: Wiley, 1972. (chap. 9)

Schiffman, H. R. *Sensation and perception: An integrated approach*. New York: Wiley, 1976. (chap. 7)

14

OLFACTION: THE SEVEN BASIC SMELLS (MORE OR LESS)
Allan L. LaVoie

Concept

While the list of the five senses has been replaced by a more exhaustive list of 11–14 basic senses, olfaction remains an enigmatic entry on all lists. Obviously an important sense and phylogenetically earlier than vision or audition, it remains poorly understood.

Introductory psychology books frequently dismiss olfaction in a paragraph or single page. But this tendency may change as more basic research results accumulate into a mass of solid data applicable to a variety of important human behaviors. For example, olfactory cues have now been strongly implicated in menstrual synchronicity, status among female primates, learning and performance, mate selection, and emotional behavior.

When I introduce the topic in my introductory courses, I focus on Amoore's (1970) theory. He postulated seven basic odors (akin to three primary colors or four basic tastes) that are determined by molecular shape and electrical charge. This stereochemical, or lock-and-key, theory has been called into qestion for a variety of reasons, but it remains the best theory extant and also makes for a variety of interesting demonstrations and exercises. For these reasons, I continue to use samples emitting Amoore's seven basic smells to introduce my classes to the reality and complexity of olfactory research.

Materials Needed

The seven smells and the chemicals that emit them are listed on the next page, with threshold concentrations and the sources from which they can be obtained (1976 prices given). In addition, you should have an array of glass-stoppered flasks to hold the solutions. (My procedure was to take the concentrated odorants to our chemistry laboratory and ask how one mixed .0007 parts of musk with a million parts of water.)

Prepare threshold concentrations of each odorant, plus two control bottles. Use only distilled water (for musky, the odorant must first be warmed, then mixed by shaking well). The control bottles, intermixed in a line with the other seven bottles, serve to estimate the contaminating effects of ambient odor. Tell the students in advance that there are only two control bottles.

It may be useful to warn other faculty in your building, especially on floors above yours, that you will be conducting the demonstration. It has been my experience that, exhaust fans notwithstanding, putrid has extraordinary penetrating power and can reach the English offices two floors above in only a few seconds. I have learned to live with their scathing epithets; you may prefer to conduct the exercise outdoors or in a properly ventilated laboratory.

Preparation of Class

This exercise can fit into a variety of topics, including psychophysics, transduction, and a general introduction to sensation and perception.

The context will determine what preparation, if any, is necessary. For my introductory class, students read a chapter on the chemical senses.

Instructions

Ask the class to line up in single file with note pads and pencils in hand. Explain that to sample each odor, they should wave the bottle stopper near their noses while gently sniffing. If they detect nothing, they can increase the intensity of their sampling by substituting the bottle for the

Seven Basic Smells

Odor	Threshold (parts per million of water)

1. Ethereal, or ether-like (1,2-dichloroethane)
  1 kg for $2.65 from
  City Chemical Corporation
  132 W. 22nd St.
  New York 10011
	29.0000

2. Camphoraceous, as moth balls (1,8-cineole)
  $1/4$ pint for $1.90 from
  City Chemical Corporation
	.0120

3. Musky (15-hydroxpentadecanoic acid actone)
  1 ounce for $6.50 from
  Givaudan Corporation
  125 Delawanna Avenue
  Clifton, New Jersey 07014
	.0007

4. Floral, as roses (d,1-B-phenylethyl
  methylethyl carbinol)
  5 gm for $10 from
  Aldrich Chemical Corporation
  Rare Chemical Division
  940 West St. Paul Avenue
  Milwaukee, Wisconsin 53232
	6.4000

5. Minty (d,1-methone)
  25 gm for $2.85 from
  City Chemical Corporation
	.1700

6. Pungent, as vinegar (formic acid, 90%)
  1 pint for $1.75 from
  City Chemical Corporation
	1500.0000

7. Putrid, as foul meat (dimethyl sulfide)
  100 gm for $4 from
  City Chemical Corporation
	.0012

Note: After this book was published, the EPA reported that this chemical is hazardous to health. Dispose of this and all chemicals appropriately.

stopper and sniffing more and more vigorously. After all of the students have sampled, record on the blackboard the number of males and females who detected each odorant.

On the note pads, the students should write the name of a common substance called to mind by each odorant. This part of the exercise leads to a discussion of the apparent inaccessibility of smells to accurate verbal labeling (you might point out that the sense of smell is unique in not having a separate area of the cortex with which it is connected and that it does not appear to have relays in the thalamus). Students frequently comment that one or more of the smells triggered a rich array of associated visual images with attendant emotion. This can lead to a later discussion of the role of olfaction as a relatively primitive survival mechanism.

Analysis

Two groups of data are to be analyzed. For the detection data, compare the percentage of males who detected the odor with the percentage of females. If you accurately mixed the solutions, you should find a significant sex difference for musky (roughly 25% of males and 85% of females in my classes detect it; see Amoore & Venstrom, 1966).

For the labeling data, the class can cooperate in calculating what percentage of the labels were accurate. Minty has proved the most easily labeled, pungent and putrid the least. I have never found reliable sex differences in the labeling data.

Discussion

If you keep the demonstration informal, there will be ample discussion without your guidance. My major objectives in devising this exercise were to focus student attention on a relatively neglected topic and to increase their critical analysis as they read in their textbooks. Hence, my discussion focuses on Amoore's evidence and on what determines whether a category is a primary smell, including criteria such as the most parsimonious description of an exhaustive odors list, a specific receptor maximally sensitive to a particular odorant, and so on.

I then focus discussion on more remote implications of smell research, for example, pheromonic control of human behavior, the use of odors as the pegs of a peg-and-hook mnemonic device, and thinking by smell (as in Galton's, 1894, "Arithmetic by Smell"). If time allows, we also use specific odors to guide a blindfolded student through a maze or to test the ability of humans to pinpoint the source of an odor by using only the nose. To indicate the astounding sensitivity of the nose, point out that students who detected the musk were detecting roughly 1 molecule per 1.4 billion molecules of water. You might then compare human smell sensitivity with that of other animals, or focus on functional explanations of the differential thresholds. In short, there are unlimited numbers of discussion topics and exercises.

Suggested Background Readings

Amoore, J. E. *Molecular basis of odor.* Springfield, Ill.: Charles C Thomas, 1970.

Amoore, J. E., Johnston, J. W., & Rubin, M. The stereochemical theory of odor. *Scientific American,* 1964, *210*(2), 42–49.

Amoore, J. E., & Venstrom, D. Sensory analysis of odor qualities in terms of the stereochemical theory. *Journal of Food Science,* 1966, *31,* 118–128.

Galton, F. Arithmetic by smell. *Psychological Review,* 1894, *1,* 61–62.

Uttal, W. R. *The psychology of sensory coding.* New York: Harper & Row, 1973.

15

BLUE-BLINDNESS IN THE CENTRAL FOVEA
William B. Cushman

Concept

Humans with normal color vision are blind to blue light (tritanopic) in an area at the center of the fovea subtending a visual angle of approximately 7–8 minutes of arc (Wald, 1967). Color vision is made possible by the action of three different receptor types, called cones because of their shape under a microscope. These receptors have a maximum sensitivity to red, green, and blue light, respectively, and the perception of *any* color can be caused by presenting the subject with a mixture of these three colors if the mixture is in the right proportions. A color television uses this principle; if you look closely at the screen you will see only red, blue, and green phosphor dots, but as you back away they mix into all the colors of the rainbow. The fact that a mixture of only three colors can produce the perception of all the others is, in fact, taken as primary evidence for the existence of only three color, or cone, receptor types. If persons are color-blind, however, they usually are missing either the red-sensitive or green-sensitive receptors and will match mixtures of only two colors to all the colors of the visual spectrum.

It is easy to imagine that these three cone types are distributed over the surface of the fovea in a homogeneous matrix, rather like the phosphor pattern of a color television, but this is not, in fact, the case. In 1967 the Nobel-Prize-winning physiologist George Wald reported that the blue-sensitive receptors in the human fovea had their maximum density at its border and decreased as one moved toward the center until, in an area subtending 7–8 minutes of visual angle, they were few or entirely missing. In contrast, both the red and green receptors followed the opposite gradient and increased in density to a maximum in the center. Tritanopea, the rarest form of human congenital color-blindness, is therefore a normal feature of the central fovea. The following experiment will demonstrate these different cone densities to a large class.

Preparation of Class

This phenomenon is easily demonstrated in the classroom by providing a small source of blue light—for example, a flashlight bulb behind a blue cellophane filter—and so arranging things that this light flashes on and off a few times per second. A flasher for the light can be made by wiring a relay like a "buzzer" and placing a large electrolytic capacitor across the coil winding. As the value of the capacitor is increased, the "buzzer" will cycle slower. Don't make the light source too large, because the idea is to approximate a "point source" as closely as possible. A piece of red or green cellophane is also useful to show the effect of changing the color.

Instructions

If the blue light is dim relative to the room light, when a subject or the whole class looks directly at it, it will seem to disappear. If, however, the subjects look a few degrees to either side of the bulb, they will plainly see

36

it flashing. Have the class try this, then repeat the experiment with a red or green cellophane filter over the light.

Discussion

The following questions may be used to guide discussion.

"Why do you suppose we used a flashing light rather than a steady one for this experiment?" (Merely to draw attention to the light, since untrained observers can rarely "attend" to something in their visual field without looking directly at it.)

"Since we know that colors like purple can be made by mixing red and blue light, what do you suppose a piece of paper with color gradients opposite that of the fovea would look like if you stared at the center? For example, a piece of paper with more and more blue as you looked toward the center and, at the same time, less and less red?" (It would look just like it was described, but this question may get the class thinking about the gradients involved.)

"If the hue of a light source is a function of the proportions of colors making it up (as, for example, purple made from red and blue), but the proportions of receptors, and their sensitivities, vary across the fovea, why doesn't a plain purple paper look something like the paper I described in my previous question?" (This one is still very much a mystery at the time of this writing; some sort of neural "filling in" must be taking place.)

In addition, you can use the demonstration to bring up the topic of color-blindness, discussing topics such as heritability factors, receptor deficits, and the ways in which people who are color-blind learn to compensate for their inability to see certain hues.

Suggested Background Readings

Hurvich, L. M., & Jameson, D. Human color perception: An essay review. *American Scientist,* 1969, *57,* 143–166.

Teevan, R. C., & Birney, R. C. (Eds.). *Color vision.* Princeton, N.J.: Van Nostrand, 1961.

Wald, G. The receptors of human color vision. *Science,* 1964, *145,* 1007–1017.

Wald, G. Blue blindness in the normal fovea. *Journal of the Optical Society of America,* 1967, *57,* 1289–1303.

16

VISUAL ACCOMMODATION: DOUBLE VISION WITH ONE EYE
W. E. Scoville

Concept

The following vision demonstrations are simple to perform, yet their results are not readily predicted. Depth perception depends on a combination of binocular and monocular visual cues. In binocular vision, one cue involves the sense of muscular strain of the eye muscles as the eyes converge. Another binocular cue is retinal disparity, which involves judgment of distance based on the differences in the two retinal images. Of the monocular cues, accommodation is effective only at short distances. This process refers to the changes in the shape of the crystalline lens of the eye, an action achieved by the ciliary muscles in the eye.

Instructions

Instruct the class as follows: "Hold your right arm out at arm's length with upstretched thumb, and put your left hand at the right elbow with index finger raised. Which image, near or far, is double when the focus of the eye is on the alternate object? When you focus on the thumb, is the double image of the index finger (at elbow distance) made into a single image by the closing of one eye? Which eye?" Appropriate diagrams could go on the blackboard. Ask, "Would it be possible for a cyclops to see double? Could you see double with one eye closed?"

Most people will readily agree that this is impossible, whereupon you present each person with a 3 × 5 card and an ordinary pin. Instruct the students to place two pinholes in the card so that there is about a width-of-a-pin distance between the two holes. Upon holding this card up close to the eye and looking at the sky or another bright surface, two *overlapping* luminous circles of light will be seen; if not, make new pinholes and adjust the width. Hold the pin by its head at arm's length so that the pin's image is seen in the overlapping area of the luminous circles. Have the students bring the pin toward the eye, and at some point (if the pin is within the area of overlap) a double image will be seen with only one eye.

Discussion

In the "two pinhole" condition, the distance cue is the change in the shape of the eye's lens. While a camera lens focuses by changing the distance to the film (and sometimes by changing the relationship between the lens elements), the eye focuses an image on the retina by changing the shape of the lens (at least for objects that are close). With use of the two pinholes we restrict the lens of the eye to two "bundles" of light. When the lens is properly focused, the pin will be seen as a single image, and when the lens is not in focus we will have double vision, since the two images will be coming to focus at a different point. As the pin is moved toward the eye, it will (at some point) come closer than the ability of the lens to accommodate. As we get older our lenses become less flexible, so the point of near vision becomes progressively further away from us. While a young person can perhaps achieve a single image as little as four inches away, an older person may find the distance a foot or more. Reading glasses (or bifocals) are required when our point of near vision is so far away that by the time we have the print far enough away to come into focus, the print is too small for us to read (or our arms are too short to hold it at that distance). The students can find their near point of vision by finding the shortest distance at which they can maintain a single image.

Suggested Background Readings

Forgus, R. H., & Melamed, L. E. *Perception: A cognitive-stage approach* (2nd ed.). New York: McGraw-Hill, 1976. (chap. 13)

Gregory, R. L. *Eye and brain: The psychology of seeing* (2nd ed.). New York: McGraw-Hill, 1973. (chap. 13)

McBurney, D. H., & Collings, V. B. *Introduction to sensation/perception.* Englewood Cliffs, N.J.: Prentice-Hall, 1977. (chap. 10)

Schiffman, H. R. *Sensation and perception: An integrated approach.* New York: Wiley, 1976. (chap. 16)

THE PULFRICH PENDULUM EFFECT: WHEN TO AND FRO IS ROUNDABOUT
Ludy T. Benjamin, Jr.

Concept

The Pulfrich phenomenon is one of the most effective demonstrations in visual perception and one of the easiest to prepare. This simple demonstration evokes a powerful illusion of movement or, more specifically, a perceived misdirection of movement. The student views an object swinging back and forth at eye level in a plane perpendicular to the line of vision. Viewing is binocular, but one of the student's eyes is covered with a sunglass lens (or some other form of light filter). The swinging object will appear to be moving in an elliptical or circular orbit rather than in a straight line. When the lens is shifted from one eye to the other, the object will reverse its direction of movement.

Materials Needed

The simplest way to demonstrate the Pulfrich effect is to attach a string to the ceiling with a weight tied to the free end. The weight should be about the size of a flashlight battery or nine-volt transistor radio battery. In fact, either of those objects will work quite well. The only problem with this technique (and it is not really a drawback for demonstrational purposes) is that one must continually restart the pendulum action when the arc begins to decrease. If motion of the object at a constant speed is important for systematic data collecting, then the pendulum should be attached to a motor. One solution is to find a motor designed for this kind of motion. For example, many motors used in window display advertising are often geared to moving an object back and forth. These motors are not usually heavy-duty, so the shaft of the pendulum and the pendulum bob must be lightweight. A ping pong ball, painted some dark color so that it contrasts well with light-colored walls, makes an excellent bob. The shaft can be a rod made of some thin metal such as aluminum. It should be light enough not to induce undue strain on the motor yet heavy enough to remain rigid in the pendulum motion.

Preparation of Class

Announce in advance that students should bring their sunglasses to class on the day of the demonstration. Other light filters can be used, such as exposed film (as long as it isn't too dark).

Instructions

Position the students toward the center of the classroom as near to the back of the room as is possible. Some may be sitting while others stand behind them. Optimal viewing distance is from 15 to 20 feet, although shorter distances can be used. In demonstrating this phenomenon the background is a critical variable. There should be ample distance (from 6 to 10 feet) between the path of the swinging object and any adjacent walls; otherwise the magnitude of the effect will be diminished. Ask students to cover their right eyes with the sunglass lenses. If a student is using an intact pair of sunglasses, the best procedure is to hold both legs of the glasses, one in each hand, with the sunglasses turned around and held in a vertical position. That is, the lenses are up and down, with the student looking through the lower lens. This allows rapid switching of the lens from one eye to another.

When students have their glasses in place, remind them that they are to view the pendulum with *both eyes open.* Start the bob swinging and instruct the students to watch the motion of the bob. After a few seconds, ask them to describe what they are seeing. They will usually say that they see the object moving in a circle or an ellipse. (With the lens over the right eye, the front part of the orbit will be seen as left to right. When the lens is switched to the left eye, the direction of the orbit reverses.) When most of the students report seeing the movement, have them quickly switch the lens to the left eye and describe the direction of the movement. Once they see that it reverses, they can shift the lens from eye to eye to repeat the effect. The darker the sunglass lens, the greater the magnitude of the illusion.

Other interesting effects can also be observed. For example, if the teacher stands to the side of the arc of the pendulum and positions one hand so that it is in front of the bob near the end of the arc, the bob will appear to pass through the hand as it makes the forward pass of its illusory orbit. Feel free to experiment with the effect. Varying the nature of the background can also change the magnitude of the effect. Placing the bob so that the arc is parallel and close to a wall causes the back portion of the orbit to flatten out.

Discussion

By covering one eye with a filter, the eye is said to be partially dark-adapted. This produces a difference in the time it takes information to be transmitted from the eye to the brain. That is, the dark-adapted eye will transmit its neural messages slower than the other eye. This delay causes the dark-adapted eye to see the bob slightly in the past. It is the difference in transmission times from the two eyes that produces the perceived illusory elliptical orbit. In other words, the brain receives information exactly like that it receives when viewing an object swinging in an elliptical orbit with *normal* binocular vision. The figure below (from Gregory, 1973) is helpful in explaining the effect and should be reproduced as a handout for students or illustrated on a chalkboard.

Pulfrich Pendulum Effect

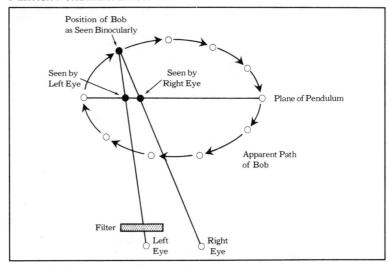

Suggested Background Readings

Gregory, R. L. *Eye and brain* (2nd ed.). New York: World University Library, 1973. (pp. 78–80)

Lit, A. The magnitude of the Pulfrich stereophenomenon as a function of binocular differences of intensity at various levels of illumination. *American Journal of Psychology,* 1949, *62,* 159–181.

Rock, M. L., & Fox, B. H. Two aspects of the Pulfrich phenomenon. *American Journal of Psychology,* 1949, *62,* 279–284.

Standing, L. G., Dodwell, P. C., & Lang, D. Dark adaptation and the Pulfrich effect. *Perception & Psychophysics,* 1968, *4,* 118–120.

ACTIVITY
18

BLIND SPOT IN VISION
John J. Duda

Concept

That area at the back of the eye where the nerve fibers from all parts of the retina collect to form the optic nerve is called the optic disc or, more commonly, the "blind spot." Indeed, that portion of the retina is functionally blind—incoming light is ineffective because there are no photoreceptors in that region. The two exercises described here provide interesting illustrations of the blind spot.

Instructions

Take a blank piece of white paper that measures $8^1/_2$ by 11 inches, and cut it in half so it is $8^1/_2$ by $5^1/_2$ inches. On one side of the paper, center and type (or print in corresponding size) a capital X and a capital Y about 4 inches apart. On the other side, center and type capitals X, Y, and Z about 3 inches apart (with Y in the center).

For the first demonstration, hold the side of the paper with the X and Y at arm's length while covering one eye with the other hand. If the left eye is covered, fixate on the X (assuming it is on the left), and vice versa. Then slowly advance the paper toward the eye. Notice what happens to the Y: At some critical distance from the eye it disappears, but as the distance from the eye is further decreased, it reappears. You should then be able to tune the Y in and out by adjusting the distance of the paper from the eye.

The second demonstration involves using the side of the paper with the X, Y, and Z, holding it at arm's length, fixating on the Y with the left eye covered, and slowly advancing the paper toward the eye. At some critical distance from the eye the Z will disappear. If the paper is then held at this point, it is possible to observe an unusual phenomenon: Shifting fixation to the X causes the Y to disappear and the Z to reappear. Thus, by shifting fixation back and forth between the Y and the X, you can make the Z and the Y alternately pop in and out of view.

Discussion

Explain that we have a blind spot in each eye, or a total of two such spots in our typical visual field. Why don't we see holes in that visual field? Partly because these holes are eliminated by eye movements that shift the parts of the visual field to different portions of the retina. In addition, our visual system tends to fill in gaps in what we see, in a manner similar to the Gestalt principle of closure. As a result, we are unaware of our blind spots and require a demonstration such as the one described above to illustrate their existence.

Suggested Background Readings

Begbie, G. H. *Seeing and the eye: An introduction to vision*. New York: Anchor Press/Doubleday, 1973.

Geldard, F. A. *The human senses* (2nd ed.). New York: Wiley, 1972. (chap. 2)

Gregory, R. L. *Eye and brain: The psychology of seeing*. New York: McGraw Hill, 1973. (chap. 4)

ACTIVITY
19

SIZE–WEIGHT ILLUSION:
A POUND IS A POUND
THE WORLD AROUND?
Clifford L. Fawl

Concept

Relativity is one of the fundamentals of psychology. Nowhere is this more evident than in the field of perception, where Gestalt psychologists, more than a half century ago, demonstrated that it is difficult at best to perceive a part independent of the whole. For example, Circle A in the figure may appear larger than Circle B, despite the fact that they are identical. And, in a (relative) sense it is: Circle A is larger relative to the context of which it is a part than Circle B is relative to its context. Circles A and B thus can be compared by absolute size, in which case they are identical, or by their size relative to context, in which case Circle A is larger. Perceptual judgments tend to be based upon the relative aspects of an object even though the assumption is that one is attending to the absolute.

This fundamental principle can be demonstrated in many facets of perception: loudness, hue, motion, or even social perception (e.g., intelligence). Wallach (1959), in an easily read article published in *Scientific American,* presented an especially impressive case showing that the perception of the motion of a figure is dependent upon the physical change in the relationship between the figure and its ground, even when it is the ground rather than the figure that is in actual motion. With effort, several classroom activities can be developed from this article.

Easier to exhibit, yet equally impressive in effect, is the size–weight illusion. It is easy to illustrate that the apparent weight of an object is profoundly affected by its context—in this case the context of its size. Below is an adaptation of a presentation found in a textbook by Krech, Crutchfield, and Livson (1974, p. 300).

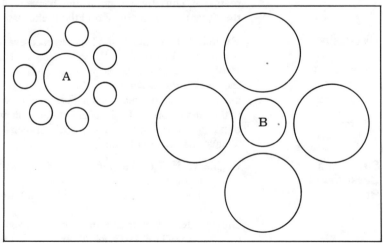

Materials Needed

A variety of materials may be utilized for this demonstration; however, the following are suggested: one large can (e.g., an empty, 46-oz. tomato-juice can) filled with sufficient sand to weigh 200 grams (hereafter referred to as the standard) and seven smaller cans of uniform size (e.g., empty, 6-oz. frozen orange-juice cans) filled with sufficient sand to produce weights of 75, 100, 125, 150, 175, 200, and 225 grams (hereafter to be called the comparison cans). Ideally, each can should have a cap to prevent visual inspection of the contents, and either a ring or knob by which it can be lifted; however, neither improvement is essential. The seven comparison cans should be coded in some way so that only the teacher will know the weight of each can.

Preparation of Class

Only one student at a time can be used for this demonstration. Nevertheless, since the procedure is brief it might be possible to allow most of the students to participate. It is a fun activity, and most students will want to try it for themselves. Have the students record their responses privately so as not to influence other students who will serve as subjects later.

Instructions

Place the eight cans in a row on a table. The larger (standard) can should be first, followed in random order by the seven comparison cans. Inform the student that the larger can weighs exactly 200 grams. Have the student lift the can in order to get a notion of how heavy 200 grams feels. Next, with the large can as the standard, have the student lift each of the comparison cans in turn and record his or her estimate in grams of what each can weighs. The student may return to the standard can if desired, but not to a previous comparison can. If the student prefers, the standard can may be lifted in one hand while lifting the comparison can with the other hand. If asked, do not reveal whether any of the seven comparison cans is equal in weight to the standard can. The recorded weights should be handed to the teacher before the next student commences.

A second procedure may be employed with either the same or a different group of students. Again, use only one student at a time. As before, arrange the seven comparison cans in a random order. This time, however, inform the student that one of the seven comparison cans weighs exactly the same (200 grams) as the standard. The student's task is to find which can it is. Once determined, he or she is to write down the code letter of the can on a piece of paper, which is then handed to the teacher. Since other students might be able to see which can was picked, rearrange the order of the comparison cans for the next student.

Discussion

Results can be displayed easily to the class. For the first procedure, post either the mean or median weight assigned to each comparison can along with the actual weight of the can. The students most likely will have estimated the comparison cans to weigh considerably more than they actually do. Some students may report even the lightest comparison can (75 grams) to be heavier than the standard.

For the second procedure, the results can be reported in two ways. First, post the frequency with which each of the comparison weights was identified as being equal in weight to the standard. Second, determine the mean (or median) weight of the comparison can that was identified as equal to the standard. The findings are usually so surprising that students may question whether the eight cans have been weighed accurately. Have a balance scale available, accurate to the nearest gram, so that you can publicly weigh each can.

Is this an illusion to which one adapts quickly? Not really. Does the illusion evaporate once one knows the right answer? Again, not really. In fact, if time permits, have a few students repeat one or both procedures. Even though the magnitude of the illusion is lessened, most students will report that the smaller can of 200 grams still feels heavier than the standard.

Students often feel "stupid" or embarrassed when they find themselves vulnerable to an illusion, especially one involving judgment such as the present one. They may be relieved to learn that Crutchfield et al. (reported in Krech, Crutchfield, & Livson, 1974) found that a group of military officers also was highly susceptible to the illusion. The officers were given two boxes: Each weighed 300 grams, but one was eight times greater in volume than the other. The officers were told the weight of the larger box and asked to estimate the weight of the smaller one. Their average estimate was an incredible 750 grams, or two and one-half times the actual weight!

Perceptual judgments of weight are in part relative, not just absolute. As in the comparison of Circles A and B discussed at the beginning, there is a sense in which the comparison can of 200 grams *is* heavier than the standard can of 200 grams. The former is heavier relative to its size than is the latter. Obviously, one is being affected by the *density* of the cans, not just their absolute weights, and density, after all, is a *relative* measure (weight per unit of volume). The best way to demonstrate the influence of size on judgment of weight is to have the students lift the cans without seeing them. Under such conditions they cannot know the size or volume and thus are more likely to respond purely upon the basis of weight, with the result that the illusion disappears.

Suggested Background Readings

Krech, D., Crutchfield, R. S., & Livson, N. *Elements of psychology* (3rd ed.). New York: Knopf, 1974.

Wallach, H. The perception of motion. *Scientific American,* Offprint No. 409. San Francisco: W. H. Freeman, 1959.

20

BALANCE SENSITIVITY
P. S. Fernald and L. D. Fernald, Jr.

Concept

Balance sensitivity involves several senses, but usually vision and the sense of equilibrium are primarily involved. The eye, of course, is the sense organ associated with vision. Equilibrium is sensed through several organs in the inner ear—the semicircular canals, which make us aware of rotary motion, and the vestibular sacs, which make us aware of position and motion in a straight line. When cues from either our vision or our sense of equilibrium inform us that we are losing balance, we make compensatory motor adjustments that return us to a balanced state. Because the adjustments are both minute and automatic, we often fail to recognize their importance except under unusual circumstances such as dizziness or inebriation. A few simple exercises like those below can call attention to the fact that the adjustments do occur. The exercises can also call attention to the sensory cues that prompt the adjustments.

Instructions

Have students stand on one foot, without support, for 20 seconds. Ask them to describe the sensations that occur in the foot and leg on which they are standing and how the sensations are related to maintaining balance. Among the sensations they should experience are increased pressure on the foot because it has assumed all their weight, and also constant contractions in their foot and leg muscles. These muscle contractions are the minute motor adjustments that bring them back to a balanced state as they start to become imbalanced.

   The foregoing exercise can be regarded as a control condition. Next, have students stand again on the one foot, but this time have them close their eyes. Again have them describe their sensations, and ask them to compare this condition with the control condition. Students should experience greater difficulty in maintaining balance with their eyes closed because they are not receiving the visual cues that are important to balance sensitivity. The greater difficulty will be apparent in students' leaning farther to one side or another before they make the necessary compensatory motor adjustments to bring themselves back into balance. The compensatory motor adjustments, although still minute, will be more extreme and require greater muscular activity.

   Finally, have students, with their eyes open, quickly spin themselves around five times and then with their eyes shut, stand again on the one foot. Ask them to describe their sensations under this condition compared to the other conditions, and encourage them to

Adapted from *Student Guidebook* to accompany *Introduction to Psychology,* 3d ed., by Norman L. Munn, Peter S. Fernald and L. Dodge Fernald. Copyright © 1972 by Houghton Mifflin Company. Used by permission.

speculate about the reasons for the difference. They should experience extreme difficulty in balancing because the spinning will interfere with their sense of equilibrium.

Discussion

It should become apparent from this exercise that although vision is important, the sense of equilibrium plays the major role in maintenance of balance. You might choose to discuss some of Witkin's research on judgments of postural verticality as related to styles of perceiving (see suggested readings).

Suggested Background Readings

Geldard, F. A. *The human senses* (2nd ed.). New York: Wiley, 1972. (chap. 14)

McBurney, D. H., & Collings, V. B. *Introduction to sensation/perception.* Englewood Cliffs, N.J.: Prentice-Hall, 1977. (chap. 9)

Witkin, H. A. The nature and importance of individual differences in perception. *Journal of Personality,* 1949, *18,* 145–170.

Witkin, H. A. The perception of the upright. *Scientific American,* 1959, *200,* 50–56.

ACTIVITY

DELAYED AUDITORY FEEDBACK
Philip G. Zimbardo and James Newton

Concept

This activity illustrates the effects of delayed auditory feedback on verbal behavior. Recommended equipment includes earphones, a microphone, a reel of tape, and a tape recorder with three heads (record, erase, and playback) and a monitor or source switch—that is, a tape recorder that can play back what is being recorded as it is being recorded.

Instructions

The procedure involves having a volunteer, who speaks into the microphone, record a passage while listening on the earphones to what he or she is saying. Because the record and playback heads on the tape recorder are slightly separated, there will be a momentary delay in the auditory feedback, which should have marked effects on the volunteer's performance. That is, the speaker will have considerable difficulty in reading aloud and will stammer and pause frequently. The length of the delay can be varied by adjusting the speed of the tape (if the recorder has speed selections) or the distance between the two heads. Optimum delay is about one fifth of a second. If a tape recorder with three heads and a monitor switch is not available, you might try placing two standard tape recorders side by side, winding the tape to record on one and play back on the other. However, using two tape recorders may so delay the feedback that the effect is minimal. Whichever method is used, it would be wise to get a volunteer in advance and test him or her. Not all people will exhibit the desired effect.

Conceal the volunteer and the equipment behind a curtain or partition. Explain to your students that they are going to hear someone (unidentified) reading aloud and that they should try to analyze the reader's problem. Then have the volunteer begin reading and the students begin analyzing. Note the gist of their comments on the chalkboard, and note mentally their spontaneous reactions: Do they laugh? Does this reaction change as they begin to believe something is really wrong with the reader?

When the students' comments begin to diminish, and while the person continues to read, turn the monitor switch off for an interval (thus stopping the delayed feedback), then on again, then off once more. (If you have the tape recorder concealed within your reach, you can inject a little flamboyance into the demonstration by stating that the person is under your control and then waving one hand conspicuously while you flip the monitor switch with the other.) Now expose the reader and explain the cause of his or her problem.

From *Psychology and Life,* Brief 9th Ed. and 9th Ed., *Instructor's Resource Book* by Philip G. Zimbardo and James W. Newton. Copyright © 1976, 1975 by Scott, Foresman and Company. Reprinted by permission.

Discussion

The demonstration can be extended to illustrate that disruption is a function of the degree to which the material to be presented is integrated and interdependent. The order of difficulty in speaking coherently should increase as the volunteer goes through the following sequence: reciting well-learned material (name, address, the numbers from 1 to 20, etc.); reading passages; answering thought questions; reciting tongue twisters; whistling a tune; and leading a few rounds of "Row, row, row your boat."

Discussion can focus first on the effects of delayed feedback in this particular situation and then be generalized to the pervasive role of feedback—for example, in learning, perception, socialization processes, and interpersonal relations.

Suggested Background Readings

Chase, R. A., Harvey, S., Standfast, S., Rapin, I., & Sutton, S. Comparison of the effects of delayed auditory feedback on speech and key tapping. *Science,* 1959, *129,* 903–904.

Yates, A. J. Delayed auditory feedback. *Psychological Bulletin,* 1963, *60,* 213–232.

ACTIVITY
22

ADAPTATION TO DISPLACED VISION
Ludy T. Benjamin, Jr.

Concept

Adaptation to displaced vision is one of the oldest problem areas of experimental psychology. A demonstration similar to the one described in this article was first reported by Hermann Helmholtz in 1867 in his *Handbook on Physiological Optics*. This demonstration illustrates the interrelationships of afferent and efferent information and how those relationships are altered when information to one of the sensory systems is distorted. In this activity, objects in the real world are laterally displaced by means of wedge prism goggles. Adaptation and readaptation may then be studied.

Construction of the Goggles

The goggles can be made from welding safety goggles. These goggles are inexpensive (usually under $10) and are especially advantageous because they permit the subject to wear prescription glasses while the goggles are in place. Select the kind of goggles with a rectangular faceplate and no center dividing bridge. Remove the safety-glass lenses and replace them with a clear piece of $1/8$-inch plexiglas. The triangular wedge prisms (two) can be cut from scrap pieces of 1-inch plexiglas. Begin by measuring the dimensions of the exposed surface of the front of the faceplate. Cut two pieces identical in size from the 1-inch plexiglas and completely cover the exposed faceplate surface. The ideal prism angle is between 20° and 30° (which provides from 10° to 15° of actual visual displacement). Polish the two large faces of each prism and then cover those faces with masking tape. Spray the three exposed edges with flat black paint to prevent light from entering those surfaces. Finally, after the paint is dry, remove the masking tape and attach the prisms to the plexiglas faceplate with a plexiglas glue such as ethylene dichloride. The prism bases should be mounted either to the right or left sides for vision to be displaced in a lateral direction. In most welding goggles the faceplate is removable; thus the direction of the displacement can be reversed by reversing the faceplate. For other perceptual effects, the prisms can be mounted on the faceplate in a variety of orientations. Making multiple pairs of goggles is nearly as easy as making one pair, and of course the extra goggles will allow you to involve more students in the demonstrations.

Instructions

Ask for a volunteer(s) to wear the goggles in front of the class. If the goggles displace the visual field to the left, that means objects will appear to be to the left of their actual location. In quickly reaching for objects, subjects will miss the objects by reaching too far to the left. Having subjects reach quickly for objects is critical if one is to observe the errors the subjects make due to the displacement. If allowed to reach slowly for objects, subjects will see their hands and arms, which will enable them to grasp or touch the objects easily. Thus it is important to have subjects make rapid hand/arm movements or to conduct the demonstration so that the subjects cannot see their hands. One procedure is to have the subject stand (or sit) next to a table or other platform whose height is about shoulder high. Place an object on the other side of the table in front of the subject. With the subject's arm under the table, ask the subject to point to the location of the object. You can even record the displacement error by measuring the distance from the actual object to the position of the pointing finger. Move the object to several locations on the table and record the magnitude of the error each time. That distance should remain rather constant if the subjects receive no feedback on their performance.

Next, have the subjects leave the table and perform a number of tasks that provide feedback about the visual field displacement and thus an opportunity for adaptation. You could draw a small circle (about 2 inches in diameter) on the chalkboard and request the subject to "hit" the target using the index finger of the right hand. Make sure that the arm movements are rapid and that the beginning of the movement takes place outside of the subject's visual field. At first the subject misses to the left of the circle, but gradually the subject adapts and after 30 seconds or so can consistently hit the circle. Draw another circle in another location and ask the subject to hit that one. Performance should be good on this task because the subject has adapted—that is, learned to make *new* motor responses with the right arm to correspond to the new visual field. At this point you should have subjects try to hit the circle with their left hands. Since the motor learning in the right arm does not transfer to the left arm, the subjects should perform like they did in the initial part of the demonstration. That is, they will miss consistently to the left. Have the subjects switch back to using the right arm until it is clear that they have adapted. Then remove the goggles, draw a new circle on the board and ask the subjects to hit it. They will miss to the right by a margin of error similar to that which existed prior to adaptation. With successive attempts they will quickly regain their accuracy, completing the process known as readaptation.

An alternative way to demonstrate adaptation and readaptation is to have the subjects stand from 15 to 20 feet away from a cardboard box and attempt to throw objects (pennies, marbles, etc.) into it. Again, the arm motion must be rapid and must start from outside of the subject's field of view. When adaptaton has occurred and subjects are hitting the box with consistency, remove the goggles and have them continue to throw, observing the magnitude of error and the time it takes for them to readapt.

Discussion

You should discuss this form of adaptation as motor adaptation, drawing on that part of the demonstration that shows the adaptation does not transfer from one arm to the other. That is, the subject does not learn to see the visual field as displaced but learns to make new motor responses that are consonant with the new visual field. In other words, the adaptation is with regard to motor processes, not visual ones. Talk about the time required for that adaptation to occur; students are usually amazed that adaptation can occur so quickly. Read the article by Kohler (1962), which describes other effects such as color fringes and the unusual movements of the visual field one experiences when making lateral and vertical head movements with the goggles in place.

Suggested Background Readings

Harris, C. S. Perceptual adaptation to inverted, reversed, and displaced vision. *Psychological Review,* 1965, *72,* 419–444.

Kohler, I. Experiments with goggles. *Scientific American,* 1962, *206,* 62–72.

Rock, I. *The nature of perceptual adaptation.* New York: Basic Books, 1966.

Weinstein, S., Sersen, E. A., Fisher, L., & Weisinger, M. Is reafference necessary for visual adaptation? *Perceptual and Motor Skills,* 1964, *18,* 641–648.

CHAPTER III
LEARNING AND
CONDITIONING

All but one of the nine activities described in this chapter are designed for use within the classroom. The first four exercises describe different methods for illustrating operant conditioning in humans. Activity 23 requires very little class time, while Activities 24, 25, and 26 are more elaborate and employ shaping procedures in which the instructor serves as the source of reinforcement. Activity 25 describes a procedure that uses all of the students in the class in an operant-conditioning demonstration. That exercise also uses a verbal punishment procedure that can be compared to the use of reinforcement. Activity 26 demonstrates an extinction procedure.

Activity 27 describes a recording procedure that can serve as a form of self-modification and discusses ways in which individuals can use operant conditioning techniques to modify their own behavior.

Three activities deal with the relationship of learning and performance and show factors that affect both. Activity 28 illustrates the importance of knowledge of results by using groups of subjects given either no knowledge, full knowledge, or partial knowledge. Activity 29 uses the Stroop Color Word Test to show how irrelevant stimuli can interrupt attention and thus affect performance. The effects of practice and negative transfer on performance are demonstrated in Activity 30.

Activity 31 describes a procedure for generating a number of learning curves for a variety of motor and cognitive tasks.

ACTIVITY

23

OPERANT CONDITIONING: ROLE IN HUMAN BEHAVIOR
Edward Stork

Concept

From infancy onward, conditioning plays a major role in our lives. Yet most of us tend to downplay that role, possibly feeling that to admit such control over our behavior would be to admit that our lives are overly determined. Often when students read in their texts about classical and operant conditioning, they tend to associate that type of learning with infrahuman animals. That is, "Dogs, rats, and pigeons are affected by conditioning, but it doesn't play any role in my behavior." This activity is designed to provide a starting point for discussion of conditioning in humans.

Instructions

While discussing operant conditioning, interrupt your lecture with "Oh, by the way, before I forget again" and then ask a question to which you know you will get either an almost totally positive or negative response. For example, if your students are primarily seniors, you might say, "I was supposed to ask, how many of you have signed for a diploma for graduation?" All students will usually raise a hand. Then tell them to hold the position they are in and ask if anyone told them to raise their hands or even mentioned raising hands.

Discussion

The usual response is a chorus of groans as the students recognize that they have been "used." Discuss the activity as an example of human conditioning. Ask students to generate other examples that describe conditioning in humans. You can use the ensuing discussion as a bridge to talking about conditioning techniques used with humans in behavior therapy.

Suggested Background Readings

Bellack, A. S., & Hersen, M. *Behavior modification: An introductory textbook*. New York: Oxford University Press, 1977.

Hulse, S. H., Deese, J. E., & Smith, H. E. *The psychology of learning* (5th ed.). New York: McGraw-Hill, 1980.

Smith, W. I. *Conditioning and instrumental learning* (2nd ed.). New York: McGraw-Hill, 1978.

ACTIVITY
24

OPERANT CONDITIONING DEMONSTRATION
Patricia Keith-Spiegel

Concept

This classroom demonstration is a simple way to illustrate the process of operant (instrumental) conditioning with a human being. (It has never failed in 14 years, although some volunteers take longer than others to "learn.")

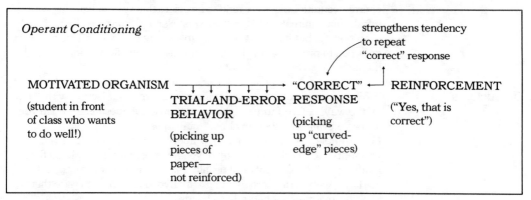

Instructions

Cut out approximately 40 pieces of paper 2 inches × 2 inches. Then cut these 2-inch squares into a variety of shapes. Twenty of the pieces should have only straight edges, and 20 pieces should have at least one curved side each. (Save them in an envelope for repeated use.) Mix up the paper shapes and spread them out on a desk or table top. Ask for a student volunteer. Tell the volunteer to start picking up the pieces of paper one at a time and place them in a box. Each time the student picks one of the pieces that has a curve on it, say "Yes, that is correct." Each time the student picks up a completely straight-edged piece, give no reinforcement at all. Usually within 10 to 15 draws, the student will "learn" what has been defined as the "correct response" and will swiftly continue picking up pieces until all of the curved pieces are gone. (The students observing usually begin to approvingly giggle as the volunteer receives rapid positive reinforcements.)

Discussion

Ask the student to tell the class what she or he has learned. Be sure to point out to the class that the *only* input given the student (aside from the initial direction to pick up pieces) was in the form of Positive Reinforcement. Nothing was said about shapes or any other facet of the task. Ask the student to relate to the class what went through his or her mind during the learning process. Various trial-and-error strategies often emerge here (e.g., "At first I thought it was the larger pieces that were correct because the first big one I picked up was correct.") The basic operant-conditioning diagram provided here is helpful in summarizing for the class what they have just witnessed.

Suggested Background Readings

Keller, F. S. *Learning: Reinforcement theory* (2nd ed.). New York: Random House, 1969.

Krech, D., Crutchfield, R. S., Livson, N., & Krech, H. *Psychology: A basic course*. New York: Knopf, 1976. (chap. 3)

Smith, W. I. *Conditioning and instrumental learning* (2nd ed.). New York: McGraw-Hill, 1978.

SHAPING BY SUCCESSIVE APPROXIMATIONS
David Watson

Concept

This activity deals with shaping—that is, reinforcing successive approximations of one behavior to the exclusion of other behaviors. The exercise helps students learn the basic principles of reinforcement and makes it possible for them to compare the effects of positive reinforcement and punishment.

Instructions

Start the exercise by showing students how shaping is done. Ask for a volunteer whose behavior you will shape. Send the volunteer out of the room while you and the class select a simple behavior to shape—for example, touching the chalkboard. Have the volunteer return, and explain the task as follows: "We've picked a particular act that we want you to do, but we won't tell you what it is; you have to figure it out. It's simple and not embarrassing. Each time you move in the direction of doing it, I will say 'Good.' If you don't move in that direction, I won't say anything. When you get a little warm, I won't keep on saying 'Good.' I'll wait for you to get a bit warmer before saying it. That way you will make progress. What I'll be doing is called 'shaping.'"

Begin shaping the volunteer's behavior by saying "Good" to any movement in the direction of the desired act. For example, if the volunteer is to touch the chalkboard, say "Good" to any glance, turn, or step toward it. Then say "Good" only to steps toward it, then to approaches of the hand toward it, etc. Eliciting the desired act takes about 10 minutes, on the average.

Now divide the class into pairs. At the outset one person in the pair should be the shaper, and one the person whose behavior will be shaped. Then roles should be switched. Have the shapers select a target behavior—remind them that it should be a simple one, not embarrassing—and then have them proceed to shape their partner's behavior. While they are working, circulate among them, coaching.

On the same day if time allows, or on another day, continue the exercise, but instead of having shapers say "Good" when their partner gets warmer, have them say "Bad" when their partner gets colder.

Discussion

End the activity with a discussion of what students have learned. Bring out the following points: that reinforcers such as the word "Good" guide behavior, that reinforcement must come quickly if it is to have an effect, and that shaping is an effective way to develop behaviors. Ask why some shapers did better than others. A shaper may have required too large an initial step, or inadvertently reinforced the wrong move, or not given enough reinforcers. Also discuss what effects the change of approach

Adapted from Teacher's Guide for *Here's Psychology* by David Watson, © Copyright 1977 by Ginn and Company (Xerox Corporation). Used with permission.

from "Good" to "Bad" had. Typically, punishment (as represented here by the word "Bad") does not teach new behaviors effectively. There are also some typical side effects: The person on whom punishment is being used will become frustrated, may become aggressive, may show disrupted behavior, and may want to escape the whole situation. Ask students for examples of shaping from real life. Point out that much shaping occurs without conscious intent. If you are really brave, you might ask your students how a class might conspire to shape the instructor's behavior.

Suggested Background Readings

Coon, D. *Introduction to psychology: Exploration and application.* New York: West Publishing, 1977. (chaps. 8, 9)

Malott, R. W., Ritterby, K., & Wolf, E. L. C. *An introduction to behavior modification.* Kalamazoo, Mich.: Behaviordelia, 1973.

Morgan, W. G. The shaping game: A teaching technique. *Behavior Therapy,* 1974, *5,* 271–272.

26

REINFORCING STATEMENTS
OF OPINION
B. R. Hergenhahn

Concept

This experiment provides an opportunity to examine the methods of operant conditioning by essentially replicating an earlier study by W. S. Verplanck (1955). If attention is reinforcing to a person, you should be able to increase the frequency of any response that is followed by attention. Also, if a "point" is important to a student, you should be able to increase the probability of a response by giving a student a "point" when that response occurs.

Instructions

Have students form experimenter–subject pairs. Orient experimenters to the experiment, out of subjects' earshot. Each experimenter will need a data recording sheet, a pencil, and a watch. Each subject will need a pencil and paper.

Have experimenters read the following instructions to subjects:

"I will ask you to begin talking. Talk on any topic you wish. I will say nothing at all. Do not let my silence disturb you. Your job is to work for points. You will receive a point each time I tap my pencil. As soon as you are given a point, record it by making a tally mark on your sheet of paper. You are to keep track of your own points. Do you have any questions? Please commence talking."

Each time the subject makes an opinionated statement such as "I think that . . ." or "I believe that . . . ," etc., the experimenter is to tap his or her pencil, thereby giving the subject a point.

Using the data recording sheet, have experimenters keep track of the number of opinionated statements in consecutive 3-minute intervals. Continue this process for 15 minutes. After 15 minutes stop giving points. This is the extinction period. Again keep track of how many opinionated statements are made. Continue extinction for 9 minutes.

Have experimenters ask subjects what they were doing to receive points. On the basis of what they say, classify them as "aware" or "unaware." Be sure not to tell them whether they were right or wrong until the entire experiment is over.

Combine data from all experimenters and plot the mean number of opinionated statements for each 3-minute interval, including extinction. Determine the percentage of subjects who were aware of the behavior that was being reinforced.

Discussion

Was operant conditioning demonstrated? Was extinction demonstrated? Describe other responses that could possibly be conditioned. Describe

From *A Self-Directing Introduction to Psychological Experimentation* (Second Edition), by B. R. Hergenhahn. Copyright © 1970, 1974 by Wadsworth, Inc. Reprinted by permission of the publisher, Brooks/Cole Publishing Company, Monterey, California.

other rewards that could be used as reinforcers. Will a reinforcer for one person necessarily be one for another person? Explain. How would you reinforce a masochist? Describe some implications of operant conditioning for teaching practices and childrearing.

Todd Risley of the University of Kansas points out some qualifying statements. Risley explains that although human verbal behavior obviously does come under operant control, it is very difficult to control the variables so that a clear cause-and-effect relationship can be established between them. In the first place, discriminating a correct response (a statement of opinion) from an incorrect one is not easy to do, and in the second place, the experimenter tends to become involved in the experiment by reinforcing the subject with other cues such as nodding, smiling, and asking questions. For elaboration of these points see the article by Azrin, Holz, Ulrich and Goldiamond (1961).

Suggested Background Readings

Azrin, N. H., Holz, W., Ulrich, R., & Goldiamind, I. The control of the content of conversation through reinforcement. *Journal of the Experimental Analysis of Behavior,* 1961, *4,* 25–30.

Greenspoon, J. The reinforcing effects of two spoken sounds on the frequency of two responses. *American Journal of Psychology,* 1955, *50,* 409–416.

Keller, F. S. *Learning: Reinforcement theory* (2nd ed.). New York: Random House, 1969.

Hildum, D. C., & Brown, R. W. Verbal reinforcement and interviewer bias. *Journal of Abnormal and Social Psychology,* 1956, *53,* 108–111.

Verplanck, W. S. The control of the content of conversation: Reinforcement of statements of opinion. *Journal of Abnormal and Social Psychology,* 1955, *51,* 668–676.

27

RECORDING AND SELF-MODIFICATION

Concept

A basic procedure in the experimental analysis of behavior is observation and recording of a selected behavior to establish a baseline of its occurrence. Once a baseline has been established, the experimental situation can be manipulated to determine the effects of selected variables on the behavior. Typically, observation and recording are done by second parties or are done mechanically, in part because observation of one's own behavior can have the effect of changing the behavior and thus distorting the baseline. However, self-observation is sometimes necessary (for example, when the behavior to be recorded is not readily observed), and it is acceptable in situations where scientific rigor is not essential. The activity that follows uses self-observation and builds on research indicating that self-observation by itself can sometimes modify the behavior being observed.

Instructions

First explain the nature of the activity to students, stressing that participation is voluntary. Then have those students who want to participate select a simple behavior they want to observe and record—a behavior they would like to increase or decrease. Some examples include punctuating sentences with "okay?" or "you know," biting one's nails, talking excessively on the telephone, watching too much television, smoking, saying "thank you," and complimenting others. Explain the methods and mechanics of observing and recording, and help students determine the best method for them to use (as described below). Then have them observe and record for an appropriate time period. Students who so desire can report to the class on the outcomes of their efforts—that is, the data they collected and whether they think observing and recording the behavior had the effect of modifying it.

Behaviors can be recorded in one of two ways: by frequency or by duration. The choice of method will depend on the nature of the behavior: If the behavior to be recorded is the habit of saying "you know," one will want to ascertain how many times the phrase is used in the course of a conversation. If on the other hand, the behavior is television-watching, the significant information is how many minutes or hours per day one engages in it. An important consideration in recording is whether the behavior is particular to a situation or is more generalized. If the former is true, the recording procedure should take it into account. For example, opportunities for a person to say "thank you" are obviously restricted to situations in which the person is the recipient of some kindness or favor. Thus, the person should record the number of times he or she actually said "thank you" relative to the number of opportunities that were presented to say it. Nail biting, by contrast, may be a continuous practice, in which case the person should note the number of times per day the behavior occurs. The recording itself can be done on a 3 × 5 card marked with appropriate recording categories (behaviors per day, behaviors per opportunities each day, etc.). For greatest reliability, the behaviors should be recorded as they occur, not stored mentally until the end of the day. How long the students conduct their self-observation will depend on the behavior involved. A week of self-observation should suffice for behaviors that occur frequently.

Discussion

Recording or charting one's behavior for a period of time can often result in dramatic changes in that behavior in the desired direction. For some people, this kind of feedback seems to be sufficient to alter behavior.

Recording some behavior, charting the results, and posting the chart in a conspicuous place can aid in the modification of one's behavior. Use an example like overeating. A number of variables might be recorded, such as number of meals (and snacks), size of portions eaten, and so forth. Although not a behavior, the easiest factor to record is your weight, which is after all the end product of your desired modification. Weigh yourself every day and keep a graph of the changes where you can see it, for example, on the refrigerator. If the curve starts to go up, that change in the chart can serve as a punisher. If it starts to go down, the change in that line may serve as an effective secondary reinforcer in helping you to lose weight. If simply charting the behavior does not eventually achieve the desired outcome, then other methods will be necessary. Students may want to work on complex behaviors or attempt self-modification using operant-conditioning procedures (see Watson & Tharp, 1972).

Suggested Background Readings

Goldiamond, I. Self-control procedures in personal behavior problems. *Psychological Reports,* 1965, *17,* 851–868.

Smith, W. I. *Conditioning and instrumental learning* (2nd ed.). New York: McGraw-Hill, 1978.

Watson, D. L., & Tharp, R. G. *Self-directed behavior: Self-modification for personal adjustment.* Monterey, Calif.: Brooks/Cole, 1972.

ACTIVITY
28

KNOWLEDGE OF RESULTS
Louis Snellgrove

Concept

Practice is important for learning, but is practice itself sufficient for learning to occur? The activity described here offers a way to assess the relative effectiveness of several kinds of practice.

Instructions

Divide the class into three groups, or if the class is large, choose 18 students, assigning six to each of three groups. Ask subjects to leave the room and to return one at a time for testing (or they can remain in the room as long as they do not observe the task). The task is to draw a line 24 inches long on the chalkboard while blindfolded. Give each subject 10 tries to draw accurately the 24-inch line (or an approximately 60-centimeter line, if you are metrically inclined). The groups will differ in terms of the feedback, or knowledge of results, that you give them. Give Group 1 full knowledge; that is, after each attempt, tell the subject the actual length of the line that was drawn. Give Group 2 partial knowledge; following each attempt, tell the subject only whether the line was too short or too long. Group 3 is the no-knowledge group. Have the subjects in this group draw 10 successive lines each, but give them no feedback on the accuracy of their performance. The results for each of the three groups should be summed across subjects for each of the 10 trials. You can plot the performance of each of the three groups, or you can look at the differential in performance on the first three trials compared to the last three trials for each of the groups.

Discussion

Of course, all three groups receive equal amounts of practice in this experiment. Group 3, the practice-only group, should show little or no improvement in drawing the line of desired length. In fact, that group should be as likely to get worse in their performance as to get better. Typically these subjects will become more consistent in drawing their lines in the later trials, but accuracy is something they cannot achieve without feedback. Both of the other groups should show marked improvement, with the full-knowledge group having the best performance. You can use this activity for a general discussion of the importance of feedback. How is feedback important for learning to control heart rate or skin temperature in a biofeedback task? What kind of feedback do we get in learning to ride a bicycle or drive a car? What kinds of feedback exist in the classroom to tell students about the progress of their learning?

Suggested Background Readings

Ellis, H. C., Bennett, T. L., Daniel, T. C., & Rickert, E. J. *Psychology of learning and memory*. Monterey, Calif.: Brooks/Cole, 1979.

Hulse, S. H., Deese, J. E., & Smith, H. E. *The psychology of learning* (5th ed.). New York: McGraw-Hill, 1980.

Logan, F. A., & Ferraro, D. P. *Systematic analyses of learning and motivation*. New York: Wiley, 1978.

29

COLOR BIND:
INTERFERENCE ON ATTENTION
Ray Brumbaugh

Concept

This exercise illustrates the Stroop effect, in which word meaning as a stimulus dimension interferes with color naming. It shows how difficult it can be to ignore irrelevant stimuli. Instructors who use this activity should be alert to the possibility of students who are color-blind.

Materials Needed

On a large sheet (about 22 × 28 inches) of white posterboard, print the words RED, BLUE, GREEN, YELLOW, and BLACK in random order four times each. Print the words large enough to be visible from any place in the room, and arrange them in five rows of four words each. Print each word in a different color than the color it names, varying the color you use. For example:

RED *(in yellow)*	BLUE *(in green)*	YELLOW *(in black)*	GREEN *(in red)*
BLUE *(in black)*	BLACK *(in red)*	YELLOW *(in green)*	RED *(in blue)*
GREEN *(in blue)*	RED *(in yellow)*	BLACK *(in yellow)*	YELLOW *(in red)*
YELLOW *(in red)*	GREEN *(in black)*	GREEN *(in blue)*	BLACK *(in blue)*
BLACK *(in green)*	BLUE *(in yellow)*	RED *(in black)*	BLUE *(in green)*

Instructions

Explain to students that you are going to present a chart of 20 words to two volunteers, in succession, and that you want the volunteers as quickly as possible to name the color in which each word is written. Then ask for two volunteers, send one out of the room, and present the chart to the other. Have a student record the time it takes the volunteer to complete the task, and have another student record errors (wrong calls, including those that are subsequently corrected). When the task has been completed, turn the chart upside down, ask the first volunteer to try once more, and again have time and errors recorded. Performance the second time should be much better because the meaning of the words is less likely to interfere with attention to the color in which they are printed.

Now bring in the second volunteer and have him or her perform the same two tasks. This time, however, present the chart upside down first, then right side up. (The second volunteer thus counterbalances any effect that practice may have had on the performance of the first volunteer.)

The demonstration can be extended to explore the effects of practice on performance by having each volunteer go through 10 trials with the chart right side up. To control for possible memorizing of sequence, the chart should be cut vertically into four panels that can then be shuffled for each trial.

Discussion

Questions for discussion include the following: Why is there interference in color naming? If instead of words, the colors were simply blocks, would the amount of time needed to complete the list be the same? Would printing the words in a foreign language (one that the volunteers had studied in school) produce partial interference? Why? If a student was color-blind, what kind of response might be anticipated? How would you know if the student were color-blind?

Suggested Background Readings

Golden, C. J. Effect of differing number of colors on the Stroop Color and Word Test. *Perceptual & Motor Skills,* 1974, *39,* 550.

Golden, C. J. Sex differences in performance on the Stroop Color and Word Test. *Perceptual & Motor Skills,* 1974, *39,* 1067–1070.

Golden, C. J., Marsella, A. J., & Golden, E. E. Personality correlates of the Stroop Color and Word Test: More negative results. *Perceptual & Motor Skills,* 1975, *41,* 599–602.

Singer, M. H., Lappin, J. S., & Moore, L. P. The interference of various word parts on color naming in the Stroop test. *Perception & Psychophysics,* 1975, *18,* 191–193.

Wise, L. A., Sutton, J. A., & Gibbons, P. D. Decrement in Stroop interference time with age. *Perceptual & Motor Skills,* 1975, *41,* 149–150.

ACTIVITY
30

PERFORMANCE
AND NEGATIVE TRANSFER
T. L. Engle and Louis Snellgrove

Concept

This exercise provides a good vehicle for practice in collecting, analyzing, and plotting data, as well as a demonstration of learning and negative transfer. It has the added virtues of (a) requiring minimal equipment, (b) providing an easy means for simultaneous involvement of all members of a class, and (c) being easily assigned as an out-of-class activity, the results of which can be tabulated and discussed in class. Required materials include a deck of playing cards, a table, a stopwatch (a watch with a sweep second hand will do), and four pieces of paper for every two students.

Instructions

Draw a club, diamond, heart, and spade on the four pieces of paper, one suit per piece. Using masking tape, divide the top of the table into four sections, and place one of the pieces in the far corner of each section. Have a student subject stand in front of the table holding a deck of cards face down. Turning the cards face up one at a time, the subject should sort the deck into the four quadrants of the table according to suit. A student experimenter should keep an accurate record of the time it takes the subject to place the cards correctly. Errors should also be tallied, including those corrected by the subject. The subject should repeat the sorting of the deck 10 times, with the experimenter shuffling the cards well between trials.

After the tenth trial, the subject should walk around to the opposite side of the table and follow the same procedure as in the first 10 trials, sorting the cards an additional 10 times from the new position. Again have the experimenter record time and errors for each trial.

If time permits, experimenter and subject should swap roles and repeat the experiment. Then have the experimenters draw four performance curves for their subjects, two curves for time on the two sets of trials, and two for errors. Plot time and errors on the ordinate (vertical axis) and Trials 1–10 on the abscissa (horizontal axis). Comparison of performance on the two sets of trials is aided by plotting both time curves on one graph and both error curves on another.

Discussion

Discussion can focus on a wide variety of learning phenomena. For example, does the subject's performance improve during the first 10 trials? What happens to the subject's performance at the start of the second 10 trials? How does it compare with his or her performance at the start of the first 10 trials? What principle has been demonstrated? Where in the sets of 10 trials was the improvement in performance greatest and

Adapted from *Psychology: Its Principles and Applications,* Fifth Edition by T. L. Engle and Louis Snellgrove, copyright © 1969 by Harcourt Brace Jovanovich, Inc. Reprinted by permission of the publisher.

where was it least? What would be the best control group to use to substantiate impressions formed in comparing the two sets of trials?

If a sufficient number of students is available to supply data, some interesting variations can be worked into the basic comparison. For example, what is the effect on performance of increasing the rest between trials in the first set? In the second set? What happens when the length of the rest period between sets is varied? In addition, retention of skills from the first set can be measured using the savings method: How does performance on the first set a second time around compare with performance on the second set the first time it was attempted?

Suggested Background Readings

Kimble, G. A., Garmezy, N., & Zigler, E. *Principles of general psychology* (5th ed.). New York: Wiley, 1980. (See Part II)

Osgood, C. E. The similarity paradox in human learning: A resolution. *Psychological Review,* 1949, *56,* 132–143.

Zimbardo, P. G., & Ruch, F. L. *Psychology and life* (9th ed.). Glenview, Ill.: Scott, Foresman, 1977. (chap. 3)

31

LEARNING CURVES
David Holmer

Concept

The nature of learning as illustrated by the shape of the classic learning curve is one of the oldest facts in the history of modern psychology. The exercises described here provide a number of verbal and motor tasks in which performance can be assessed. The exercises include throwing darts, typing, negotiating a finger maze, memorizing poetry, and memorizing nonsense syllables or numbers. Each exercise can be assigned to a group of students, some of whom successively perform the task while others record performance or accuracy as a function of trials or length of practice. The chart below can be used to record data.

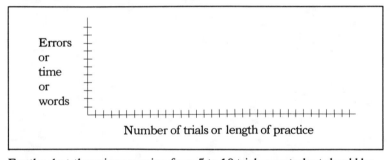

Errors or time or words

Number of trials or length of practice

Instructions

For the dart-throwing exercise, from 5 to 10 trials per student should be sufficient to yield a significant curve. Each trial should consist of the student throwing five darts. Recorders should plot average error for the trial, error being defined as distance from the bull's eye. The curve should show a decrease in average error as a function of trials.

In the typing exercise, each student should type steadily for 15 minutes, with a recorder sampling performance every 3 minutes for a 1-minute period. Performance should be recorded in number of words per minute as a function of length of practice. The curve should show an initial increase in words per minute followed by a gradual leveling off.

Performance in negotiating a raised finger maze (which the students can easily construct with small wooden dowels from a picture of a rat maze) can be plotted in terms of errors as a function of trials or time per trial. Errors here are defined as entries into a cul-de-sac or blind alley. In either case the curve should show a decrease as a function of trials. Trials should be continued until the curve reaches an asymptote.

For poetry memorizing, short rhyming poems should be used, one per student. Give each student 1 minute's practice (silent reading), then have him or her recite the poem. Repeat the practice/trial sequence five times. Plot number of words recalled as a function of length of practice. The curve should show an increase followed by a gradual leveling off. The same procedure can be used for memorization of nonsense syllables or numbers and should yield a similar curve.

Discussion

The variety of learning tasks covers quite a range, including tasks that are primarily motor learning (or perceptual-motor learning) and those that are largely cognitive. The data you collect in these exercises can be used to compare the course of learning in each task. Are there differences across tasks? If so, why? Do individuals who learn rapidly in one kind of learning task also learn rapidly in the others? Discuss the role of associations in learning. For example, why use nonsense syllables to measure learning? What advantages do they offer as material to be learned? Rhyming verse was used in one of the tasks. What would acquisition have looked like if prose had been used instead? What if you had chosen a prose passage written in a foreign language with which the students were unfamiliar?

Suggested Background Readings

Ellis, H. C., Bennett, T. L., Daniel, T. C., & Rickert, E. J. *Psychology of learning and memory.* Monterey, Calif.: Brooks/Cole, 1979.

Hulse, S. H., Deese, J. E., & Smith, H. E. *The psychology of learning* (5th ed.). New York: McGraw-Hill, 1980.

Zimbardo, P. G. *Psychology and life* (10th ed.). Glenview, Ill.: Scott, Foresman, 1979.

CHAPTER IV
MEMORY AND COGNITION

The 16 activities in this chapter are designed for use in the classroom. All but one of the activities involve the entire class simultaneously. Memory, language, problem solving, transfer, and creativity are among the topics covered by demonstrations and experiments in this chapter.

Activity 32 illustrates a number of memory phenomena, including forgetting curves, serial position effect, and the effects of emphasis, repetition, and meaningfulness on retention. Activity 33 looks at memory storage and the reconstructive nature of memory that becomes apparent when missing details are added in recall. Activity 34 contrasts the two most commonly used methods for measuring retention—recall and recognition.

Four activities stress the importance of meaningfulness for memory: Activity 35 demonstrates the enhancement of recall, Activity 36 shows the importance of context for interpreting and recalling material, Activity 37 illustrates the role of association value in memorization, and Activity 38 demonstrates how emphasis can make nonmeaningful material impossible to forget.

Retroactive and proactive inhibition are components of Activity 39, which looks at interference in learning and retention. Activity 40 illustrates transfer in a mirror-tracing task and leads to discussion of transfer in other forms of learning.

Three activities describe problem-solving demonstrations: Activity 41 investigates the effectiveness of problem solving by individuals versus groups, Activity 42 looks at set as an aid and a hindrance to problem solving, and Activity 43 provides an example of the Zeigarnik effect relating memory to success and failure in a problem-solving situation.

The final four activities focus on other phenomena within the field of cognition. Concept learning using Greek-letter trigrams is described in Activity 44. Activity 45 illustrates the meaning of the word *language* and its role in communication. Various aspects of creativity are explored in Activity 46, which is designed to enhance student creativity. Activity 47 uses a semantic clustering technique to demonstrate the role of unconscious processes in categorization in a recall task.

ACTIVITY

32

MEMORY AND FORGETTING
Michael Wertheimer

Concept

This simple pencil-and-paper experiment can demonstrate a number of principles of memory and forgetting including the forgetting curve, meaningfulness, repetition, emphasis, and the serial position effect.

Instructions

At the beginning of a class session, divide the class into four approximately equal groups. Ask the students to take out a blank piece of paper and to write their group number (1, 2, 3, or 4) on it. Then tell the class that they are to memorize a list of items, which you will read to them twice. The following list works reasonably well: envelope, bex, nav, Carter, ruj, fet, textbook, nav, Nixon, fulfill, GEF, mandate, fet, 47, tal. Present the items slowly and distinctly, with a uniform interval of a second or two between successive items; both pronounce and spell the nonsense syllables (e.g., bex, B - E - X); and shout at the top of your lungs when you read GEF. Try to make your second reading of the list as similar to the first reading as possible.

As soon as the second reading is finished, ask Group 1 to write down as many of the items as they can remember. Tell the remaining students not to write down any items until asked. Conduct class as usual for the rest of the hour, but about 3 minutes after you ask Group 1 to recall the list, ask Group 2 to do so; some 5 minutes after that, ask the same of Group 3. Then wait until the end of the hour (approximately 45 minutes or so after memorization) to ask Group 4 to recall all of the items they can.

Discussion

The mean number of items correctly recalled by each of the four groups typically shows a classical, negatively accelerated forgetting curve. Averaging for percent recall of each item across groups demonstrates additional principles. Thus, more meaningful material is better recalled than less meaningful material (familiar names average best, words come next, and nonsense materials are recalled least well). Repeated nonsense syllables are remembered better than nonrepeated ones. Items that stand out perceptually (the two-place number and the shouted syllable) are typically better remembered than their control counterparts (the nonrepeated nonsense syllables). The serial position effect (items just past the middle of the list are less well remembered than items near the end, and items near the beginning are remembered best of all) usually appears in both the nonrepeated nonsense syllables and in the words.

This demonstration can be varied in a number of ways, of course, by using different items, different numbers of repetitions, and so on. You can also ask the class, perhaps 2 weeks later, to recall as many items as they can. Many will be surprised at how much they can remember that long after the original learning, that is, at how flat the forgetting curve is after the initial, fairly steep drop. You may also get creative errors in recall (such as nave, DEAF, gaff, towel, grudge, football, or vex).

Suggested Background Readings

Glanzer, M., & Cunitz, A. R. Two storage mechanisms in free recall. *Journal of Verbal Learning and Verbal Behavior,* 1966, *5*, 351–360.

Gruneberg, M. M., Morris, P. E., & Sykes, R. N. *Practical aspects of memory.* New York: Academic Press, 1978.

Hunter, I. M. L. *Memory.* Baltimore: Penguin Books, 1964.

ACTIVITY

RECONSTRUCTIVE NATURE OF HUMAN MEMORY
Richard A. Kasschau

Concept

Two views have long been held as to how we humans store information for later use. We might view memory as analogous to a series of mailroom sorting bins in which a series of entire memories are stored *in toto,* to be pulled out and used as necessary. This is the *reappearance* notion—that each act of remembering is simply the arousal of something that already exists. However, the work of Loftus and Palmer (1974) and other studies of eyewitness testimony have suggested that this is not the case. A newer view suggests that for any past event, what we tend to store is just a few elements or rules or facts which will allow us to reconstruct the memory as necessary—the *utilization* view. If this is true, then one obvious question concerns how it is that we come to sense the need to reconstruct a particular memory. More specifically, does the nature of a question that we are required to answer influence in any way how we reconstruct our memory of a past event? The following data and demonstration bear on this question.

Instructions

The figure on the next page includes several pieces of information. Reproduce each drawing in Column A so that each drawing fills a single sheet of paper large enough to be seen anywhere in your classroom. You should also create two "answer sheets" by copying all the terms on List 1 and List 2 in Column B onto separate sheets of paper, arranging each list down the left side of the paper with enough room between each word so a student can draw the indicated figure. You will also need either a stopwatch or a watch with a sweep second hand.

Present each figure, one at a time, for 10 seconds, and ask your class to look at it and try to remember it without having any paper in front of them. Then pass out either a copy of List 1 or List 2 (as reproduced from the figure) to each student. Do *not* tell your students until the experiment is completed that different cues are being used on each list, but pass out equal numbers of both lists. Allow your students five minutes to recall and draw as many of the stimulus figures as they can, and then collect all the answer sheets, separating them into stacks of List 1 and List 2.

Discussion

Loftus and Palmer (1974) had subjects view a movie of a minor, fender-bender accident. After viewing, the subjects were asked a series of questions, one of which varied critically in how it was expressed. The question was, "About how fast were each of the cars going when they *(verb)ed* each other?" Loftus and Palmer found that when more and more violent verbs were used in the question, the mean speed estimate

Adapted from *Teacher's Guide With Tests to Accompany Psychology: Exploring Behavior* by R. A. Kasschau. Copyright 1980 by Prentice-Hall Publishing Company. Reprinted by permission.

Stimulus figures, word lists, and sample reproduced figures to be used in demonstrating the reconstructive nature of human memory.

	(a)	(b)	(c)	
	LIST 1	LIST 2	SAMPLE 1	SAMPLE 2
⊙—⊙	Eyeglasses	Dumbbells		
	Bottle	Stirrup		
	Crescent Moon	Letter "C"		
	Beehive	Hat		
	Curtains in a Window	Diamond in a Rectangle		
7	Seven	Four		
	Ship's Wheel	Sun		
	Hourglass	Table		

(Adapted from L. Carmichael, H. P. Hogan, & A. A. Walter, "An Experimental Study of the Effect of Language on the Reproduction of Visually Perceived Form." *Journal of Experimental Psychology*, 1932, *15*, 73–86.)

increased. And even more impressive was their finding that in response to later questions which were identical, different subjects gave different answers as a result of which question they had previously been asked. Specifically, in response to the question "Did you see any broken glass?" 16% of those previously hearing "smashed" responded yes, and 34% said no. But for those who had previously heard "hit," only 7% responded yes, and 43% said no. Using a more violent verb in a preceding question more than doubled the number of persons who indicated they had seen broken glass even though there was none!

In this context you can now analyze your class's responses. While presenting each of the original stimulus forms again, read the two cues that were offered, and examine each stack of answer sheets to find evidence as to whether the clue offered on List 1 caused some students to remember the form differently than those responding to List 2. Again, your data should indicate the reconstructive nature of memory and the impact of retrieval cues on the "memory" actually recalled. Column C in the figure includes some sample drawings from an early study of this process (Carmichael, Hogan, & Walter, 1932).

What are the implications of this research for how to obtain the most accurate "eyewitness testimony"? Seemingly, the most accurate recall is elicited by the most neutral possible question.

Suggested Background Readings

Carmichael, L., Hogan, H. P., & Walter, A. A. An experimental study of the effect of language on the reproduction of visually perceived form. *Journal of Experimental Psychology*, 1932, *15*, 73–86.

Loftus, E., & Palmer, J. Reconstruction of automobile destruction: An example of the interaction between language and memory. *Journal of Verbal Learning and Verbal Behavior*, 1974, *13*, 585–589.

ACTIVITY

34

RECALL VERSUS RECOGNITION
Marty Klein

Concept

There are three general methods for measuring retention: recall, recognition, and relearning (also called the savings method). This activity compares the first two techniques.

Instructions

You will need about 15 miscellaneous objects for this activity—for example, chalk, stapler, coin, tape, light bulb, spoon, screwdriver, and so forth. You will also need a mimeographed listing of these 15 objects interspersed with approximately 25 additional objects. Pass out the mimeographed list (of 40 items) *face down* to half of the students in the class (every other person if possible). Give the other students a piece of blank paper. Tell the students that you will present a variety of items that they will be asked to remember. The items to be presented should be hidden from view under a cloth or in a paper bag or box. Present the objects one at a time for 3–5 seconds each (in random order), and then remove them from view. Announce the name of the object as you display it. After all of the items have been presented, ask the people with the mimeographed list to turn their papers over and circle those items that they saw (recognition group). Ask the remainder of the class to list as many items as they can remember (recall group). On the chalkboard, prepare a table of three columns labeled "Item," "Recall," and "Recognition." Show each item again and record the number of students (show of hands) in each group that remembered the item.

The recognition group should perform significantly better than the recall group. Alternatively, you could collect the data sheets for both groups, compiling the results yourself and reporting back at the next class period. You could even use a *t* test to assess whether performance in the two groups differed significantly (see Appendix A).

Discussion

Why is recognition said to be a more sensitive measure of retention than recall? What is relearning and how does it compare to the other methods in measuring retention? What does this demonstration say about testing—for example, multiple-choice versus essay questions? Would you study differently if you knew your test would require only recognition rather than recall?

If some particular items were remembered much better than others, this fact can lead to discussion of some of the principles of memory. You might want to select objects that are likely to show sex differences. To demonstrate some principles of long-term memory, you might ask the class to recall or recognize the same items several days later or several weeks or months later.

Suggested Background Readings

Bahrick, H. P. Retention curves: Facts or artifacts? *Psychological Bulletin,* 1964, *61,* 188–194.

Cofer, C. N. On some factors in the organizational characteristics of free recall. *American Psychologist,* 1965, 20, 261–272.

Crowder, R. G. *Principles of learning and memory.* New York: Halsted Press, 1976.

Mussen, P., Rosenzweig, M. R., et al. *Psychology: An introduction* (2nd ed.). Lexington, Mass.: D. C. Heath, 1977. (chap. 15)

ACTIVITY

35

MEANING ENHANCES RECALL
James Jenkins

Concept

The activity that follows shows how "meaning" can aid memory and "nonmeaning" can hinder it. The activity also illustrates the recall method as a research technique, shows how memory depends mostly on what people are doing during information processing, and illustrates experiments in which each subject is used as his or her own control.

Instructions

Make a list of 20 common nouns that are not related to each other in any obvious ways. Some should be one syllable; some should be two syllables or more. Write each noun on a 3 x 5 card. On 10 of the cards write the letter A after the word, and on the rest write the letter B. Shuffle the cards so that the A's and the B's are well intermixed. Now you are ready for the class.

Have each student take a sheet of paper and number down the side from 1 to 20. Tell the students that they are going to hear a list of words that you will ask them to recall later but that first you want them to rate the words on two judgments. The letter that follows the word will tell them the judgment you want. If the word is followed by an A, you want them to write down how many syllables there are in the word. If the word is followed by a B, you want them to write whether it is pleasant or unpleasant (P for pleasant and U for unpleasant). You can put this information on the chalkboard as a reminder.

Read the list of words at the rate of one word every 4 seconds or so. For example, "Table (pause), B (count 1, 2, to yourself), Ocean (pause), A." When you have read the whole list, ask the students to turn over their papers, to try to recall all of the words they have just heard in any order they want, and to write down the words in a straight column. (Your purpose here is to provide a little delay and to make the data easy to handle.) In 3 or 4 minutes they will have written all the words that they can recall.

Let the students score their own papers. Sort out the A cards and read the words to the class. Have each student total how many he or she recalled. Then make a frequency distribution on the board. Ask the class how many recalled all 10 of the words, how many recalled 9, 8, and so on. Now, score the B words. Make a frequency distribution right beside the first one. Some students will recall 8 or 9 of these 10 words, and the average is likely to be twice as high for the pleasant–unpleasant words as for the syllable-counted words.

Discussion

To demonstrate the use of subjects as their own controls, find out how many students recalled more A words than B words and how many recalled more B words than A words. Often no one falls in the first group, and everyone falls in the second. Ask the class how to generalize from this. What other tasks would work this way? What tasks would be good for remembering, and which would be poor? Those that require thinking about the *meaning* of the word are generally good for recall: Is the word important or unimportant? What adjective goes with the noun? Would it be pleasant or unpleasant on a desert island? Tasks concentrating on the form of the word are bad for memory: Is it spelled with an e? How many letters are in it? Give me a word that rhymes with it. If you have more word lists ready, it is easy to test the students' ideas immediately. Finally, ask what the implications are for how one ought to study!

Suggested Background Readings

Cofer, C. N. Constructive processes in memory. *American Scientist,* 1973, *61,* 537–543.

Klatzky, R. L. *Human memory, structures and processes* (2nd ed.). San Francisco: W. H. Freeman, 1979.

Miller, G. A., & Selfridge, J. A. Verbal context and the recall of meaningful material. *American Journal of Psychology,* 1950, *63,* 176–185.

ACTIVITY
36

CONTEXT AND MEMORY
Marty Klein

Concept

Memory is affected by a number of variables, some that enhance retention and some that promote forgetting. Perhaps the most important factor in learning and memory is the meaningfulness of the material involved. One way to increase the meaning of material is to place that material in context. This activity illustrates that principle.

Instructions

Give half of the students in your class a piece of paper that contains the statement, "The context is kite flying." Indicate to these students that they are not to reveal the contents of this message to their classmates. Then read the following paragraph aloud, very slowly:

"A newspaper is better than a magazine. A seashore is a better place than the street. At first it is better to run than to walk. You may have to try several times. It takes some skill but is easy to learn. Even young children can enjoy it. Once successful, complications are minimal. Birds seldom get too close. Rain, however, soaks in very fast. Too many people doing the same thing can also cause problems. One needs lots of room. If there are no complications it can be very peaceful. A rock will serve as an anchor. If things break loose from it, however, you will not get a second chance."

Ask all the students to take out pencil and paper and write down as much of the paragraph just read as they can recall. Have those students who had been given the contextual statement in advance mark their papers so that you will be able to identify their responses. Collect the responses and compare the recall of each half of the class on a line-by-line basis. If you want to quantify the two sets of papers for a more accurate assessment of differences between the two groups, you should plan on providing the results at the next class meeting and holding discussion over until that next session. In that event, you should use the first part of this activity—that is, the actual recall task—at the close of a class period so that you collect the responses at the end of class.

Discussion

Obviously, knowing the context adds meaning to material that might otherwise appear as a set of unrelated statements. The context makes organization of learning possible. If organized properly, "one thing leads to another." What does this principle suggest about study strategies? If you wish, you might extend the discussion to the importance of context in perception and how it serves to enhance perceptual abilities.

Suggested Background Readings

Crowder, R. G. *Principles of learning and memory.* New York: Halsted Press, 1976.

Houston, J. P., Bee, H., Hatfield, E., & Rimm, D. C. *Invitation to psychology.* New York: Academic Press, 1979. (chaps. 6, 8)

Miller, G. A., & Selfridge, J. A. Verbal context and the recall of meaningful material. *American Journal of Psychology,* 1950, *63,* 176–185.

ACTIVITY

37

MEANINGFULNESS AND MEMORY
P. S. Fernald and L. D. Fernald, Jr.

Concept

This exercise effectively demonstrates the impact of meaningfulness or association value on the ease of memorizing items important to us all—telephone numbers.

Instructions

Which kind of "numbers" should be assigned to telephones—all digits, prefixed (mixed), or all letters? To collect data helpful in deciding which form is best, present the three lists below to students. First, expose the all-digit list on the chalkboard or screen for 30 seconds. Then allow students 30 seconds to write down as many of the seven number sequences as they can remember, in any order. Repeat the procedure with the all-letter list and then with the prefixed list.

645-2685	OIL BOTL	SE2-6455
363-6422	EME NIBB	TR6-5447
825-9746	HAL YRIN	BY4-3977
732-6455	SEA MILK	MI5-2685
876-5447	TRO KHIS	HA5-9746
294-3977	BYG FYSS	EM3-6422

Have students score their performances on each list, and then compute a class mean for the three types of numbers. Memory for the prefixed numbers should exceed memory for the all-digit numbers, and the all-letter "numbers" should be the most easily recalled. Point out that the three lists are comparable for dialing instructions, since the prefixed and all-letter lists were derived from the numbers on the all-digit list. (The numbers represent a random selection.)

Discussion

Discussion questions might include the following: If you were advising the telephone company, which form of numbers would you recommend? Why? Why are the all-letter "numbers" easier to remember? This point can lead to a discussion of association values and the difficulty of controlling for association values when using so-called "nonsense" syllables in studies of memory. How would you code the telephone number 732-6455 into letters so that it would be easily remembered? So it would be difficult to remember? Here tell the students which letters accompany the various numbers on the telephone dial: 2—ABC, 3—DEF, 4—GHI, 5—JKL, 6—MNO, 7—PRS, 8—TUV, 9—WXY.

Students may ask why telephone companies do not use letters. There appears to be no reasonable basis for not changing, other than that

Adapted from *Introduction to Psychology,* 3d ed., *Instructor's Manual,* by Norman L. Munn, Peter S. Fernald, and L. Dodge Fernald. Copyright © 1972 by Houghton Mifflin Company. Used by permission.

ACTIVITIES HANDBOOK

the present system, like any well-established pattern of behavior, is not easily replaced. Dvorak's improved typewriter keyboard never has been widely accepted, and pigeons are not used as pill inspectors although they inspect with greater accuracy than humans.

Suggested Background Readings

Noble, C. E. An analysis of meaning. *Psychological Review,* 1952, *59,* 421–430.

Noble, C. E., & McNeely, D. A. The role of meaningfulness (m) in paired-associate verbal learning. *Journal of Experimental Psychology,* 1957, *53,* 16–22.

Silverman, R. E. *Psychology* (2nd ed.). New York: Appleton-Century-Crofts, 1974. (chap. 7)

Zimbardo, P. G., & Ruch, F. L. *Psychology and life* (9th ed.). Glenview, Ill.: Scott, Foresman, 1977. (chap. 4)

38

MEANING AND MEMORY: AN ASSIGNMENT TO BE FORGOTTEN
Ludy T. Benjamin, Jr.

Concept

This exercise is intended to illustrate the importance of meaning as a factor in retention. The procedure purportedly originated with the magician Harry Blackstone.

Instructions

For this activity, you will need a chalkboard, a piece of chalk, an eraser, and some facility at acting, including the ability to keep a straight face. This activity requires from 10 to 15 minutes (depending on how longwinded you choose to be) and should be conducted at the close of a class period. It represents a particularly good way to introduce your class to the topic of memory. End your lecture (or other activity) early and announce to the class that you are about to give them a homework assignment. A possible script is as follows:

"I am going to give you a homework assignment that I expect you to have successfully completed by our next class meeting. This assignment will require no writing or reading. In fact you don't even have to do any thinking. Nevertheless, it is an important assignment, one that I believe is critical for your performance in this course. Frankly, I am concerned that some of you will not take this assignment seriously. You will no doubt view it as a trivial activity and will therefore put out little or no effort in an attempt to complete it. If you are in that category, then I suggest you seriously consider why you are taking this course. It could be that you are wasting your time. On the other hand, there are those of you who will work extremely hard on this assignment and for that effort I am very grateful." (etc., etc.)

Your speech should be serious in tone as well as content, and your face should project that concern as well. Time your "message" to end approximately one minute before the end of the class period. At that point, go to the chalkboard and write a three-digit number (107 for example). Make large numbers so they are clearly visible in the back of the room. Step to the side in order not to obscure the view of the students. Keep looking at the numbers (not at the students) for about 5 to 10 seconds. Then erase the numbers. Turn toward your class and announce, "Your assignment for our next class meeting is to forget the number you just saw." In a few seconds you should begin to observe some smiling faces (hesitantly at first) and then laughter as more and more of the students realize what has happened. Indicate that you have attempted to demonstrate how meaning can be attached to an otherwise meaningless number. You might ask for a show of hands from those students who believe they will be unable to complete the assignment. Most of the students (if not all of them) will usually raise their hands.

Discussion

At the next class meeting, ask for a show of hands from those students who were unable to forget the number and from those students who were able to forget. Ask them to verbalize why they were or were not able to forget. You can then lead the discussion to a number of related topics on the importance of meaning in learning and memory—the use of nonsense syllables, grouping of material (chunking), mnemonic systems or devices, learning material in an unfamiliar language compared to learning the same material in your native language, and so forth. This discussion presents a good opportunity to talk about the ease of learning and remembering material that is highly valued by an individual. For example, many people seem to have incredible memories on certain topics: batting averages in baseball, mintage figures for coins, a myriad of facts about old movies and movie stars, and details about Civil War battles. Get the class to speculate about the nature of learning and forgetting in situations like those described.

While it is likely that the emphasis you attached to the number is the reason it was remembered, it is also possible that the retention was due to rehearsal. That is, in attempting to forget the number, the student was forced to think of the number and thus rehearsed it many times in an attempt to consciously forget it. Although this explanation seems less plausible, it can provide some interesting discussion about what really happens to prevent one from forgetting the number.

Suggested Background Readings

Cofer, C. N. Constructive processes in memory. *American Scientist,* 1973, *61,* 537–543.

Gruneberg, M. M., Morris, P. E., & Sykes, R. N. *Practical aspects of memory.* New York: Academic Press, 1978.

Hunter, I. M. L. *Memory.* Baltimore: Penguin Books, 1964. (especially pp. 110–123)

Klatzky, R. L. *Human memory, structures and processes* (2nd ed.). San Francisco: W. H. Freeman, 1979.

39

RETROACTIVE AND PROACTIVE INHIBITION
John K. Bare

Concept

Retroactive inhibition refers to difficulties with the retention of previously learned material caused by the interference of more recently learned material. Proactive inhibition describes the difficulties in learning and retention caused by the interference of previously learned material. Both forms of inhibition can be demonstrated with this activity.

Instructions

Read list M_1 (see table) to students five times (allowing 2 seconds between words and perhaps 4 seconds between repetitions). At the end of the fifth reading, engage students in a task for 5 minutes to help prevent rehearsal (for example, have them count backwards from 2000 by 7s and write down the numbers). Then ask them to recall as many of the 10 adjectives as possible and record their scores.

Next, using the same reading procedure, have the students learn list O_1 and immediately thereafter list P_1, at which point they should resume the diversionary task begun earlier and pursue it for another 5 minutes. Ask then for a recall of list O_1, and again have students record their scores.

Several options are now open. The procedure can be reversed, as follows: Learn list O_2, learn list P_2, rest, recall list P_2; learn list M_2, rest, recall list M_2. The experimental design would thus include counterbalancing. Or one might stop, analyze the data, and ask for criticisms of the design, anticipating that someone will suggest the reversal. Alternatively, proactive inhibition can be demonstrated using the second set of lists and the following design (and its reverse): Learn list M_2, rest, recall list M_2; learn list O_2, learn list P_2, rest, recall list P_2.

Students can convert their scores into percentage measures of retroaction by subtracting their O scores from their M scores, dividing the differences by their M scores, and multiplying by 100.

Word Lists for Learning and Recall

LIST M_1	LIST O_1	LIST P_1	LIST O_2	LIST P_2	LIST M_2
middle	parched	thirsty	pretty	lovely	golden
mixed	clumsy	aware	missing	unsought	direct
sleepy	afraid	rigid	nervous	active	slavish
stylish	creased	fearful	polite	civil	elfish
honored	stalwart	brawny	funny	absent	dusky
untrue	conscious	awkward	unasked	restless	neuter
mongrel	severe	folded	ailing	sickly	heavy
piercing	joyous	happy	lively	comic	elder
futile	tiresome	humdrum	smaller	minor	unsound
muddy	stained	soiled	living	vital	pearly

Discussion

The demonstration seldom fails, particularly because the P lists contain synonyms of the O lists. Retroactive inhibition is greater when synonyms are used. You could set up an experiment to test that assertion by using lists without synonyms for one group and lists with synonyms for the other. How does this demonstration relate to studying for two exams in different subject areas?

Suggested Background Readings

Bilodeau, I. M., & Schlosberg, H. Similarity in stimulating conditions as a variable in retroactive inhibition. *Journal of Experimental Psychology,* 1952, *42,* 199–204.

Keppel, G. Retroactive and proactive inhibition. In T. R. Dixon & D. L. Horton (Eds.), *Verbal behavior and general behavior theory.* Englewood Cliffs, N.J.: Prentice-Hall, 1968.

Thune, L. E., & Underwood, B. J. Retroactive inhibition as a function of degree of interpolated learning. *Journal of Experimental Psychology,* 1943, *32,* 185–199.

Underwood, B. J. Proactive inhibition as a function of time and degree of learning. *Journal of Experimental Psychology,* 1949, *39,* 24–34.

ACTIVITY
40

TRANSFER OF TRAINING: STAR TRACK
Ray Brumbaugh

Concept

This activity tests whether there is positive transfer of training from one hand to the other in a mirror-tracing task. The procedure described here uses a mirror-tracing device; however, a television camera and monitor will also work if you have students trace a pattern guided by its image on the television monitor.

Materials Needed

Tracing sheets, a short pencil, mirror-tracing equipment, a timer, and graph paper.

Instructions

To prepare a master tracing sheet, on $8^{1}/_{2} \times 11$ inch paper draw a six-pointed star that measures about 8 inches from top to bottom. Inside that star, draw another star about one-quarter inch smaller. The result should be a star with double borders about one-quarter inch apart. Subjects trace the star by drawing between the parallel lines. Mirror-tracing equipment can be readily fashioned from a mirror and a cardboard box. The box should be about 10 inches wide, 10 inches long, and 5 inches high, and the mirror should be at least 7 inches high and 10 inches wide. Cut two parallel 10-inch sides out of the box, and place it on a table so that one open side will face a seated subject. Prop the mirror to face the other open side. Position the tracing sheet inside the box so that the top of the box blocks the sheet itself from view but the mirror reflects the image of the star to the subject.

Introduce the activity by explaining the concept of transfer of training. Then ask for volunteer subjects from the class. You will need at least 10 but can use more if you have time. Divide the subjects evenly into two groups—experimental and control—and instruct them as follows: "Start at the point indicated and trace along the path of the star until you return to the starting place. Try not to let your pencil point even touch the borders of the path. If you do cross a border, don't continue forward; trace back to the point at which the error occurred and then proceed. Make the trip along the path as rapidly as you can, consistent with the avoidance and correction of errors." When subjects are tracing with their right hands, they should move clockwise, starting at the V between the two left points of the star. When they are tracing with their left hands, they should move counterclockwise, starting at the V between the two right points.

As a preliminary test, have each subject in both groups trace the star five times using the nonpreferred hand. Time each trial, and plot the times and trials on a separate graph for each subject (trials on the abscissa, times on the ordinate). Mark this curve "N(1–5)" to represent performance with the nonpreferred hand on the first 5 trials. Next, train each subject in the experimental group by having him or her trace the star 10 times with the preferred hand, again timing and plotting performance on each trial. Mark this curve "P(1–10)." Finally, have each subject in both groups trace the star 5 more times with the nonpreferred hand. Time and plot performance, and mark the curve "N(6–10)."

For each group, compute the average time on trials N(1–5) and N(6–10), figure the difference between the two averages, and divide it by the average time on trials N(1–5). Then compare the results for the two groups.

Discussion

Performance on the last five trials should be significantly better in the experimental group. That is, training with the preferred hand should transfer positively to the nonpreferred hand.

This activity can be used as a basis for a discussion of transfer in general, for example, positive versus negative transfer, conditions that facilitate or hinder transfer, theories of transfer, transfer in animals (see Harlow, 1949), and so forth.

Suggested Background Readings

Goss, A. E. Transfer as a function of type and amount of preliminary experience with task stimuli. *Journal of Experimental Psychology,* 1953, *46,* 419–427.

Grose, R. F., & Birney, R. C. (Eds.). *Transfer of learning.* Princeton, N.J.: Van Nostrand, 1963.

Harlow, H. F. The formation of learning sets. *Psychological Review,* 1949, *56,* 51–65.

ACTIVITY

41

PROBLEM SOLVING: GROUPS VERSUS INDIVIDUALS
Wilbert J. McKeachie, Charlotte Doyle, and Mary Margaret Moffett

Concept

Problem solving is a subject that has concerned psychologists as well as politicians and administrators. One of the important questions they all ask is, "Under what circumstances are groups more effective than individuals at solving problems?" Two all-important variables in answering the question—that is, in assessing effectiveness—are the quality of the solution and the implementation of the solution. The latter variable is particularly critical; research indicates that people cooperate more in implementing a solution if they participated in reaching the solution. Certain other variables—such as the nature of the task, group size, and group processes—relate to performance in problem solving and hence to the quality of the solution. The activity described here is designed to introduce students to problem solving as a subject of scientific investigation and to help students explore some of the variables that affect the relative problem-solving capabilities of individuals and groups.

Instructions

For the activity you will need a stopwatch and a handout—enough for the whole class—that reads as follows:

Nine men play the positions on a baseball team. Their names are Brown, White, Adams, Miller, Green, Hunter, Knight, Smith, and Jones. Determine from the following information the position played by each man.

(a) Brown and Smith each won $10 playing poker with the pitcher.

(b) Hunter is taller than Knight and shorter than White, but each weighs more than the first baseman.

(c) The third baseman lives across the corridor from Jones in the same apartment house.

(d) Miller and the outfielders play bridge in their spare time.

(e) White, Miller, Brown, the right fielder, and the center fielder are bachelors, and the rest are married.

(f) Of Adams and Knight, one plays an outfield position.

(g) The right fielder is shorter than the center fielder.

(h) The third baseman is a brother of the pitcher's wife.

(i) Green is taller than the infielders and the battery (i.e., the pitcher and catcher), except for Jones, Smith, and Adams.

(j) The second baseman beat Jones, Brown, Hunter, and the catcher at cards.

(k) The third baseman, the shortstop, and Hunter made $150 each speculating in General Motors stock.

(l) The second baseman is engaged to Miller's sister.

(m) Adams lives in the same house as his sister but dislikes the catcher.

(n) Adams, Brown, and the shortstop lost $200 each speculating in grain.

(o) The catcher has three daughters, the third baseman has two sons, but Green is being sued for divorce.

Tell students that they are going to participate in an experiment to determine whether groups or individuals are more effective at problem solving. You will present them with a problem, and they will try to solve it within a 20-minute time limit, working either as an individual or as a group member. Tell students also that their participation is not likely to cause them any embarrassment. Those who wish to decline to participate may do so freely and quietly, without penalty.

Have students count off one, two, one, two, etc. Group the Ones randomly into clusters of five or six students; tell the Twos they are to work individually. Locate each of the groups in as isolated a spot as possible so that the other groups and the students working individually cannot overhear information. Distribute the handout, asking students to keep it face down until you signal them to turn it over. Tell students that the handout presents a problem that they have 20 minutes to solve; if any of them solve it in less time, they should report to you. Then have them turn over their handouts and start working. Start the stopwatch.

While students are working, write the following on the chalkboard:

Number of Positions Correct

Groups	Individuals
#1 _____	(Initials) _____
#2 _____	(Initials) _____
#3 _____	(Initials) _____
etc.	etc.
Total number _____	Total number _____
Group average _____	Individual average _____

If any group or individual finishes early, mark the time to completion in minutes and seconds, reading from (but not stopping) the stopwatch. Call time at the end of 20 minutes. Read the correct answers, and have individuals and groups enter the number of positions that they have correct at the top of their handouts. Groups or individuals who finished early should get extra credit—1 point for every 30-second interval between their completion time and the 20-minute limit. Thus, if a group finished 2 minutes and 49 seconds early and had all the positions correct, it would get 14 points—9 points for the positions plus 5 points for the five full 30-second intervals in the 169 seconds that it had remaining before time was called.

The correct answers are as follows: Jones, pitcher; Smith, catcher; Brown, first baseman; White, second baseman; Adams, third baseman; Miller, shortstop; Green, left fielder; Hunter, center fielder; Knight, right fielder.

Record group and individual scores in the appropriate columns on the chalkboard, total the columns, and compute the means. Then compare the results.

Discussion

Discussion can focus on why the individuals or the groups (depending on the results) worked more effectively on the problem that was presented. The nature of the task is important here. Groups tend to be more effective at solving problems that depend on a correct answer or clever contribution because the probability is greater that a group will contain an expert than that an individual will be an expert. In the present problem, recognition of the need for a matrix to organize information represents such a contribution. Groups also tend to be more effective at solving problems that everyone has an equal chance at, like estimating the number of beans in a bottle. Having more than one person making estimations results in overestimations and underestimations compensating for each other and yielding an average closer to reality. On the other hand, individuals tend to be more effective at solving problems in which less able persons control the pace. Mountain climbing provides an analogy here; a team can only go as fast as the slowest member.

Among factors that may affect a group's performance is its size. On a task that requires skills to be combined in an additive manner, as the number of members in a group increases, the additive effect is progressively diminished by a "process loss." To use an analogy, although two persons may be individually capable of pulling 50 pounds, their combined pulling power is not 100 pounds, but more like 90. This process loss increases disproportionately with additional numbers. Thus, three persons together might only be able to pull 120 pounds. Finally a point is reached when the loss is about equal to the gain. To get around such an effect in large groups, group facilitators often form a small, representative group to solve the problem, seat the members in the center of the larger group, and put some extra chairs in the circle. As they feel inclined, members of the larger group then use the extra chairs to join the core group and inject their ideas or opinions.

Suggested Background Readings

Davis, J. H. *Group performance.* Reading, Mass.: Addison-Wesley, 1969.

Schmuck, R. A., & Schmuck, P. A. *Group processes in the classroom* (2nd ed.). Dubuque, Iowa: Wm. C. Brown, 1975.

Steiner, I. D. *Group processes and productivity.* New York: Academic Press, 1972.

42

PROBLEMS OF SET
Louis Snellgrove

Concept

The following activities illustrate the concept of set—hidden assumptions that most often help but can also hinder problem solving. The first example comes from Louis Snellgrove and the second from A. S. Luchins.

Instructions

Copy the following numbers one at a time in a column on the board (the sum of the numbers *is not to be given*): 10, 1,000, 40, 1,000, 30, 1,000, 20, 1,000, 10 = (4,110). As each number is written, ask the class to keep a running total in their heads. Have them write the final total down. Then ask them to add the columns now on the board and write the answer down a second time. Quite often they will arrive at a different sum. Finally, add the 1,000s (total of 4,000) and then the two-digit numbers (total is 110) to show that the grand total is 4,110.

For the second activity, give students a series of problems for which you tell them, "You are to obtain an exact amount of water from a large tank, but you only have certain empty jars to measure with. You can empty and fill the jars as much as you like." The problems are listed below:

Problem	Quart capacity of empty jars used			Total number of quarts to be obtained
1 (illustrative)	29	3	0	20
2	21	127	3	100
3	14	163	25	99
4	18	43	10	5
5	9	42	6	21
6	20	59	4	31
7	23	49	3	20
8	15	3	3	18

To illustrate set, divide the class into two groups. Give the first group a piece of paper you have prepared with all 8 problems on it. Diagram the solutions to Problems 1 and 2 on the paper. In addition, explain them in words: "For example, in Problem 1 you fill the 29-quart jar and subtract 3 quarts three times, leaving 20 quarts; in Problem 2 you fill the 127-quart jar and take out 21 quarts once and 3 quarts twice, leaving 100 quarts." Then ask the group to finish the problems in order. Give the second group a piece of paper with Problems 1, 3, 4, 5, 7, and 8 on it. Illustrate Problem 1 for them also, and then ask them to finish their problems in order.

The method that works in Problems 2 through 6 will also work on 7 and 8, but Problems 7 and 8 can be solved more directly: Problem 7 =

$23 - 3$; Problem $8 = 3 + 15$. The first group, which had "training" on Problems 2 and 6, should give far fewer direct solutions than the second group.

Discussion

With reference to the first activity, ask the class why it was so difficult to arrive at the correct answer. Explain that correct addition is difficult because one expects to add 1,000 each time in the latter part of the columns (usually with the 20). In both activities you might have the class speculate about why some students were influenced by the set while others were not. Ask the students to give examples of set or expectancy as an aid or hindrance to problem solving. What role does set play in perception? Discuss the concept of functional fixedness.

Suggested Background Readings

Adamson, R. E., Functional fixedness as related to problem solving: A repetition of three experiments. *Journal of Experimental Psychology,* 1952, *44,* 288–291.

Bruner, J. S. On perceptual readiness. *Psychological Review,* 1957, *64,* 123–152.

Harlow, H. F. The formation of learning sets. *Psychological Review,* 1949, *56,* 51–65.

Luchins, A. S. Classroom experiments on mental set. *American Journal of Psychology,* 1946, *59,* 295–298.

Haber, R. N. Nature of the effect of set on perception. *Psychological Review,* 1966, *73,* 335–351.

43

THE ZEIGARNIK EFFECT:
SUFFERING TO SERVE THE PSYCHE
Allan L. LaVoie

Concept

Repression is described as the expulsion from the conscious mind of painful or threatening experiences. The events live in the unconscious but remain unavailable to direct recall. The Zeigarnik effect, in contrast, refers to the highlighting in memory of certain events that could be seen as painful or threatening. Originally described by Bluma Zeigarnik in an achievement setting, the effect was seen when students tended to better recall tasks at which they had failed than tasks at which they had succeeded.

Instructions

Four versions of a task booklet are needed (samples are available from the author). Version A should consist of 20 pages, 1 task per page. Ten of the tasks should be completable within 45 seconds (success tasks) and 10 not completable (failure tasks). Version B should be the mirror image of Version A; for example, if the first task in Version A is a completable pencil maze, in Version B it should be an uncompletable maze. Version C should contain the same tasks as Version A, but in a new random ordering. And Version D should be the mirror image of Version C. The four versions are necessary to eliminate the effects of task attractiveness and serial position on later recall.

The tasks may be very simple in concept: anagrams, digit-letter substitutions, listing cities that begin with C, counting letters, rearranging sentences, and so on. But each task must have self-explanatory directions and must be available in a short (success) form and a long (failure) form. Two examples of such tasks are included below.

Example of an incompletable task:
1. Cross out the punctuation marks in the paragraph below.
2. Draw a line through the two-letter words.
3. Copy the four-letter words on this sheet below the paragraph.
4. Words having more than four letters may now be eliminated by drawing a line through them, unless they end with "d."
5. Now draw a circle around the 1st, 18th, 21st, and 32nd words in the paragraph.
   Now is the time for all good men to come to the aid of the party. Are you coming? Why are so many hours of practice necessary before one is a finished typist?

Example of a completable task:
Draw a small circle around each number "6" in the following series of numbers.

5 4 3 6 7 8   6 6 5 8 9 2   5 4 3 7 6 8 9

9 8 7 6 6 5   6 5 7 4 3 2 6 9 6

To obtain the Zeigarnik effect, it is important that the test be presented in a high achievement setting so that students will be highly and personally involved. One way to accomplish this is to tell the students that they will be given an important test and that it is therefore necessary that they do their best. (The real purpose of the test, however, should be explained to the students *following* completion of the recall task described below). Distribute the booklets face down to each student and explain that no one should begin until told to do so. The task will be more ego involving if the booklets are distributed so that each student is near a student with the opposite booklet, a situation that creates a competitive atmosphere (i.e., one will succeed while another is still working and vice-versa). When ready, call time, and after 45 seconds call "Stop!" Ask students to mark the page "S" if they think they succeeded on the task, and "F" if they believe they failed on the task (subjective success is critical here, not objective success). Do not allow students to return to earlier tasks, or to go ahead in the booklet, to insure that each student has 45 seconds' exposure to each task. Continue until all 20 tasks are done, reminding students at each page to mark "S" or "F."

Then ask students to put aside their booklets and give them a substitute activity for 3–5 minutes (e.g., writing the alphabet backwards or upside down). At the end of the filler period, instruct students to write brief descriptions, on a separate piece of paper, of each task in the booklet. They needn't recall them in order; you may tell them, however, that there were 20 tasks. Allow 3 minutes for the recall task (my experience has been that longer periods weaken the Zeigarnik effect). Before proceeding further, explain to the students the real purpose of the test booklet.

Ask the students to go through their booklets and count and record the numbers of successes and failures. Then have them mark each recalled task as an "S" or "F" task. Count and record the numbers of "S" tasks and "F" tasks recalled. Calculate and record percentages of "S" tasks recalled and "F" tasks recalled (e.g., if 10 "S" tasks and 3 "S" tasks are recalled, the percentage of "S" recall = $^3/_{10} \times 100 = 30\%$).

Calculate individual Zeigarnik ratios by dividing the percentage of "F" recall by the percentage of "S" recall.

Collate the class data on the board, using three rough categories: greater than 1, approximately 1, and less than 1. List each student's ratio under the appropriate heading. Then calculate category averages and a total class average—these will serve as the data for discussion.

Discussion

Begin with the three column averages. Typical means will be 2+, 1, and .5. A ratio of 2.0 indicates greater recall of failures. In discussing this average, consider the functional value of "overremembering" one's failures—for example, to insure later success by rehearsing a problem until it's solved.

The next point to discuss is the third mean, .5. This can be taken as an index of repression. Perhaps these students find failure very threatening, and the ego defends itself by putting the memory out of consciousness.

Then consider the mean of 1.0, which can be taken as an index of lack of concern with achievement strivings or ambivalence about achievement tasks. There are data to support each of these interpretations; hence the discussion isn't entirely a post facto explanation. Further, the students will find it easy to identify their own feelings about achievement and will typically supply ample anecdotal support for each interpretation.

Finally, consider the total average, usually about 1.2, and discuss how misleading this mean is in describing individual tendencies to recall successes and failures. Raising this point always leads to a discussion by the students of the importance of considering the individual rather than just the group. You may also generalize the results to other motives. For example, will there be a Zeigarnik effect for power strivings? Affiliative strivings? Sexual strivings?

Suggested Background Readings

Atkinson, J. W. The achievement motive and recall of interrupted and completed tasks. *Journal of Experimental Psychology,* 1953, *46,* 381–390.

Ellis, W. D. (Ed.). *A sourcebook of Gestalt psychology.* New York: Harcourt Brace, 1938.

Heckhausen, H. Achievement motive research. *Nebraska Symposium on Motivation,* 1968, *16,* 103–174.

Tudor, T. G., & Holmes, D. S. Differential recall of successes and failures. *Journal of Research in Personality,* 1973, *7,* 181–185.

Weiner, B., Johnson, P. B., & Mehrabian, A. Achievement motivation and the recall of incomplete and completed exam questions. *Journal of Educational Psychology,* 1968, *59,* 181–185.

Zeigarnik, B. On finished and unfinished tasks. In W. D. Ellis (Ed.), *A sourcebook of Gestalt psychology.* New York: Harcourt Brace, 1938.

ACTIVITY

44

CONCEPT LEARNING
Ludy T. Benjamin, Jr.

Concept

In our everyday lives we deal with a great variety of concepts acquired in previous learning—from simple concepts such as "cat" and "apple" to more complex concepts such as "animal," "fruit," "generosity," "intelligence," and "a good night's sleep." We learn concepts because they are extremely useful as a shorthand form of learning. Concept learning allows us to apply the same label to a number of objects or events based on the recognition of a property common to those objects and events. This activity describes a concept-learning task that can easily be performed in the classroom with any number of students. The demonstration is usually more effective if students have read the section on concept learning in their texts prior to participating in this task.

Instructions

Prepare a set of stimulus materials and multiple copies of a scoring sheet for student use. My preference for stimulus materials is slides, since they can be easily presented to a large class and the time of their exposure can be controlled. Good stimulus materials (or objects) for this activity are a number of Greek-letter trigrams such as $\Delta\Theta\Gamma$ or $\Sigma\Phi\Delta$, because they are low in association value (as long as you don't select trigrams that signify fraternities, honorary societies, and so forth) and are not readily pronounceable in a short amount of time. To make the slides, I recommend making Thermofax transparencies and then cutting those items to size for mounting in slide mounts.

Procedure for making slides: Obtain a typewriter with interchangeable elements and a symbol element with the letters of the Greek alphabet (chemistry and mathematics departments are likely to have such symbol elements). Type your trigrams on plain typing paper, spacing them far enough apart to provide an appropriate border for mounting as slides. Construct 36 trigrams half of them containing the letter Θ (theta) and the other half containing the letter Φ (phi). In no instance should these two letters appear together in the same trigram. In addition, it will be necessary to prepare a set of answer slides—18 of which should say True and 18 of which should say False. When you have typed the trigrams and answer words, run the typed pages through a Thermofax copier to produce the transparencies (use a heavier transparency stock if available, since it will make better slides). Then cut out the words and trigrams and seal them in slide mounts (available at most camera supply stores—use either the 135 or 126 size).

Arrange the slides in three sets in the slide tray; each set should consist of 12 trigrams (half with theta, half with phi) and 12 answer slides (half True, half False). The True slides should be placed after the trigrams containing theta, and the False slides following the trigrams containing phi. Randomly order the trigrams in each of the three sets. The 72 slides will easily fit the tray capacity of most slide projectors.

Leave one or two blank spaces between each of the three sets of slides to mark the end of one series.

Prepare answer sheets for the students consisting of a single sheet of paper marked off in 8 columns by 12 rows. Number the columns at the top of the page 1 through 8. Twelve blank boxes should appear below each number.

Provide the following instructions for the class: "You are going to participate in a concept-learning task. In a moment I will show you some slides that contain three Greek letters forming a trigram. Some of these trigrams are true, while others are false. Your task is to learn which ones are true and which ones are false, by learning what characteristic of the trigrams determines their truth or falseness. That is the concept you are to learn. I will present the trigrams in trial blocks of 12, showing them to you one at a time. Each trigram will be followed by an answer slide indicating whether the previous slide was true or false. Look at the answer sheet I have given you. Begin with Column 1, marking your answers down the column. The task will proceed as follows: A Greek-letter trigram will appear on the screen very briefly, for approximately 5 seconds. As soon as you see it, you are to decide whether it is true or false and then mark either the letter T or F in the first box under Column 1. The next slide is an answer slide and will tell you if you were correct. If the answer slide indicates you were not correct, circle that box on your answer sheet and be ready for the next trigram. Note that the task will proceed very rapidly. All slides, both trigrams and answers, will appear on the screen for approximately 5 seconds each. Thus you must work very rapidly."

"When you have learned the concept, you should keep that knowledge to yourself. Let your neighbors learn on their own. I will define learning in this task as two successive trial blocks without an error (that is, 24 correct responses in a row). When you reach that criterion you should sit quietly at your desk until the completion of this demonstration. We are ready to begin." (Note: At this point many students will have a puzzled look on their faces, feeling that you have forgotten to tell them something. Some may even ask, "How do we tell whether the trigrams are true or false?" Simply indicate that you have given all of the information necessary for the task.)

Show the first trial block of 24 slides, which will require approximately 2 minutes. At the end of that block ask for a show of hands from those who got them all right. Rarely does anyone get them all right at this point. Begin the second trial block and at the end call for a show of hands. Usually there are several people who have mastered the task by this time. Run through seven or eight complete trial blocks (or less if you have less time). I have found that after seven trial blocks, approximately 60%–75% of the students have had at least one totally successful trial block. (Note: Since there are only three sets of slides, have students fold their answer sheets after the completion of the first three trial blocks so that Columns 1–3 are no longer visible.)

When you finish the last trial block, caution the students not to talk, as the demonstration is not concluded. Go to the chalkboard and write a 20-digit number on the board. Tell the students that you are reasonably confident that none of them has ever seen that number before. Then ask them if the number is odd or even. How do they know that since they have never seen that particular number before? This illustration provides a lead-in to discussion of the concept-learning task just demonstrated. On the board draw the following trigram: $\Delta\Theta\Phi$. Tell the students that this is a trigram they have not seen and that you want those who reached the learning criterion in the concept-learning task to vote on this new trigram. Is it true? Is it false? Or is it ambiguous? Ask for a show of hands on each question and record the number on the board beside the labels True, False, and Ambiguous. Usually there will be students who raise their hands for each category.

Tell the students that they have actually participated in a double concept-learning task. That is, there were two concepts—theta means true, phi means false. Those students who learned both concepts voted that the new trigram was thus ambiguous. Yet students who learned only one of the concepts were able to perform perfectly in the concept-learning task. For example, students who answered "true" to the new trigram learned that trigrams which contained a theta were true and that trigrams without theta were false. Those who answered "false" learned the opposite concept.

Discussion

Discuss the shape of the learning curve one obtains in a concept-learning task (especially when the stimulus objects are not repeated). The curve would initially show performance around the chance level, but once the concept was discovered, performance would be at the 100% success level. Is this an example of gradual learning or is it indicative of one-trial learning? Get the students to talk about the strategies they employed in attempting to learn the concept. What false hypotheses did they test before arriving at the correct one?

Talk about concept learning as an aid to human functioning. Get the students to give examples of this facilitative process. Discuss concepts that are learned that hinder us in our perceptions, judgments, and so forth. For example, stereotypes are a type of concept learning in which we learn to label a number of people based on our belief that they share common qualities or attributes.

Concept learning is usually viewed as a strictly human activity. Can subhuman animals form concepts? See Harry Harlow's article on learning sets and the other background readings for a discussion of these and other questions on concept learning.

Suggested Background Readings

Brainerd, C. J. Cognitive development and concept learning: An interpretive review. *Psychological Bulletin*, 1979, *77*, 919–939.

Cofer, C. N. Experimental studies of verbal processes in concept formation and problem solving. *Annals of the New York Academy of Sciences*, 1961, *91*, 94–107.

Harlow, H. F. The formation of learning sets. *Psychological Review*, 1949, *56*, 51–56.

Morgan, C. T., King, R. A., & Robinson, N. M. *Introduction to psychology* (6th ed.). New York: McGraw-Hill, 1979. (chap. 6)

45

LANGUAGE AND COMMUNICATION: DEFINING LANGUAGE CAN LEAVE YOU SPEECHLESS

William J. Hunter

Concept

Much important research is currently being done in language acquisition, psycholinguistics, and related areas. Many psychologists have come to regard linguistic behavior as a most important, if not unique, component of both human behavior and cognition. The verbal learning studies of bygone days have been giving way to studies of sentence construction, sentence memory, the use of syntax, the role of semantics, and so forth. If any of this literature is to be meaningfully discussed, students should have a clear understanding of what is meant by the word *language* (though, as is so often the case, researchers and theorists do not always agree about which features define *language*).

Instructions

Enter the classroom a minute or two late so that there is likely to be some conversation and/or noise when you are ready to begin the lesson. *Without speaking,* demand quiet (e.g., clap hands, or books, together loudly and place finger over lips; if absolutely necessary, but only then, write QUIET in large letters on the board). As the students begin to quiet down, begin giving simple nonverbal directions; for example, indicate that students in one row should move their desks over, or gesture that a student (or students) should stand, turn around, or clap three times. Without speaking, have the class form discussion groups. Secure quiet. Do a brief mime routine. Finally, either speaking or on the board, ask, (1) What is communication? (2) What is speech? and (3) What is language? Allow the students to discuss in small groups and then ask each group to report.

Discussion

End the demonstration with either a question-and-answer approach or lecture focused on a definition of language that *you* can work with. For example, "Language is a system of abstract symbols which can be combined using a limited set of rules to communicate meaning." For closure, or as a follow-up, ask students to resolve questions like the following ones: Is mime language? Is mime communication? Is American Sign Language *really* a language? Do animals communicate? Do animals have language?

The spectacle of a nonspeaking teacher is so far outside most students' personal experience that this lesson has mystical and humorous effects. Nevertheless, I have always found it to lead to a pointed, constructive discussion that is a good preliminary to giving (or guiding the students in producing) a definition of language useful in discussing language acquisition, chimpanzee studies, and some of the literature on cognition.

Suggested Background Readings

Brown, R. *Words and things*. Glencoe, Ill.: Free Press, 1958.

Miller, G. A. Some psychological studies of grammar. *American Psychologist,* 1962, *17,* 748–762.

Palermo, D. S. *The psychology of language*. Glenview, Ill.: Scott, Foresman, 1978.

Rumbaugh, D. M. (Ed.). *Language learning by a chimpanzee: The Lana project*. New York: Academic Press, 1977.

Terrach, H. S. How Nim Chimpsky changed my mind. *Psychology Today,* June 1979, pp. 65–76.

Weitz, S. (Ed.). *Nonverbal communication* (2nd ed.). New York: Oxford University Press, 1979.

46

CREATIVITY
Allan L. LaVoie

Concept

Students often think that creativity, like size or eye color, represents a fixed attribute—the genetic dice predetermine your creative potential, and there is nothing more to be said or done about it. This exercise can change such beliefs and in addition will stimulate student excitement and enthusiasm for days to come.

Most forced-creativity techniques share the assumption that reality, especially social reality, inhibits originality. When we succeed in suspending reality, we are all truly creative, as in our dreams.

A second assumption underlying many such different techniques concerns the creative mechanism: Metaphorical or analogical thinking seems to be at the core of creativity. Discovering what two things have in common forces you to consider how the first thing *might* share other attributes of the second, which leads to new insights.

Instructions

Divide the class into groups of 4–5 people. A college-level dictionary is needed for each group. Try to equate the groups with respect to such variables as conventionality and extraversion. Give them their task in terms such as these:

"Today you are going to try to devise significant new improvements for an everyday object, namely a (mousetrap, teapot, car, book, etc.). To help you think of creative improvements, you will make a list of 10 stimulus words. Please take turns opening the dictionary at random and selecting a common noun at random from the page. When you have written the 10 words your group will be using, each of you should write brief definitions for all 10 words.

Now that you have 10 stimulus words, I would like you to apply each one to the improvement of a _____ . Sometimes there will seem to be no relation, but if you allow yourselves to get silly, you will find some connection. Don't worry about what others in your group think: Bizarre is beautiful in this exercise."

Each group should have a facilitator/recorder who can keep ideas flowing, urge quiet members to share their ideas, and record each different idea. Your task is to circulate among the groups, cross-fertilizing where appropriate, encouraging the suspension of criticism, and rewarding unconventional ideas. When the groups have exhausted the potential of the 10 stimulus words, reorient the task as follows:

"Recorders, please read each idea you have listed so that group members can elaborate, revise, or develop new ideas. Be sure to note changes." Finally:

"Now that you have a list of your best ideas, I would like you to design a new _____ , incorporating as many of your ideas as you can. When you have a *practical* new design, draw it on paper, then select one of your members to draw and label it on the board."

For the word *practical,* you can substitute economical, attractive, fantastic, efficient, etc. As each group draws their final design on the board, the rest of the class can circulate to examine the work of the other groups. Typically, as the students circulate, you will hear them giving interesting and innovative suggestions to improve other designs. You might harness the flow of these ideas by directing the class to focus their collective attention on each design to give new suggestions; I prefer to keep it spontaneous.

Discussion

Try to keep discussions focused on the two assumptions addressed earlier: To increase creativity, you must suspend your critical faculty while increasing your use of metaphorical thinking. When students have been successful in postponing critical analysis, they usually express astonishment at how creative everyone has been. A fairly frequent response is "Are you sure this is really creative?"

At this point, introduce various definitions of *creative* and *originality;* I use those provided by Arieti (1976), Davis (1973), Koestler (1964), Torrance (1962), and Webster's Unabridged Dictionary. There are many others you can use. There does not seem to be an objective reason for preferring one definition over another, so after a relatively brief discussion, reach a consensus and move on to the next question.

Individual differences in creativity can be attributed to a variety of sources, such as varying abilities or practice in metaphorical thinking, willingness to accept unusual solutions, motivation to develop new ideas, and so on. Torrance (1962) identifies many others. After considering some of these, lead into the question of how one may become more creative. The response will follow from a consideration of individual difference factors. For example, how can you become more motivated to seek and accept innovative practices? How do you become better able to suspend disbelief?

On the rare occasions that we have class time left, I follow up the discussion by referring to such related matters as creative problem solving (Koestler, 1964) and dream control for problem solving. I may also offer a second group-creativity exercise, such as bionics, synectics, or morphological synthesis (Davis, 1973).

Suggested Background Readings

Arieti, S. *Creativity: The magic synthesis.* New York: Basic Books, 1976.
Davis, G. A. *Psychology of problem solving.* New York: Basic Books, 1973.
Koestler, A. *The act of creation.* New York: Macmillan, 1964.
Torrance, E. P. *Guiding creative talent.* Englewood Cliffs, N.J.: Prentice-Hall, 1962.

ACTIVITY
47

SEMANTIC (CATEGORY) CLUSTERING
Allan L. LaVoie

Concept

Most instructors find it relatively easy to convince students that the unconscious exists, but the student's conviction relies primarily on clinical evidence, for example, on case studies of hysterical blindness, glove anesthesia, the fugue state, and repression. To *demonstrate* that the unconscious exists, and can work constructively, this adaptation of Bousfield's (1953) semantic clustering experiment serves admirably.

Clustering occurs when subjects are asked to recall, in any order, a list of words read to them previously that were selected to represent several categories (hence the alternative term, category clustering). In Bousfield's 1953 study the categories were animals, vegetables, professions, and people's names. Free recall tends to produce clustering in fits and starts, so that a subject might recall a few vegetables, several animals, then a group of names, a cluster of professions, a few more animals, and so on. Subjects report that they do not consciously try to organize the material into categories, though when instructed to do so they exhibit even stronger grouping tendencies. Hence the organization occurs at a nonconscious level and clearly serves to demonstrate that the unconscious mind can assist the conscious.

Subsequent research expanding on Bousfield's work has identified, in addition to semantic clustering, clustering based on the modality of the word presentation (e.g., words read aloud versus words presented visually), clustering based on associative interrelationships, and clustering based on emotional characteristics. See Adams (1976) for an excellent discussion of organization in free recall.

Instructions

Explain to the class that for today's memory demonstration, they should listen carefully to the list of words you read.

Explain that after reading the list, you will give them a task to work on for a few minutes and that you will then ask them to write down all the words they can recall, in any order, in 5 minutes. At this point ask the students to find a partner, and have them sit together.

Read the list in slow, measured tones, with 5 seconds between words. Wait 10–15 seconds, then have the pairs of students alternately count backwards by 3 from 402 (i.e., Student 1 says 399, Student 2 says 396, Student 1 says 393, etc.). Give them about 4–5 minutes for this task, exhorting them to count faster and faster; then ask for recall, reminding them that order isn't important. Allow 5 minutes for recall.

If some of your students have the same classroom habits as mine, check during the reading of the word list to insure that none of them is taking notes, as note-taking vitiates the clustering effect.

For this activity, students will need paper and pens. You will need a list of stimulus words designed to illustrate whichever aspect of the phenomenon interests you. For example, for the basic semantic clustering phenomenon, I use this list:

1. barn	2. sparrow	3. blue	5. smooth
4. silo	9. canary	6. yellow	7. rough
8. crops	12. pigeon	15. orange	10. silky
11. corral	14. finch	17. red	13. scratchy
16. stable	18. robin	20. green	19. cold
23. hay	21. chicken	24. white	22. uneven
26. tractor	28. cardinal	27. pink	25. sharp

The words are listed in columns by semantic categories; the numbers refer to the order of presentation as determined by a random numbers table, with the constraint that no category be sampled twice consecutively. You may note two ambiguous words: Chicken has to do with farms and birds; cardinal is a color and a bird.

Other lists may be compiled as you wish. (An emotional clustering list, based on semantic differential research, is available from the author.)

Discussion

Phenomenological exploration may take place immediately. Ask the students what strategies they used, whether they noted anything unusual, and what effect the counting had on their memory rehearsal (see below). Inquire whether anyone was successful in rehearsing the words while counting backwards.

Begin numerical analysis by asking students to note how frequently category members were recalled together. Each pair earns one point, each triplet two points, etc. Obtain a total score. The total scores can be compared against scores obtained by chance, though the phenomenon is striking enough to make it unnecessary.

Determine informally the extent to which students felt they consciously controlled the words they recalled. The counting task should have effectively prevented conscious rehearsal, making more plausible the concept of unconscious semantic processing as the explanation for the clustering.

There are always several students who claim they should receive a point for including chicken as a farm word. While pointing out that the other farm words are nonanimals, capitalize on the question by pointing out the implications of the confusion for better understanding of the underlying memory network. To illustrate briefly, while chickens undeniably belong to farms, they are also definitely birds. But birds should fly; since chickens don't, they belong more appropriately to another category, such as food or farm (see Collins & Quillian, 1969, for a more sophisticated discussion of semantic networks).

By this time you should have convinced most of the class that automatic semantic processors exist. Mention again that alerting the students to look for categories beforehand enhances the clustering effect.

To conclude the discussion, focus on the utility of conscious and unconscious processes. The fact that a conscious strategy enhances recall indicates one way in which consciousness may aid adaptation and survival. My experience has been that students quickly become engaged in discussion of the issues and require little direction. This demonstration also ties in nicely with a variety of other topics, such as Hilgard's "divided mind," psychoanalysis, human information processing, and a discussion of free will.

Suggested Background Readings

Adams, J. A. *Learning and memory: An introduction*. Homewood, Ill.: Dorsey Press, 1976.

Bousfield, W. A. The occurrence of clustering in the recall of randomly arranged associates. *Journal of General Psychology*, 1953, *49*, 229–240.

Collins, A. M., & Quillian, M. R. Retrieval from semantic memory. *Journal of Verbal Learning and Verbal Behavior*, 1969, *8*, 240–247.

CHAPTER V
DEVELOPMENTAL PSYCHOLOGY

The activities in this chapter span human development from infancy through the aging process and even include an exercise on development in subhuman animals. Five of the nine activities are proposed for classroom use.

Two activities involve investigations with human infants; Activity 48 examines object permanency in infants between 2 and 12 months old, and Activity 49 looks at sensory stimulation in infants around 8 months old. If access to human infants is not available, Activity 50 involves the students in observing a litter of rat pups from birth to 4 weeks.

Following the work of Jean Piaget, Activity 51 describes a procedure to assess conservation ability in preschool children.

Three exercises focus on general issues across the span of development. Activity 52 illustrates the distinction between developmental changes and those due strictly to maturation. Activity 53 looks at life span development in an exercise based on Erik Erikson's eight stages of development. The topic of life span development is also the emphasis of Activity 54, which has students associate tasks, behaviors, attitudes, and so forth with various ages by decade.

Activity 55 is a demonstration of attitudes toward and beliefs about old age, and Activity 56 is an exercise on death and dying related to the theory of dying proposed by Elisabeth Kubler-Ross.

ACTIVITY
48

OBJECT PERMANENCE IN INFANCY:
OUT OF SIGHT, OUT OF MIND?
Deborah L. Coates and Peter M. Vietze

Concept

Psychologists have historically been interested in how adults acquire perceptions and notions about their world. The study of infant behavior has been essential in developing a body of knowledge on the origins of individual perception of both social and inanimate objects. Adult's and children's perceptions of the reality of objects are not influenced by whether the object is within the visual field or whether it is hidden from view. It is often assumed that infants share this "constant" perception of an object and that they also share the perception that the object exists whether it is within the visual field or hidden from view. This has not been demonstrated to be the case. Research has shown that there is an orderly progression of events which underlies the infant's ability to recognize that the existence of objects is permanent and transcends both time and space.

This perception of the "constancy" or real existence of a social or inanimate object, whatever its location in time or space (e.g., within or not within the visual field), is called object permanence. Several researchers have attempted to document the acquisition of this ability in infants. The development of object permanence in infancy has been related to the development of other cognitive abilities and skills (Phillips, 1975; Sherrod, Vietze, & Friedman, 1978).

Systematic observation of infants' behavior with objects has revealed that younger infants typically respond to objects differently than do older infants. The behavior of these younger infants, unlike that of older infants, seems to indicate that they do not understand that objects exist even when they disappear from view. The acquisition of "object constancy" progresses from an early stage in which an infant will follow an object moving in his or her visual field but stop when it disappears from view, to a later stage in which an infant will actively search for a hidden object even when he or she hasn't seen it being hidden. The existence of this developmental process has been challenged (Bower, 1974). However, the results of studies that have sought to demonstrate that even very young babies have object permanence are somewhat inconclusive.

This exercise demonstrates the developmental progression of the acquisition of object permanence. It also allows students to observe infants' responses and learn to appreciate the meaning of their behavior. Very young infants (about 4 months old) will follow an object with their eyes—for instance, a finger before their face—but don't seem to notice when the object disappears from view. Somewhat older infants (8-month-olds) will track the object while it is in the visual field but will also actively search for the object or note its disappearance by some expression. Still older infants (16-month-olds) will search for a hidden object even if they have not seen the object being hidden. The following exercise also demonstrates some of the methodological problems inherent in observing and measuring infant behavior.

Materials Needed

Pairs of students will need to have access to an infant between 2 and 12 months old. They will also need coding forms, small hand-sized toys (e.g., wooden car, miniature stuffed animal), two large handkerchiefs or dinner-napkin-sized cloths, and a 4 × 6 index card.

Preparation of Class

The class should read basic introductory readings on development in infancy and the relationships of experience to behavior (see chap. 6 in Sherrod et al., 1978).

Instructions

Divide the class into two groups and designate one group the 2–6-month group and the other the 6–12-month group. Pairs of students in each group should be instructed to secure access to an infant of an appropriate age for their group assignment in order to play some hiding games with the infant and to observe its behavior. One student in each pair will manipulate objects while the other records the infant's behavior; both students will be responsible for observing the infant's behavior. Students should be instructed as follows (be sure the students practice the procedures several times before they work with the infants):

1. Record the sex and age of the infant you are observing.

2. Have the mother hold the infant in her lap or seat the infant in a highchair facing a table. The infant should be able to reach the table.

3. Tracking: Hold the toy in front of the infant's face and, when the infant seems to see it, move the toy slowly in a horizontal direction until the infant has to turn its head to keep the object in view. Do this three times. Record what the baby does.

4. Barrier: Hold the card about 12 inches in front of the infant's face with one hand. Hold the toy to one side of the card and start moving it slowly toward the card when the infant seems to be looking at the object. Move the toy behind the card. Wait a few seconds, move the toy out from the other side of the card. Repeat this going the other way. Alternate directions and do this three times. Record what the infant does.

For the rest of the tasks have the mother hold the infant's hands *only* while you hide the toy.

5. Partial toy hiding: While the infant is focusing attention on a toy that has been placed on the table, partially cover the toy with a cloth so that only half of the toy is visible to the infant. Do this three times. Record what the infant does.

6. Complete hiding—one screen: Again, while the infant is focused on the toy, cover the toy completely with one of the cloths. Do this on the left side of the table and then move the object to the right side of the table and do it again. Do this once on the right and twice on the left.

7. Complete hiding—two screens: Place the second cloth on the other side of the table and then hide the toy completely under the first cloth while the infant is looking. After you have hidden the toy, adjust the second cloth in order to try to distract the infant. Alternate hiding the toy under one of the two cloths, each time remembering to touch or adjust the cloth not covering the toy. Do this three times.

In order to encourage students to observe the infants, do not tell students beforehand what the passing behaviors are for each task. Once the students have assessed the infants and recorded their responses to each of the five tasks, they should bring their observations to class and be given criteria to determine whether their infants passed each task. If the baby was observed to engage in the following behaviors two out of three times on a task, then the baby should be scored as having passed that task: tracking—watching toy in complete, smooth visual arc as it moves; barrier—watching for the toy at the other side of the card; three types of toy hiding—reaching for and obtaining the toy.

Analysis

Student pairs should report on the age and sex of the infant observed as well as describe the behaviors elicited by the tasks performed. You should describe what behaviors indicate that an infant has passed a task. Then have students score their protocols and indicate how many tasks their infants passed. The number of tasks passed should be aggregated by age (in months), and the average number of tasks passed for each age group of infants should be recorded as shown in the following figure:

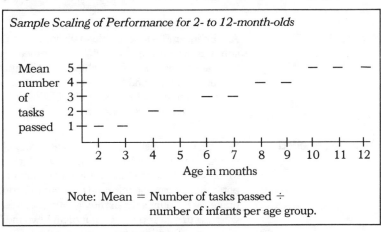

Sample Scaling of Performance for 2- to 12-month-olds

Note: Mean = Number of tasks passed ÷ number of infants per age group.

Discussion

The results of the behavioral observations can easily be displayed for the class, and the array of averages for each age (in months) can be compared to the hypothetical scale shown in the figure. You should pursue a discussion on whether or not the observations made by the class fit a developmental scale. In the discussion you may want to stress the importance of the early growth of cognitive processes in infancy and the concept of what growth involves. For example, the array of infant behaviors observed can be discussed in terms of whether or not they represent the infant's ability to perform more or less complex tasks.

You may also want to involve the class in a discussion of their experiences as observers of infant behavior. This will allow an opportunity to discuss the methodological complexities of observing and recording infant behavior (see Sherrod et al., 1978, pp. 7–14).

Suggested Background Readings

Bower, T. G. R. The object in the world of the infant. *Scientific American,* 1971, *225,* 30–47.

Bower, T. G. R. *Development in infancy.* San Francisco: W. H. Freeman, 1974.

Harris, P. L. Development of search and object permanence during infancy. *Psychological Bulletin,* 1975, *52,* 332–342.

Miller, D., Cohen, L., & Hill, K. A methodological investigation of Piaget's theory of object development in the sensory-motor period. *Journal of Experimental Psychology,* 1971, *11,* 366–375.

Phillips, J. L. *The origins of intellect: Piaget's theory* (2nd ed.). San Francisco: W. H. Freeman, 1975.

Sherrod, K., Vietze, P., & Friedman, S. *Infancy.* Monterey, Calif.: Brooks/Cole, 1978. (pp. 100–101; 110–116)

Uzgiris, I., & Hunt, J. McV. *Assessment in infancy.* Chicago: University of Illinois Press, 1975.

49

SENSORY STIMULATION AND INFANT DEVELOPMENT
Louis Snellgrove

Concept

Are infants more susceptible to visual and auditory stimulation when the stimulus objects are manipulated by someone else or when the infants themselves manipulate the objects? Although there is some evidence that as adults we tend to prefer activities that are self-initiated, do infants prefer activities that someone else begins or activities that they begin? This exercise provides one way of partially answering this question.

Materials Needed

Several pieces of strong string and a variety of objects that are safe to use with infants are needed; no object should (a) have sharp edges or corners, (b) be small enough to be swallowed by an infant, or (c) be able to potentially harm the infant in any way. In addition, the objects should make slight sounds when they gently touch each other. A stopwatch, or a watch with a sweep second hand, and two individuals to record separate responses of the infants are also required.

Instructions

Secure permission for the observation of several infants in their homes. Infants should be about 8 months old or slightly older. Provide a relatively quiet, informal setting for observation. It would be preferable to have the infants perform in a familiar environment such as their own beds and with a familiar person present (preferably their mothers).

Select several small objects that can be tied together with a string so that they move freely and can gently hit one another. The objects should be arranged to form a sort of mobile. Suspend the mobile over the bed of the infant, close enough so that the infant can see and hear the objects when they gently touch each other. For one group of infants, have the individual familiar to the infant move the mobile. For a second group of infants, place the mobile close enough so that the infant's random movements will cause the mobile to move.

For each infant under study, have two observers stand in the background so that they will not distract the infant. One observer should record the *number* of times the infant looks at and touches the mobile while it is moving. The other observer should record the *length of time* the infant looks at and touches the mobile while it is moving.

Because the total length of time infants are individually observed will be related to the number and length of contacts with the mobile, all data should be changed into percentages or ratios. For example, if an infant was observed for a total of 100 seconds and watched the mobile for 20 seconds, he or she watched it 20% of the total time. If an infant touched the mobile for a total of 15 seconds out of the 100 seconds, he or she touched it a total of 15% of the time. If an infant touched the mobile 10 times in 100 seconds of observation, then his or her ratio is 10:100, or 1:10.

Discussion

Discussion should center around comparison of the data for the two groups of infants. Comparisons can be more easily made if a table is constructed to illustrate the data. Did one group—and if so, which one—touch the mobile more than the other? Look at it longer? What responses other than length of time and number of times the infants touched or looked at the mobile could be used as measures of whether infants respond more to self-initiated actions or to actions initiated by a familiar person?

Suggested Background Readings

Bower, T. G. R. *Development in infancy.* San Francisco: W. H. Freeman, 1974.

Cratty, B. J. *Perceptual and motor development in infants and children.* New York: Macmillan Company, 1970.

Piaget, J., & Inhelder, B. *The child's conception of space.* New York: W. W. Norton, 1967.

White, B. L. *Human infants: Experience and psychological development.* Englewood Cliffs, N.J.: Prentice-Hall, 1971.

ACTIVITY
50

ANIMAL OBSERVATION: THE MAMA RAT PROJECT
Barbara F. Nodine

Concept

Few creatures are more appealing than puppies, kittens, foals, and babies. Watching the young of a species develop is engaging and illuminating. Conceptual material on development and ethology is traditionally presented in lectures for introductory psychology students. But lectures and readings are passive ways of learning material that could be better taught with some student participation. Psychology instructors find that student observation of the birth and development of a litter of rat pups enriches the teaching of concepts of development and ethology.

This activity requires students to make 4 weeks of observations of the birth, development of motor skills, socialization, and weaning of a litter. Students then organize their observations and summarize them in a paper relating them to the concepts taught in the course. Concepts that might be taught in conjunction with the observations are the trends or directions of motor development—cephalocaudad, proximodistad, and mass-specific—exemplified by crawling, walking, running, and jumping. Species-specific behaviors might be observed to occur in nest building, retrieving young, feeding, grooming, or weaning. After making observations of this growth for 4 weeks, students will have detailed personally collected descriptions that make the concepts taught in the course meaningful and real. The purposes of this activity are to have students (a) learn to make objective, detailed observations, (b) learn to prepare a written summary of those observations, and (c) learn to write an interpretation of those results using concepts from development and ethology taught in the course.

Besides being a worthwhile teaching technique, this activity has some very practical appeal for the instructor. Rats mature rapidly enough for use in this type of course. It is important for the student to see the mother give birth to a litter of totally dependent, blind, hairless pups and 4 weeks later to observe her litter looking fully developed, running, jumping, and eating solid food. The activity is also well suited to introductory courses because the requirement for apparatus is minimal. As many as 100 students can easily observe one litter cage because they can determine their own flexible observation schedules. In addition, sophisticated research skills are not needed by the student—only skills of observation. Admittedly, simple observation is more difficult than it

From *Writing in the Arts and Sciences* by Elaine P. Maimon, Gerald L. Belcher, Gail W. Hearn, Barbara F. Nodine, and Finbarr W. O'Connor. Copyright © 1981 by Winthrop Publishers, Inc. Reprinted by permission.

Professor Bernard Mausner, Chair of the Department of Psychology of Beaver College, designed this project to be a part of the introductory psychology course. The project has been taught annually for 15 years with numerous variations.

seems, but the student will be developing a basic skill useful in psychology as well as other subjects.

Preparation of Class Materials needed include a pregnant female rat, a large, clear plastic cage for mother and litter when delivered, and a room with see-through mirrors or windows. Using a window or some other barrier will prevent students from being tempted to tap on or open the cage to awaken the animals or disturb them in any way. Also, to keep distraction to a minimum, a darkened room with a red light over the cage would allow the animals to behave as though they were in their natural setting yet allow student observation.

Preparation of students for participation in this activity will take only a few minutes of lecture time, and all observations will be made on the student's time. The student handout reproduced on the next four pages explains the activity completely with the exception of the text material or readings for your course. The specific focus of the activity will depend on what you emphasize in your lectures and on the reading you select. For example, you may wish to limit the potential wealth of observations by having students concentrate on the mother's behavior, or motor trends, or the socialization of the pups. Cross-species comparisons might be made by using gerbils or hamsters.

Student papers can be modified to meet your own goals. You might want to require graphs or tables of results. Library search and use of references beyond those required could be encouraged. Length limits for the paper of two or three pages are feasible, as are longer papers. Usually, the students must select some of their observations and reject others in order to write coherent papers.

Be sure that your students read the statement from the American Psychological Association entitled "Principles for the Care and Use of Animals" (see Appendix D of this book). You may want to request a free copy of that statement to post in your classroom or in the animal observation room. Write: Scientific Affairs Office, American Psychological Association, 1200 Seventeenth Street, N.W., Washington, D.C. 20036.

(Activity continued—please turn page.)

Introduction. One of the major goals of this project is to show how the course of development follows an orderly sequence both in humans and other mammals. Another is to observe the behavior of mothers before birth and with their pups. You are probably more interested in children than rats, but children develop much too slowly for the time we have available. Rats go through childhood in 6 weeks and are sexually adult in 12 weeks; the developmental process is short in length but is similar in many respects to that exhibited by humans. As you watch baby rats develop, you will gain experience in making behavioral observations, relating those observations to theoretical principles, and writing a short paper describing your observations and conclusions.

The theoretical interest of the project lies in two areas. The first is that of "instinct," or species-characteristic behavior. One of the readings on ethology gives you some background for the ideas you will be examining in this area. Maternal behavior is often given as an example of an instinct. You will have a chance to watch a rat mother preparing for the birth of her pups and caring for them. You will then be able to check what you see against the criteria for species-characteristic behavior in the readings.

The other area is development. You will have a chance to observe the orderly changes in appearance and behavior of the pups as they get older and to check these observations against the principles of development described in your readings and in class.

Instructions for observation. You will observe the external anatomy and behavior of a litter of rat pups from the time they are born until they are weaned about a month later. You will also observe the behavior of the mother from the last few days of her pregnancy until weaning. Pregnant rats usually build nests a few days prior to parturition. With luck, you

may be present while a female is delivering.

You should observe the rats for 15 minutes per day, 3 days a week, for 4 weeks—that is, 12 observation periods lasting a total of 3 hours. If all of the rats are asleep, you will have to stay longer than 15 minutes or come back at another time. The animals are located behind a one-way viewing window in Room _____ . Rats are most active during the night, so we are maintaining them on a reversed light/dark cycle. Since they are relatively insensitive to red light, such illumination simulates their nighttime, which begins at 8:00 a.m. and ends at 5:00 p.m. Try to make all of your observations at about the same time each day. Do not turn on the lights in the observation room. You must allow a few minutes for your eyes to adapt to the very dim light in the room.

The most useful way to record your observations is to make a large table or chart on several pages of your notebook with columns for each behavior. An example of the format for such a chart is shown below. During each period you should be sure to record descriptions of at least several of the items about mother or pups from the list on Table 1. The more information you record, the easier it will be to write your final paper. Date every observation so that you see a progression and know the milestones, such as birth, eyes opening, beginning walking, first eating solid food, or weaning.

It sometimes helps to discuss your observations with someone else in the class to increase the precision of your descriptions. You may find that you did not notice some details. After talking with someone else you may be able to record your next observations with greater exactness.

Observation of mothers. Your observation periods will be divided between watching the mothers and watching the pups. In observing

Sample Chart

Date of observation	Mother's behavior	Pups' physical development	Locomotion	Sensory development	Social behavior	Miscellaneous

Table 1   *Behavioral Categories for Description of Mother Rat and Pups*

Mothers	Nest building
	Grooming self, grooming pups (especially anal licking)
	Exploration
	Nursing
	Retrieving
	Rejecting pups at weaning
	Walking
	Feeding
Pups	Sleeping (solitary, social)
	Feeding
	Suckling
	Solid food—eating behavior
	Drinking
	Locomotion: Stages include trunk movements or wiggling, twitching, freezing, sniffing, orienting, hopping, crawling with forepaws, righting movements, rising to erect position, walking, running, climbing, rising and swaying, jumping.
	Sensory behavior: Describe indications of response to visual, auditory, odor, and tactile cues.
	Elimination: urination, defecation, anal licking.
	Vocalization: quality of sounds (if audible), stimuli to sound production
	Grooming: face washing, licking, scratching (which paws, location of area scratched)
	Exploration: sniffing objects, making lateral head movements, digging in nesting materials
	Social behavior: Describe at each stage—huddling, mutual sleeping postures; fighting over nursing position; general social activity such as running, jumping, chasing, wrestling, mutual grooming; fighting, including description of posture, length of encounter, acting of "victor" and "loser"; pseudo-sexual behavior, sniffing and licking of genitals, mounting.

Stages of growth and physical development should be outlined on the basis of exact descriptions of skin (later fur), appearance of coloration, apparent length and weight, and time of opening of eyes.

the mothers you should look for the following categories of observations (as listed on Table 1): nest building, retrieving the young, grooming the young, self-grooming, nursing, sleeping, feeding, walking. The last four activities you should observe simply to see the postures and movements characteristic of an adult rat so you can compare those behaviors in the pups. The mothers' behaviors of major interest are those that involve the litter (nest building, retrieving, grooming, and nursing). You should see changes in those behaviors during the 4 weeks because at the end of that period the litter will be weaned and may be living away from the mother.

When you observe a behavior such as

grooming, record in as much detail as you can exactly how the mother does it. How does she hold the pups? Does she hold them differently at different ages? What parts of the body are involved? Is this grooming similar to her grooming of herself or to the pups' grooming of one another? When observing nursing you should also record details such as how much time it takes, what postures are displayed, what the ages of the pups are, and what the method of weaning is. Each behavior that you observe will present many aspects that you should describe precisely. If possible, try to establish your own set of subcategories for these behaviors. Remember that besides obtaining a complete description of the behavior, you are also interested in describing changes in that behavior over the 4-week period. Examples of criteria for several categories of behavior are given in Table 2.

Observation of pups. Spend two thirds of each observation period observing the pups in any single cage. Observe the same cage during all 12 observation periods so you gain an appreciation of the behavioral and anatomical development of rat pups. Table 1 provides a partial list of items to observe. For each item you must record in careful detail the components of each behavior. How do they sleep? In what position? Related to the litter in what way? How does walking develop? What parts of the body make what kind of movements? Do the pups walk the way the mother walks?

Be careful not to record your feelings or interpretations; simply record what *you see.* "The mother is taking time for herself" or "She hates her babies now that they are older" are *not* good observations. "Mother is sleeping on opposite side of cage from nest" or "Mother walks away from pups during nursing" are appropriate observations because they do not project human ideas onto the animals.

Instructions for paper. Your paper has two components: (1) a chronological summary of your observations and (2) an interpretation or discussion of the important concepts demonstrated by your observations. Assume that your paper will be read by another member of the class who could not do the observations but who read the same material you did.

Summary. In making your summary, first arrange all 12 observations of mother and pups in order and read through them to see the chronology of feeding changes, mobility, grooming, condition of the nest, and so forth. You are to summarize material both about the mothers and the pups. A summary requires the omission of some of the details and the selection of more important observations. If your 12 observation periods show a continuous, detailed picture of growth for only some of the behaviors listed on Table 1, then emphasize those behaviors and ignore others. You will see that the quality of your summary depends on the quality of your observations. A graphic or tabular summary of your observations is helpful to the reader. Remember, there are many details to be read about and understood, so give the reader all the help you can.

Also remember that you are providing scientific data rather than a report on your own feelings. For example, even if you had a strong emotional reaction to seeing a mother rat give birth, you should not include a report on that in this paper (you might want to write an entirely different kind of essay for your English class on your feelings of pity, terror, or sympathy as you watched a mother rat give birth).

Table 2   Sample Criteria for Behavioral Categories

Nest building	Mother rat pushes bedding material with nose, holds it in forepaws, heaps it in corner of cage (How high? How tidy or regular? What proportion of the bedding materials in the cage is included in the heap?). Mother lies on heap creating a depression in the center. Mother works at edges of heap. Mother picks up her tail and encircles her body with it.
Grooming self	Mother lies on back, paws extended, licks and bites at fur (Where?). Mother scratches at head behind ears with fore or rear paws (Which?). Mother rubs against sides of cage. (Describe as precisely as possible position of mother while she is licking.)
Feeding behavior	Mother lies on side, belly extended (describe position exactly). Pup struggles for position on mother's belly with wriggling movements of trunk and treading movements of forepaws. Pup holds on to nipple, engages in coordinated sucking movements and treading of forepaws. Pup struggles to maintain position, squeals if displaced by mother's movements or by other pups. (Time the length of suckling for several pups.) Describe actions as pup disengages when it is sated.

Interpretation. The purpose of this section of the paper is to link the observations you have described in the summary with the theoretical ideas and concepts discussed in the readings and in class. In a sense you are telling the reader why it was worthwhile to have made these observations. You should take several of the theoretical concepts about trends in development or about species-specific behavior and look for data in your observations that would help to explain or illustrate these concepts. One example might be the concept that motor behavior progresses from mass responses to specific or differentiated responses. Look at your observations. Can you find examples of mass responses? (Generalized twitching might be one.) Can you find examples of specific responses? (Handling solid food is one.) Now check the frequency with which mass responses and specific responses occur early in the pup's development and later in development. Does the concept fit your observations? Are there more mass responses early and more specific responses later?

Do something like this for two or three other concepts. The more ably you relate observations to concepts, the more you will understand how scientists are able to draw conclusions of importance from observational data.

ACTIVITY

5l

CONSERVATION ABILITY IN CHILDREN
J. Russell Nazzaro

Concept

The term *conservation* refers to the cognitive ability to recognize that changing the physical dimensions of an object does not change its mass, its weight, or its volume. Children in what Piaget calls the preoperational stage of cognitive development, from ages 2 to 7, typically cannot grasp this notion. Taller usually means more, regardless of relative width. However, by about age 7, as children enter the concrete operational stage of cognitive development, they are gradually able, in successive order (about a year apart), to conserve mass, weight, and volume. The various demonstrations in this activity afford adolescents an opportunity to observe differences in the cognitive abilities of young children that are characteristic of different age ranges and corresponding stages of cognitive development. They may also encourage students to take a greater interest in other behaviors of young children and the related psychological theories.

Instructions

For subjects, ask some students to bring their younger siblings (of appropriate ages) to class for a day, being sure that parents are informed about and consent to the reason for the visit. The contrast in cognitive abilities would likely be demonstrated if you were to use just two children, one of preschool age, and the other a grade schooler (second grade or above). However, the contrast and its relationship to age would be more striking with more subjects in each age group. Indeed, with some range in the ages of the grade schoolers, the gradual development of the ability to conserve—first mass, then weight, then volume—might also be demonstrated.

To test a child's ability to conserve mass, shape two equal amounts of clay into balls of the same size. Ask the child whether he or she considers them to contain the same amount of clay. Then manipulate one into a distinctly different shape such as a sausage or pancake and, with the ball as a reference, check the child's perception of whether the two objects contain the same amount of clay.

Ability to conserve weight can also be tested with two clay balls. Place them on a scale and show the child that they are of equal weight. Then again manipulate one into another shape and inquire about their relative weights.

Ability to conserve volume can be tested by starting with two identical containers holding equal amounts of liquid and then pouring the contents of one into a different-sized container that is perceptibly taller, shorter, wider, or narrower.

As Krech, Crutchfield, Livson, and Krech (1976) indicate in their discussion of the conservation concept, "Questioning is by no means a simple matter. [In a test of volume conservation, for example,] one cannot ask even a bright six-year-old, 'Is the quantity of liquid in the two containers the same?' The inquiry must be appropriate to the child's development level. Instead, we may ask, 'Suppose you are very thirsty and want to drink the water in one of the bottles. Is there just as much water in each bottle?'" Thus the questions and procedures must be carefully planned and rehearsed. Use some of the suggested readings to prepare for this exercise.

Discussion

You can use the demonstrations for a discussion of Piaget's views on intelligence and child development in general. Terms to be covered should include *reversability* and *transitivity*. Note that Piaget views the development of conservation as largely a maturational process. That is, conservation will occur when the cognitive structures mature to that level. Thus in Piaget's opinion, training is not likely to accelerate the onset of conservation. Yet other factors are obviously involved. For example, research in other countries has shown that children achieve conservation at different ages (Greenfield, 1966). You could discuss a variety of studies that have attempted to accelerate intelligence, as well as studies that point to the importance of critical early experiences for the development of intelligence (see White, 1971).

Suggested Background Readings

Goldschmid, M. L., & Bentler, P. M. The dimensions and measurement of conservation. *Child Development,* 1968, *39,* 787–815.

Greenfield, P. On culture and conservation. In J. S. Bruner et al. (Eds.). *Studies in cognitive growth.* New York: Wiley, 1966.

Krech, D., Crutchfield, R. S., Livson, N., & Krech, H. *Psychology: A basic course.* New York: Alfred A. Knopf, 1976. (chap. 5)

Piaget, J., & Inhelder, B. *The psychology of the child.* New York: Basic Books, 1969.

White, B. L. *Human infants: Experience and psychological development.* Englewood Cliffs, N.J.: Prentice-Hall, 1971.

52

MATURATION VERSUS DEVELOPMENT
Richard A. Kasschau

Concept

It is difficult to discuss developmental psychology without talking about the development *of* . . . social processes or language skills or some other skill or behavior. And interlaced through most studies of developmental processes is the traditional distinction between inherited and learned influences of human behavior. One source of confusion here may attend the distinction (or lack of it in the minds of your students) between *developmental* changes and those attributable strictly to *maturation*.

Preparation of Class

In a discussion format, create definitions of *development* and *maturation*. Development can be defined as all the processes of change through which a person's potential behaviors evolve. These developmental changes may occur as new qualities (e.g., social grace), abilities (e.g., social skills), or traits (e.g., the increasing reliability of older children). These changes include positive influences from growth and maturational processes as well as learning. These, you will note, are *qualitative* changes in behavior.

Maturation can be defined as changes in behavior that result exclusively from physiological growth and change as predisposed by heredity and precipitated or enabled by the environment. These lead to *quantitative* changes in behavior brought about by changes in size, physical structure, and proportion.

Instructions

You can illustrate the difference between maturational and developmental changes by using examples. How many behaviors can your students think of that they learned to perform primarily through practice after certain critical maturational changes have occurred? A number of examples suggest themselves: (a) Learning to climb the large rope that hangs from the rafters during gym class. As the ratio of arm strength to body weight increases, this becomes much easier. (b) Learning to water- or snow-ski or to ride a bicycle. (c) Changing tastes regarding what is good to eat or drink—ask how many of your students enjoy asparagus or spinach now and how many did so while in elementary school. Even the drinking of coffee, liquor, beer, or wine—for those who *do* develop the habit—is an acquired taste, probably enabled by the changing sensitivity of our sense of taste.

In contrast, how many examples of developmental changes in behavior can be cited? All sorts of examples should suggest themselves. (a) How about social behavior? Infants don't care who they play with, children during late childhood strongly prefer same-sex playmates,

Adapted from *Teacher's Guide With Tests to Accompany Psychology: Exploring Behavior* by R. A. Kasschau. Copyright 1980 by Prentice-Hall Publishing Company. Reprinted by permission.

whereas teenagers and adults usually prefer mixed-sex activities. (b) Ask any student in your class to describe how the ideal activity for a date has changed in the time since they started dating. Do they still enjoy doing the same things now as in junior high school? (Or as in high school for college students?)

In comparing the examples that are cited, note that physical factors play a prominent role in maturational changes. For example, the increased interest in sex is caused by hormonal changes occurring during adolescence. In contrast, social and learned changes play a much more significant role in influencing developmental changes in our behavior.

Discussion

A primary point to be drawn out in the discussion is the interactive nature of inherited and learned influences on human behavior. Heredity or environment? Nature or nurture? No, it's both—a lesson that can be demonstrated in many ways ranging from those factors that influence intelligence to those affecting our choice of same- or opposite-sex companions as we age.

Suggested Background Readings

Hurlock, E. B. *Developmental psychology: A life-span approach* (5th ed.). New York: McGraw-Hill, 1980.

Newman, B. M., & Newman, P. R. *Development through life: A psychosocial approach*. Homewood, Ill.: Dorsey Press, 1979.

Stone, L. J., & Church, J. *Childhood and adolescence: A psychology of the growing person* (5th ed.). New York: Random House, 1979.

ACTIVITY
53

THE LIFE CYCLE
Peggy Brick

Overview

A unit on the life cycle utilizing Erik Erikson's eight stages of development provides many opportunities for students to become more actively involved in exploring the development of human behavior. Following are some activities I use during this 8-week unit. These activities are in constant interaction with the more traditional presentation of information through books, lecture/discussions, and audio-visual materials. The activities are divided into categories appropriate for different age groups, to better organize the presentation of the unit. (Please note that the titles used do not represent specific labels for Erikson's stages of development.)

As I outline Erikson's eight stages on the blackboard, students are asked to include in their notes the name of a person they know personally who is at each stage. Immediately the theory becomes less abstract and more meaningful. Throughout the unit, students can check theory against the reality of their living person. Students next examine the life cycle in terms of their own lives by constructing a "life line" in their Journal (a separate private section in their notebooks). Turning the notebook paper lengthwise, students draw a line across the middle of the page and label their birthdate on the far left and a projected death date on the far right. They place the day's date several inches from the far left and note on the line important events during their first 5 years. An accident, a family move, a birthday party, a certain holiday, or the beginning of school might be examples of such events. They then recall elementary school years and early adolescence. We then begin to look at the future. Students note what they would like to have accomplished 1 year from today, in 5 years, in 10 years, when they will be middle-aged, and when they reach the age of retirement. Finally, they note other things they want to do before they die. This exercise, so demanding and so absurd, is greeted with a combination of seriousness and mirth as students divide into pairs to discuss those items they choose from their life lines. Later, as a full class, students share what they learned during the exercise.

Early Development

After the overview, we begin the study of early child development. Each student arranges a 1-hour observation of a child 5 years old or under. Observation techniques are practiced by observing a film on young children.[1] I then have the class observe my behavior for 5 minutes, writing down everything they see. By comparing notes after both exercises, the students begin to understand that some of the smallest details may reveal important data. After their child observation experiences, the students write a report that includes their notes, as well

---

[1] "How Babies Learn." Available on a rental basis from Indiana University, Audio Visual Center, Bloomington, Indiana 47401.

as a discussion of the verbal, motor, and social development of the child they observed. After parent interviews, they also report factors such as illness, family moves, or recent sibling births that may have affected the child's development.

Middle Childhood

To illustrate the next stage, a child between 5 and 8 years old is invited to class for several Piaget-type demonstrations. The students take detailed notes as I interact with the child. Questions in the beginning probe basic knowledge: counting, defining words, drawing a self-portrait, describing his or her family. Then I ask which glass has the most liquid in it as colored water is poured from a tall glass into a shorter, wider glass and which ball is bigger as a ball of clay is moulded into an oblong. Finally, to demonstrate moral development, I tell the following story. One boy was baking a cake with his mother and when he went to the refrigerator to get eggs, he dropped the whole carton and broke 12 eggs by accident. Another boy's mother told him *not* to go into the refrigerator, but he went in to get some soda and as he opened the door, one egg fell out and broke. Which boy was naughtier? This question determines whether a child considers motivation in determining if an act is "good" or "bad." After I finish, students ask questions. They are certain to uncover attitudes toward school, favorite TV programs, foods, and activities. For homework, students use all of the data collected to write a tentative portrait of the mental development of a child of that particular age, based on this one limited observation.

Latency Period

As other units on development commonly do, this unit underemphasizes the latency period. However, a number of the students do independent projects in which they observe elementary school children. The procedure for these projects, required in all other units but elective in this one, is established at the beginning of the year. Students present a research question, a hypothesis, and a research design for approval before proceeding to gather data. Typical projects have examined the importance of sex role scripting in determining children's sense of mastery; a content analysis of sexism in elementary textbooks; comparison of classroom behavior in boys and girls; and observation of teacher's language and behavior expressed to boys and to girls. These projects are reported to the class, and both methodology and results are explained.

Adolescent Period

Role play and a "career search" are major activities in the study of adolescence. For the role play, students anonymously submit problem situations that they would like to see acted out (i.e., conflicts with parents, with teachers, with peers). After the role play, the class discusses the transitions and considers alternative behaviors. We frequently role play particular actions several times, seeking the best approach to enhance communication and resolve the conflict.

The "career search" is designed to be suggestive and not at all definitive. First students take a self-inventory that elicits their personal strengths and weaknesses. Then they take a values inventory that has them rank their priorities for a job: making a lot of money, being promoted, being with interesting people, having good vacations, etc. Next they research a variety of career education materials to discover a vocation that might combine their personal strengths and work values.

Early Adulthood

A parenting simulation provides a review of earlier discussions on child rearing and gives students an opportunity to imagine themselves in one of the major roles of Erikson's next stage. Students are divided at random into pairs (we do not assume that every child is brought up by a male/female couple). These dyads are presented, one at a time, with 10 child-rearing situations representing at least one type of problem for each year of life. Situations might include the following: Your baby is newborn, will you breast-feed it? Your child is 18 months old and has started to bang its head when you put it to bed. Your child is 3½ and throws food on the floor, refusing to eat anything except peanut butter sandwiches. Your child is 5 and has regressed to wetting the bed following the birth of a sibling. The students discuss each parent's responsibility in these situations. Are the roles equal? If not, what are the differences? After the "parents" have made their decisions, they share them with the class. Just like real parents, some are insecure and ready to change their behavior when challenged, while others are secure about their methods and are ready to defend them.

Old Age

Although middle age is given short shrift in our study, student attitudes toward old age are improved dramatically by three activities: an interview with a person over 60; the movie, *Peege;*[2] and a simulation in which students "become old." We prepare carefully for the interview. First, a time line labeled "All in One Life Time" and dated from 1900 to 1980 is drawn the length of the blackboard. Together we fill it with major events and inventions that have had an impact on people living through those years. With this background, students divide into groups to write questions they want to ask older people. The questions are consolidated into one list that includes inquiries into early childhood; courtship, marriage, and family; career; the effect of world events; changes in life-style; attitudes toward society and youth; interviewees' wishes for their own lives; and their advice to the student. Students are free to revise this list for their particular interview.

Preparation also includes role playing the interview. After a demonstration in front of the class, we discuss the strengths and weaknesses of the interviewer's procedure. Then, in pairs, the students practice interviewing. The interview itself, reported in a paper, is a profound experience for many students, who gain new respect for the meaning of a life, often their grandparent's.

The impact of the interview is reinforced by the movie *Peege,* which shows a family's frustrated attempt to communicate with a senile grandmother in a nursing home at Christmas. Many students realize their own failures to communicate with older people and believe they now know how to try.

The final assignment, greeted with noisy protest, is for students to simulate being old for 4 hours and to record their feelings. Students choose how they will "be old": the age, the ailments, the living conditions. Most students cannot bear to confine their lives for 4 hours but will try it for 1 or 2 hours. Some slow down their movements, wear blindfolds, put waxed paper over their eyes, place cotton in their ears, and bind their fingers. Others can't reach up or bend down or will take 5 minutes coming down the stairs only to find that the telephone has stopped ringing before they can get to it! Several students write their reports with "arthritic" fingers. Class discussions reveal a new awareness of having a body that is severly limited in its responsiveness. This unit ends with a subunit on death and dying, but that's another story!

Suggested Background Readings

Erikson, E. H. *Childhood and society* (2nd ed.). New York: Norton, 1963.

Hurlock, E. B. *Developmental psychology: A life-span approach* (5th ed.). New York: McGraw-Hill, 1980.

---

[2] Available from the New Jersey State Museum, Film Loan Service, Trenton, NJ 08625.

54

LIFE SPAN DEVELOPMENT
Freda G. Rebelsky

Concept

Most of us have stereotyped ideas about people at various ages, that is, about teenagers, individuals in their 20s, people in their 60s, and so forth. This exercise is intended to illustrate the kinds of behaviors, tasks, attitudes, and beliefs that people associate with various ages. It is in fact a kind of word association task, but in this case the stimulus is not a word, but an age decade.

Instructions

Give each of the students a sheet of paper that lists 10 decades with three blank spaces beside each decade.

Decade			
0 – 9	_____	_____	_____
10 – 19	_____	_____	_____
20 – 29	_____	_____	_____
30 – 39	_____	_____	_____
40 – 49	_____	_____	_____
50 – 59	_____	_____	_____
60 – 69	_____	_____	_____
70 – 79	_____	_____	_____
80 – 89	_____	_____	_____
90 – 99	_____	_____	_____

Tell the students that they are to think of three words that seem appropriate to each decade and to write those words in the blanks beside that particular decade. Instruct them, as an example, to think of someone's life (in the abstract) from the ages 30 to 39 and to ask themselves what words come to mind when they think of such a person. Give them 15 minutes to work on the word list. At the end of that time tell them to stop and to put the letter E next to the decade for which it was easiest to find words and the letter H next to the decade for which it was hardest to find words. Then chart the E and H results on the chalkboard by listing how many students judged each decade as easiest or hardest.

Discussion

Rarely, if ever, will you get a distribution that equally represents all decades. Ask the students to speculate about the nature of the distribution. Why were some decades harder or easier than others? You might also point out how difficult it is to select 30 words in 15 minutes. Ask the students to read out some of their words for a particular decade. Note what similarities and differences exist. The variety of words usually achieved in this exercise is useful for showing students how differently the same thing can be seen by others. If you can spend some time on this topic in the next class period, collect the students' sheets and calculate a frequency distribution of words by decade for the whole class. Distribute copies of that listing the following day as a basis for discussion. What words are most commonly associated with a particular decade and why? Are there decades for which there is little uniformity in associations? If so, why is that the case? Depending on the nature of the words, you can use them as the basis for discussing a number of topics such as ageism, developmental tasks, and life crises. As a variant you could ask half the class to complete the exercise thinking of a female at each decade, while the other half thinks about a male at those ages. In making such an assignment, you might want to make sure you have an equal number of males and females in each of the two groups. Thus, in analyzing the responses you could look at the class data as a whole, look at the words for the hypothetical female versus the words for the hypothetical male, or reduce these two categories still further by looking at responses for each from males and females in the class. This variation would allow you to see what perceived differences exist based on the sex of the hypothetical individual and the sex of the individual making the associations.

Suggested Background Readings

Hurlock, E. B. *Developmental psychology: A life-span approach* (5th ed.). New York: McGraw-Hill, 1980.

Newman, B. M., & Newman, P. R. *Development through life: A psychological approach*. Homewood, Ill.: Dorsey Press, 1979.

Rebelsky, F. G., & Dorman, L. *Child development and behavior* (2nd ed.). New York: Alfred A. Knopf, 1973.

55

AGE-OLD BELIEFS
Robert A. Goodale

Concept

What are our attitudes toward and beliefs about old age, and how do they fit the reality of old age in America? There is an increasing proportion of persons who are old—that is, over 65—in the United States. In 1970 the approximate figure was 9–10% of the population. That percentage is going to increase at least through the year 2000. Also, the likelihood is that students who participate in this activity will themselves experience old age. In other words, old age is a major fact of life around us and for us. One aspect of old age that many gerontologists have argued is important is our beliefs about old age. Although there is some controversy, most gerontologists would suggest that there is a strong negative evaluation of old age and old people. For example, in a national survey of a representative sample of persons 18 years old and over, the National Council on Aging (1975) found that the seventh decade and beyond were most often cited as the worst years of life and that the public generally overestimated the financial, social, health, and other problems of old age. In the study, old persons were described as being not very adaptable, not very bright and alert, and not very good at getting things done. Also, respondents overestimated the percentage of time that old people spend watching television, doing nothing, and sitting. The following activity is designed to introduce students to the subject of aging, to explore their peer group's beliefs about aging, and to see how their peer group's beliefs square with popular stereotypes of old age and findings on the reality of old age.

Preparation of Class

Tell students that you want their assistance in gathering material for a class discussion of young and elderly persons' views of old age. Their participation is not likely to cause them any embarrassment. They are to find two people to participate in a project. They should give these participants the same information that you have given them about the project and the discussion. All people whose participation is sought should be free to decline participation.

Instructions

Several days before the class period scheduled for the discussion, ask each student to find two people to participate in the project—one their own age and one elderly. They should give each of their participants a sheet of blank paper, asking their peer to draw a picture that represents a typical scene in the life of an elderly person, and asking the elderly person to draw a typical scene *in his or her own life*. They should tell their participants that artistic merit is not important, only what the participants see as a typical scene.

On the scheduled day, have students bring the drawings to class. Tape the drawings to the walls and chalkboards, grouping all those by young persons and all those by elderly persons. Have students examine the drawings for about 15 minutes, noting what the young persons consider to be typical of the elderly and what the elderly consider to be typical of themselves.

Discussion

The following questions can be used to guide discussion:

"How well does the content of the pictures drawn by your peers match the content of the pictures drawn by the elderly persons?"

"Is there evidence of age-norm pressures in the pictures?" (Explain that age norm means the age at which the majority of people experience certain major life events, such as marriage, retirement, or grandparenthood, or the age at which certain behaviors are regarded as appropriate.)

"How might beliefs about old age affect a person's interactions with elderly persons or their own experience of old age?"

"Why do misconceptions about old age arise? What can be done to alter them?"

Ask students to imagine what their own old age will be like, and have them contrast their expectations with their views of old age. Introduce the concept of "ageism," relating it to sexism, racism, and other manifestations of stereotyped thinking.

The discussion could be enriched by your selecting some questions from the survey instrument used by the National Council on Aging, having students answer them anonymously, and presenting the results. Projects that might be assigned to students as follow-up activities are to have students watch selected television programs and describe the images of old age presented there or to have students list some of their beliefs about old age and then do research to see if their beliefs correspond to reality. A good source for the latter project is Atchley (1977).

Note: I have found that the students' peers' drawings typically reflect the elderly as sedentary. This "rocking-chair" stereotype is not the way in which the elderly view themselves, however. They portray themselves involved in a large variety of activities.

Suggested Background Readings

Atchley, R. *The social forces in later life.* Belmont, Calif.: Wadsworth, 1977.

Bennett, R., & Eckman, J. Attitudes toward the aging: A critical examination of recent literature and implications for future research. In C. Eisdorfer & M. P. Lawton (Eds.), *The psychology of adult development and aging.* Washington, D.C.: American Psychological Association, 1973.

Croom, B. J. Aging education for the high school student. *Social Education,* 1978, *42,* 406–408.

McTavish, D. G. Perceptions of old people: A review of research methodologies and findings. *Gerontologist,* 1971, *11*(4, Pt. 2), 90–101.

National Council on Aging. *The myth and reality of aging in America.* Washington, D.C.: Author, 1975.

Northcott, H. C. Too young, too old—Age in the world of television. *Gerontologist,* 1975, *15*(2), 184–186.

Pratt, F. A. *Teaching about aging.* Boulder, Colo.: Social Science Education Consortium, 1977.

56

THE STAGES OF DEATH AND DYING
Robert A. Goodale

Concept

Death and dying have recently become topics of wide interest, and among the most widely referred to observations on the topic is Elisabeth Kübler-Ross's stage theory of dying (Kübler-Ross, 1970). According to Kübler-Ross, the news of impending death sets into motion a dying person's coping mechanisms, and the major defense the person throws up identifies where that person is in the process of coming to grips with his or her own death.

As outlined by Kübler-Ross, the stages of death and dying are (1) denial and isolation, (2) anger, (3) bargaining, (4) depression, and (5) acceptance. In the first stage, the person suddenly feels very vulnerable after a lifetime of overcoming obstacles, looks for evidence that some mistake has been made, and denies that acceptance is required of him or her.

During the anger stage, individuals become perturbed that all of their plans are about to be cut short, and they lash out at everyone and everything that reminds them that soon they will no longer participate in the normal course of events.

When an individual turns to changes in diet, reduces his or her smoking, takes meals or medicine more faithfully, gets rest, and becomes more pleasant to others formerly ignored or scowled at, then that individual has entered the bargaining stage—holding out for the hope that being good along some guiltridden dimension will be rewarded with enough time to reach an emotionally important goal.

Following the stage of bargaining is the stage of depression—depression over the impending loss of all love objects, and then depression due to felt impotence and the inexorability of the nearing end. After that comes acceptance—not a brightening of the individual in the face of the inevitable, but a quiet expectation, void of feelings and filled with resignation.

The present exercise provides an opportunity for students to experience some of the emotions that characterize the stages of death and dying identified by Kübler-Ross and to observe a progression of changes over a rather short time span.

Materials Needed

A hat and one slip of paper for each student in the class. Number the slips from one to however many class members there are, or leave the slips blank, to be filled in by the students themselves.

Preparation of Class

It is expected that this exercise will be used in the context of studying about death and dying and specifically when considering Kübler-Ross's stage theory.

Since not all students can be expected to deal comfortably with such subject matter, it is important that the class be made aware that anyone made uncomfortable by any class activity or discussion on death and dying, whether contrived or accidental, may refuse to participate at any point in the process without penalty or disapproval.

Instructions

As soon as class begins (a) assign a number to each student in the class, (b) have students write their numbers on the small slips of paper that you then pass out to each one of them, and (c) collect all the slips and put them into the hat. In a serious voice announce to the class that someone in the room must die and that at the end of the class hour you will reach into the hat and pull out a number—the number of the person who must die by the end of the class. Return to your desk, put the hat with the slips in it in a conspicuous place, and take notes on the comments made by students over the next 30–40 minutes. If discussion lags, ask leading questions: "_____ , would you like the number to be yours?" "_____ , how will you feel if it's _____'s number that I pull out of the hat?" "_____ , if you knew for sure I was going to pick your number, is there anything you would want to do between now and the end of the class?"

If the class is slow to take the activity seriously enough, take on a more serious demeanor, glance at the clock, remind them how little time remains, shake the slips in the hat, and ask a leading question such as those suggested above. If the class begins to get heavy, lighten it up by reminding students that it is only an exercise, that you are glad they have taken it seriously, but that it is, of course, only an exercise.

Discussion

Terminate the activity at whatever point makes sense to you, but in no case should the class end before you get a chance to adequately explain the purpose of the exercise. You may choose to end the exercise by picking a number out of the hat, but in my own classes I have found that step gratuitous by the end and so I omit it.

Draw the students' attention to Kübler-Ross and her theory of the stages of death and dying. Review comments that were made during the exercise that fit into her theory. For example, comments like "This is a joke," "Why do we need to do this?" and "This isn't funny!" could be expected to emerge in the first few minutes of the exercise as the students deny that it is a meaningful activity. Comments like "Why me?" "But I'm so young!" as well as more obviously hostile and aggressive statements fit into Kübler-Ross's second stage. Third-stage comments center on ways to get a little more time to complete something before the time is up, and depression comments echo sentiments of sadness and disillusionment.

In an exercise this short students won't necessarily generate comments appropriate to all five categories, but usually comments for the first three categories will emerge.

Discuss with the students how they were feeling. Ask them how they would feel if a particular class member really did get the news that they had only a few weeks to live. Point out that young people do die from one cause or another whether we like it or not and that although death seldom occurs on a lottery basis, it does occur within a context of never knowing when your number is coming up. Besides the lessons to be learned from Kübler-Ross's stage theory, other points to be made include (a) that death does occur, (b) that we prefer to act as though it doesn't, and (c) that the need to find a meaning for our death can be the stimulus for living.

Suggested Background Readings

Kavanaugh, R. *Facing death*. Baltimore: Penguin Books, 1974.

Kübler-Ross, E. *On death and dying*. New York: Macmillan, 1970.

Lifton, R. J., & Olson, E. *Living and dying*. New York: Bantam Books, 1975.

Wilkenfeld, L. *When children die*. Dubuque, Iowa: Kendall/Hunt, 1977.

CHAPTER VI
SOCIAL PSYCHOLOGY

This chapter contains 14 exercises, four of which are designed for projects outside of class. Four activities deal with the concept of stereotyping, each focusing on different aspects of that process. Activity 57 looks at the relation of sex role stereotypes and judgments of good mental health. Activity 58 examines stereotypes in a decision task and contrasts individuals and groups as decision makers. Activities 59 and 60 illustrate the prevalence of ethnic stereotypes. (A statement of caution is warranted in regard to the latter two activities. Both require that students either exhibit ethnic stereotyped attitudes or be able to role play those attitudes. Such activities may prove discomforting for students and instructors unless the participation and explanations are handled with a great deal of sensitivity.)

Obedience to authority is demonstrated in two exercises. Activity 61 shows obedience to the instructor, and Activity 62 illustrates cooperation with perceived authority in the completion of a public opinion poll.

The other activities span the diverse phenomena of social psychology: the psychology of humor (Activity 63); sexism as it occurs in the classroom (Activity 64); an analysis of advertising appeals and how they produce changes in attitudes (Activity 65); cooperation and competition in daily activity (Activity 66); smiling as a response to social stimuli (Activity 67); the effects of group interactions on the maintenance of self-concept (Activity 68); body language as nonverbal communication (Activity 69); and assigned roles as they influence group dynamics in a problem-solving situation (Activity 70).

ACTIVITY
57

SEX ROLE STEREOTYPES AND MENTAL HEALTH

Concept

Everyone has heard about the double standard with respect to sex, but did you also realize that there is a double standard for mental health? That double standard is the focus of this activity. The idea comes from Broverman, Broverman, Clarkson, Rosenkrantz, and Vogel (1970), who asked clinically trained persons—psychologists, psychiatrists, and social workers—to describe a mature, healthy, socially competent, adult "male," "female," or "person." These authors found that the characteristics judged healthy for an adult person (presumed to show the "ideal standard of health") resembled those behaviors judged normal and healthy for men but not for women. That is, they found that what was considered normal for a woman was not the same as what was considered normal for a person.

Instructions

Give each student a sheet of paper with the following instructions. "Think of a normal adult (_____). Check each item that describes a 'mature, healthy, socially competent adult' (_____)." For one third of the students put "male" in the blank space, for one third put "female," and for the other third put "person." Below those instructions, provide the following list:

____ not at all aggressive	____ easily influenced
____ conceited about appearance	____ very objective
____ very ambitious	____ very self-confident
____ almost always acts as a leader	____ has difficulty making decisions
____ very independent	____ dependent
____ does not hide emotions at all	____ likes math and science very much
____ sneaky	
____ cries easily	____ very direct
____ very active	____ very passive
____ very logical	____ knows the way of the world
____ not at all competitive	____ excitable in a minor crisis
____ feelings easily hurt	____ very adventurous
____ not at all emotional	____ very submissive
____ very strong need for security	____ not uncomfortable about being aggressive

Tabulate the number of times each phrase is checked when a female, a male, and a person are considered. Is an adjective that is frequently used to describe a normal healthy adult more often checked when a male is at the top of the page than when a female is at the top of the page?

Discussion

Discuss the implications for females who are taught that by being normal, healthy people they are not normal. This double standard of mental health can also be discussed with respect to what mental health means. Does it mean adjustment to society? Is it healthy to adjust if society is "sick"? If sometimes it's healthy to adjust and other times it's not, what makes the difference? If therapists have a double standard of mental health, what does this imply about therapy? If the students do not have a double standard of mental health, then the discussion can focus on why. Is the class size too small to detect differences? Are the students younger than the clinicians used in the original article and thus less prejudiced?

Suggested Background Readings

Broverman, I. K., Broverman, D. M., Clarkson, F. E., Rosenkrantz, P. S., & Vogel, S. R. Sex role stereotypes and clinical judgments of mental health. *Journal of Consulting and Clinical Psychology,* 1970, *34,* 1–7.

Broverman, I. K., Vogel, S. R., Broverman, D. M., Clarkson, F. E., & Rosenkrantz, P. S. Sex role stereotypes: A current appraisal. *Journal of Social Issues,* 1972, *28,* 59–79.

Campbell, D. T. Stereotypes and the perception of group differences. *American Psychologist,* 1967, *22,* 817–829.

Clancy, K., & Gove, W. Sex differences in mental illness: An analysis of response bias in self-reports. *American Journal of Sociology,* 1975, *80,* 205–215.

Tavris, C., & Offir, C. *The longest war: Sex differences in perspective.* New York: Harcourt Brace Jovanovich, 1977.

ACTIVITY
58

GROUP DECISIONS AND STEREOTYPES
Joel Goodman

Concept

The Fallout Shelter exercise has proved to be an exciting, provocative, and involving way for students to examine and clarify their values (see Raths, Harmin, & Simon, 1966). It can also be used as a springboard for students to explore basic concepts in role and stereotype theory, the dynamic processes that operate in groups, the psychology of language, the nature of attitude and value acquisition, as well as research on moral development.

Instructions

Spin the following story to your students: "Imagine that our country is under threat of imminent nuclear attack. A person approaches you and asks you to make an independent decision concerning a nearby fallout shelter that can accommodate 6 people but has 12 people vying to get in. Based on the following information about the 12 people, which 6 would you choose to go in the shelter? The group includes a 40-year-old male violinist who is a suspected narcotics pusher; a 34-year-old male architect who is thought to be a homosexual; a 26-year-old lawyer; the lawyer's 24-year-old wife who has just gotten out of a mental institution—they both want to go in together or stay out together; a 75-year-old priest; a 34-year-old retired prostitute who was so successful that she's been living off her annuities for 5 years; a 20-year-old black militant; a 23-year-old female graduate student who speaks publicly on the virtues of chastity; a 28-year-old male physicist who will only come into the shelter if he can bring his gun with him; a 30-year-old female MD who is an avowed bigot; a 12-year-old girl who has a low IQ; and a high school student."

After your students have individually written down their choices, hit them with this challenge: "I would like you to form groups of six and, within 15 minutes, try to see if your group can come up with a *consensus* decision on which 6 people should be admitted into the shelter." This almost always results in stimulating and lively encounters. Groups can rarely reach consensus.

Discussion

There are any number of ways to follow up the exercise. (a) Ask the students to role play (or write a script for) the 12 characters and present their cases for admission to the shelter. A look at the assumptions students make can lead to an examination of role theory and stereotype formation. (b) Have students respond to questions like these: In the group consensus discussion, did you stand up for what you believed? Did you feel pressure to conform? If so, who or what caused it? How did the group reach decisions? Did you feel part of those decisions? These questions can then be tied into an investigation of group process theory as well as the dynamics underlying conformity (Solomon Asch's work would be perfect here). (c) Suggest that your students apply Charles Osgood's semantic differential to each of the characters as a way of leading into a study of the psychology of language. (d) After students have responded to the question "What values were you protecting in your own list?" they could investigate the research on attitude and value formation (including the work of Milton Rokeach and Herbert Kelman, Fritz Heider's balance theory, and Leon Festinger's cognitive dissonance theory) and moral development (e.g., Lawrence Kohlberg's developmental theory).

Suggested Background Readings

Allport, G. W. *The nature of prejudice*. Reading, Mass.: Addison-Wesley, 1954.

Campbell, D. T. Stereotypes and the perception of group differences. *American Psychologist*, 1967, *22*, 817–829.

Raths, L. E., Harmin, M., & Simon, S. *Values and teaching: Working with values in the classroom*. Columbus, Ohio: C. E. Merrill, 1966.

Tajfel, H. Stereotypes. *Race*, 1963, *5*, 3–14.

STEREOTYPING

Concept

This activity is an adaptation, for demonstration purposes, of a study done first by Katz and Braly (1933) and replicated by Gilbert (1951). It is to be used as a springboard for a discussion of stereotyping.

Instructions

Provide students with the following list of racial and national groups: Americans, Chinese, English, Germans, Irish, Italians, Japanese, Jews, Negroes, and Turks. Have students individually rank these groups in order of preference. Then distribute the following list of adjectives and have students match the characteristics with the racial and national groups: artistic, cruel, extremely nationalistic, ignorant, imitative, impulsive, industrious, intelligent, lazy, loyal to family ties, materialistic, mercenary, musical, pleasure-loving, pugnacious, quick-tempered, reserved, scientifically minded, shrewd, sly, sportsmanlike, superstitious, tradition-loving, and very religious. More than one adjective may be used to describe a group, and adjectives may be used more than once.

When this task is completed, have students keep their papers. Then read and compare the following results obtained by Katz and Braly in 1933 (given in terms of the two characteristics receiving the highest percentages of agreement):

Americans	industrious (48%) and intelligent (47%)
Chinese	superstitious (34%) and sly (29%)
English	sportsmanlike (53%) and intelligent (46%)
Germans	scientifically minded (78%) and industrious (65%)
Irish	pugnacious (45%) and quick-tempered (39%)
Italians	artistic (53%) and impulsive (44%)
Japanese	intelligent (45%) and industrious (43%)
Jews	shrewd (79%) and mercenary (49%)
Negroes	superstitious (84%) and lazy (75%)
Turks	cruel (47%) and very religious (26%).

Next share the results of the 1951 Gilbert replication:

Americans	materialistic (37%) and intelligent (32%)
Chinese	loyal to family ties (35%) and tradition-loving (26%)
English	tradition-loving (42%) and reserved (39%)
Germans	scientifically minded (62%), industrious (50%), and extremely nationalistic (50%)
Irish	quick-tempered (35%) and very religious (30%)
Italians	very religious (33%), artistic (28%), and pleasure-loving (28%)
Japanese	imitative (24%) and sly (21%)
Jews	shrewd (47%) and intelligent (37%)
Negroes	superstitious (41%) and musical (33%)
Turks	cruel (12%), ignorant (7%), and sly (7%).

Discussion

Did students agree in their rankings of ethnic groups? Is there any stereotyping evident in the ranks assigned? What is a stereotype? How is a stereotype generated? Is there substantial agreement on stereotypes? What is the basis for stereotyping groups? What changes are taking place in our society with respect to stereotypes? Are new stereotypes replacing the old?

Suggested Background Readings

Allport, G. W. *The nature of prejudice*. Reading, Mass.: Addison-Wesley, 1954.

Brigham, J. C. Ethnic stereotypes. *Psychological Bulletin*, 1971, *76*, 15–38.

Gilbert, G. M. Stereotype persistence and change among college students. *Journal of Abnormal and Social Psychology*, 1951, *46*, 245–254.

Katz, D., & Braly, K. Racial stereotypes of one hundred college students. *Journal of Abnormal and Social Psychology*, 1933, *28*, 280–290.

ACTIVITY
60

STEREOTYPES
T. L. Engle and Louis Snellgrove

Concept

This activity illustrates the preconceived attitudes and beliefs held about different groups of people and the relative consistency of those beliefs.

Instructions

On a sheet of paper list the following behaviors:

1. _____ are musical
2. _____ drive Cadillacs
3. _____ have more fun
4. _____ are great lovers
5. _____ cause civil disorders
6. _____ are good athletes
7. _____ are flighty
8. _____ are on welfare
9. _____ all look alike
10. _____ are absent-minded
11. _____ are shrewd and crafty
12. _____ live off other people
13. _____ have hot tempers
14. _____ are more fun

(You might want to expand the list to reflect the prevailing stereotypes of the students in your geographical region.)

Now have your students fill in the blanks with the name of the group of people to whom they believe each statement best applies. When all the blanks are filled in, the students should hand in their answers on separate sheets of paper without including their names. You may want to include other information that could be used for comparison, for example, sex of student. The frequency of answers is then tabulated.

Discussion

What similarities were there in each answer? Were there few, or different answers to each item? Does it sound like an answer you might have thought of? If not, why not? Does the class resent any request to classify persons at all? If so, why? What kinds of situations can you think of that tend to stereotype people (e.g., the role of women on television commercials)? How did these beliefs in stereotypes evolve? What can the class, as individuals and as a group, do to lessen or avoid stereotyping? Why does stereotyping persist? Is it ever useful?

A variation of this activity is to duplicate the statements and have the students gather data from different age groups. The responses of the

Adapted from *Psychology: Its Principles and Applications,* Sixth Edition, Teacher's Manual by T. L. Engle and Louis Snellgrove, copyright © 1974 by Harcourt Brace Jovanovich, Inc. Reprinted by permission of the publisher.

different age groups can later be compared. You might also want to compare differences between male and female responses, etc.

Suggested Background Readings

Allport, G. W. *The nature of prejudice*. Reading, Mass.: Addison-Wesley, 1954.

Brigham, J. C. Ethnic stereotypes. *Psychological Bulletin,* 1971, *76,* 15–38.

Campbell, D. T. Stereotypes and the perception of group differences. *American Psychologist,* 1967, *22,* 817–829.

Tajfel, H. Stereotypes. *Race,* 1963, *5,* 3–14.

ACTIVITY
61

OBEDIENCE TO AUTHORITY
William J. Hunter

Concept

Obedience to duly constituted authority is an essential prerequisite for an orderly society, yet it can be overdone. Real-life examples of totalitarianism should be known by students as a result of social studies instruction, but today's students may consider these examples to be as distant to them as the Civil War was to their parents. Stanley Milgram's experimental studies constitute a dramatic demonstration of the paradox of obedience stated in the first sentence above, but they may seem artificial to students. I have had students who refused to believe the results obtained or even that the study was done, even after seeing filmed reenactments. This demonstration is intended to give the concept of obedience and its attendant dilemmas a more personal meaning.

Instructions

The instructor should enter the class after the students have had time to be seated. It is not necessary that the instructor be the regular teacher of the course; indeed, unless it is the first day of class, it is desirable that the instructor *not* be the regular teacher but another adult not likely to be recognized by the students. If necessary, the instructor should begin by requesting that everyone be seated and then continue with:

"Now could I have everyone move up and fill the empty seats toward the front, please. I find it difficult to speak loudly enough to be heard in the back. (Pause until this request has been honored. If necessary, request individual students to move: "I'm sorry, but could you please take that seat up there?") Thank you."

"Now please remove everything from your desks and place your hands flat on the desk so that I can see when everyone is ready. (pause) Good. Thank you."

"Now could I have the first three people in this row exchange places with the last three people in that row? (pause) Yes, that's good."

Now I'd like everyone with blond hair to stand for a moment. (If necessary, say, "I'd call your hair blond, would you stand, please?") (pause) Okay."

"And people who are wearing a watch, would you raise the hand your watch is on?" (pause)

"Now, those who are standing, turn and face the back. Those whose hands are up, stay as you are. Everyone else, give them a round of applause. (Start clapping; when it appears that all are clapping, stop and continue talking.) Thank you. Now everyone be seated and relax.

Discussion

If someone other than the teacher has been playing the role of instructor, the teacher should return to lead the discussion. Begin by asking, "Why did you do all that?" Pursue the question until students clearly indicate that they ascribed authority to the instructor. Then ask, "But why does he (she) have authority, or why did you think so?" Keep a list on the board of attributes of authority figures. Ask the following questions: Why do you obey authority? (Try to get them to avoid circularity here.) Should you always obey people in authority? (If not, what conditions warrant or justify disobedience?) How does a person get to have authority? What would the world be like without authority? What would the world be like if everyone *always* obeyed authority?

In either the same class or a subsequent one, the teacher should next describe the Milgram studies, emphasizing the differences between people's beliefs about what they would do and the actual behavior of subjects. Students who find the results incredible should be reminded of their own compliance in the demonstration. Some will point out the different nature of the tasks (a realization for which they should be praised), which may lead nicely to a discussion of ethics. In such a discussion, students should be urged to weigh the importance of Milgram's findings against the apparent cruelty of the procedure.

As indicated earlier, this demonstration can be useful as a first lesson. Used in this manner, it can (a) serve as a focusing exercise for a discussion of class rules and regulations; (b) introduce an examination of the teacher and student roles in the classroom; and (c) introduce the concept of *control* and provide a framework for the discussion of psychology as the scientific study of behavior seeking to *explain, predict,* and *control.*

The lesson may, however, be used as part of a unit on social behavior or moral development, or even as a closing demonstration to show how knowledge of scientific psychology can, in fact, enable one (the teacher, in this case) to predict and control behavior.

The teacher should be prepared to deal with questions regarding the ethics of this lesson. Some students will feel embarrassed by their behavior; others may be angry when they perceive that they have been manipulated. Unless the teacher is prepared to answer those questions in the same context that he or she would discuss the ethics of Milgram's studies, the demonstration should not be employed. Handled with sensitivity, such questions can lead to a fuller appreciation of the dilemma of obedience to authority and the peculiar ethical problems faced by researchers who employ human subjects.

Suggested Background Readings

Cartwright, D., & Zander, A. *Group dynamics: Research and theory* (3rd ed.). New York: Harper & Row, 1968. (chaps. 3, 4)

Frank, J. D. Experimental studies of personal pressure and resistance. I. Experimental production of resistance. *Journal of General Psychology,* 1944, *30,* 23–41.

Milgram, S. Behavioral study of obedience. *Journal of Abnormal and Social Psychology,* 1963, *67,* 371–378.

Milgram, S. Some conditions of obedience and disobedience to authority. *Human Relations,* 1965, *18,* 57–76.

Milgram, S. *Obedience to authority.* New York: Harper & Row, 1974.

PUBLIC OPINION POLLS AND COOPERATION WITH AUTHORITY
Louis Snellgrove

Concept

How often do we cooperate with individuals primarily because they represent an authority? Do we cooperate more, or less, if we believe that an authority figure asks us to do so? Do we believe that others cooperate more, or less, with someone they believe is an authority? This activity demonstrates how procedures can be used to bias public opinion polls and shows how different degrees of authority may influence who answers questions in such a poll.

Instructions

Instruct your students as follows:

"Make up a list of five questions dealing with the same topic. You may choose any topic area. All questions should begin with 'Do you agree or disagree?' Type the questions on a sheet of paper so they appear 'official.' Ask the questions of subjects under the three different conditions described below.

"*Always* select your subjects in a highly safe public place during daylight hours only. It is preferable to have one or two other persons with you as a safety precaution. Select your subjects at random from passersby, such as every third person who is *alone*. Record whether or not a subject stops and answers your questions, and record the answers of those who do. At the end of the questions, always thank the subjects for helping you. Use at least 10 subjects for each of the following conditions."

"For Condition 1, memorize this introduction: 'I am doing a survey for my psychology class. Would you take a minute to answer five questions?'

"For Condition 2, memorize this introduction: 'I am writing an article that will be published in our local paper. Would you take a minute to answer five questions?'

"And for Condition 3, memorize the following introduction: 'I am assisting Dr. (use a ficticious name) in collecting data for an article to be published in a scientific journal. Would you take a minute to answer five questions?' In all three conditions, if the subject agrees, then ask your questions. If the subject does not agree, say 'Thank you anyway' and walk away."

Have students complete the following table after collecting data:

Condition	Number of subjects asked to answer the questions	Number of subjects who stopped and answered questions	Percentage of subjects who answered questions
1			
2			
3			

Although the specific answers to their questions are not the primary data in this experiment, you might want to help students analyze the responses they collected.

Discussion

Discussion should center around, but not be limited to, the following questions: (1) Was the percentage of subjects answering questions highest in Condition 1, Condition 2, or Condition 3? (2) As "authority" increases from Condition 1 to Condition 3, is there a corresponding increase in the percentage of subjects answering questions? (3) Would using a different type of introduction, such as the one used in this activity, bias *who* stops and answers questions? Would this result in a bias of answers to a poll? (Hint: Would a particular characteristic of individuals, such as being more susceptible to authority, influence *how* they answered the questions?) (4) Would the sex of the subjects influence whether or not they stopped to answer questions? (5) Would the sex of the person asking the questions influence who stopped and answered the questions? (Note: If you are interested in answers to these last questions on the sex of the subjects, you may wish to repeat this activity and vary the sex of the subject and the one who asks the questions.)

Suggested Background Readings

McNemar, Q. Opinion—Attitudes methodology. *Psychological Bulletin,* 1946, *43,* 289–374.

Milgram, S. *Obedience to authority.* New York: Harper & Row, 1974.

THE PSYCHOLOGY OF HUMOR
Robert A. Goodale

Concept

Consider the following joke: "Did you hear that the _____ (Italians, French, Polish, etc.) can't make ice anymore?" Answer: "No, why not?" "Because the woman who knew the recipe died!" Or yet another joke: "Mommy, mommy, can we get another dog?" Mother: "No, we haven't finished eating this one yet." Jokes such as these are referred to as ethnic jokes and sick jokes, respectively. Other classes of jokes are so-called "dirty" jokes, elephant jokes, puns, in-jokes, and so forth.

What is a joke? Why does it make us laugh? Does psychology have anything to say about humor and laughter? As a matter of fact it does, and two popular theories of humor in psychology today are those of Sigmund Freud (1905/1960) and Arthur Koestler (1964).

Freud reduced humor to expressions of sex (any form of pleasure) and aggression (any form of attack). Ethnic jokes put some other nationality down (aggression), and sick jokes derive pleasure from someone else's perversity or predicament. Sex jokes are obvious examples of Freud's theory, as are jokes that include humiliation, embarrassment, stupidity, or prejudice.

Unlike Freud's theory, which seeks to explain *why* we create humor, Arthur Koestler's theory attempts to explain *how* we create humor. For Koestler, laughter is an explosion—an explosion of emotion that results when two or more ideas brought together clash as opposed to fusing (as in creative problem solving) or simply juxtaposing (as in aesthetic appreciation). If we apply Koestler's theory to the first joke given above, it is obvious that no national group can be so stupid as to need a recipe for making ice, and so the two ideas—(a) ethnic group and (b) recipe for making ice—clash and explode in a burst of laughter. In the second joke, the image of an innocent child earnestly pleading to have its former pet replaced clashes with the bizarre rejoinder from the child's mother.

How adequate are these two theories in explaining the dynamics of a joke? As a modest attempt to answer that question, the present exercise applies the theories of Freud and Koestler to a representative sample of present-day jokes.

Instructions

As with Izaak Walton's famous observation on beginning a rabbit stew, the first thing you need to procure is a sample of jokes. These can be retrieved from your own long-term memory, from family and friends, from joke books found in the library, from popular magazines such as *Reader's Digest,* or by requiring each student to be prepared to tell a joke to the rest of the class on an appointed day. The latter method has a few things going for it, namely, a sample appropriate to the intended audience, mitigated selection bias, observation of a side of students not often rewarded in the academic setting, and the potential for a rip-roaring class.

Whatever the method of sampling, write the two most obvious themes from as many jokes as you can reasonably fit on the blackboard given your own time and space constraints. Explain to the class Freud's theory of *why* we create jokes and Koestler's theory of *how* we create them, as outlined above. Examine each joke with the class and tally whether or not Freud's and Koestler's theories adequately explain the motive and structure of each joke summarized on the blackboard. In applying Freud's analysis, remember that the forms of sex and aggression take on many disguises (e.g., competition, double entendre), so look for the subtle possibilities when the obvious content appears to negate the theory. In applying Koestler's analysis, look for at least two ideas that clash and bounce away instead of fusing or standing juxtaposed for values analysis.

Discussion

How completely does each theory explain the how and why of jokes? Where does each theory provide some insight and where does it fall short? How far can the theories be extended to provide insight into other forms of humorous expression such as slapstick, pantomime, cartoons, and games? If the class as a whole or individual class members are not impressed by the completeness or appropriateness of either theory, what modifications or corrections can they supply which either make the theories more complete or provide a better explanation? Examine "old" jokes that are no longer funny and jokes that still bring out howls of laughter even though we have heard them before, and see if the class can discover why some jokes get old but others do not. Compare jokes that were funny at an earlier age level but no longer are to jokes that are funny at the present age level, and try to gain some understanding of what the difference in the humor is at the two age levels. Finally, consider current concern for displays of violence and aggression in children's television programming. How would children's cartoon comedy TV shows be affected if expressions of aggression as humor were banned from children's programs?

Potential Projects

1. One value of the experimental method is that it enables us to establish cause and effect relations. In the present application, a complete theory of humor should allow an investigator to mix the proper ingredients and predict laughter in every case. Challenge the class to generate a recipe that guarantees laughter with reasonable success. For further insight into the solution, observe a few stand-up TV comedians and analyze their jokes, since such individuals make a living at being successful joke tellers.

2. Can a computer be programmed to create jokes? Take 10 cartoons from a popular magazine. Cut the captions from each cartoon and either on a random basis or on a permutation basis match any caption to any cartoon. Tally how often something (a) as funny, (b) funnier, or (c) less funny results when compared to the original cartoon–caption pairing. Since a computer could be programmed with cartoons and captions and instructed to pair them on some rational basis, what is the outlook for such a technique? What modifications of this simple approach might increase the hit rate?

3. Ask the individual members of the class to indicate on a sheet of paper whether they consider themselves to possess an (a) average, (b) above average, or (c) below average sense of humor. If the class is too small for meaningful analysis, consider having the students conduct a survey of the question on a sample of 100–200 students. Tally the

answers. The surprising result is that usually more than 50% of people surveyed say that they have an above average sense of humor (Eysenck, 1958). Such a conclusion is a logical impossibility, of course. What does it mean to say that someone has an above average sense of humor? What does it mean that most people believe their own sense of humor to be above average?

Suggested Background Readings

Chapman, A. J., & Foot, H. C. *Humour and laughter: Theory, research and application*. New York: Wiley, 1976.

Eysenck, H. J. *Sense and nonsense in psychology* (2nd ed.). Baltimore: Pelican Books, 1958.

Freud, S. *Jokes and their relation to the unconscious* (A. A. Brill, Trans.). New York: Norton, 1960. (Originally published, 1905)

Koestler, A. *The act of creation*. New York: Macmillan, 1964.

ACTIVITY
64

SEXISM IN THE CLASSROOM
David L. Cole

Concept

Throughout the learning of psychology there is a tenuous relationship between academic learning and the application of that learning to one's own life. While students are eager to "learn about themselves," it is not immediately obvious that either they or their instructors are necessarily much changed in their day-to-day behavior by the findings and theories of psychology. This interface of learning and doing can be brought into focus by leading a class discussion on manifestations of sexism in American society and then afterward turning the class's attention to its own behavior during the discussion. By having an observer (a) record, unknown to the class, various aspects of verbal (and possibly nonverbal) interaction and behavior during the discussion of sexism and (b) subsequently report on them to the class, it is possible to demonstrate how thoroughly sex role prescriptions influence our behavior without our awareness.

Instructions

The students should be assigned readings on sexism and sex roles in American society. The readings can vary with what is available but could include an appropriate chapter in the course text, any of several paperback books, or articles from professional journals and/or popular media such as *Psychology Today*. Because of its emphasis on nonverbal behavior, Henley's (1977) paperback *Body Politics* is particularly useful, but many other alternative books would be quite acceptable.

After completing the reading, the class should engage in a discussion of the reading. Clearly the group must be of a size that makes discussion possible, so large classes should be broken down into, small discussion groups. These can be run simultaneously if space is available and time in short supply. No group should have more than 15 members, and it is crucial that each group have roughly equal numbers of men and women.

The focus of the discussion can vary with the sophistication of the class. For example, the focus can be on student reactions to the assertions in the reading, on sexism as they experience it or do not experience it, on how one would go about testing the validity of assertions made in the reading, or on how one would raise children to avoid sex stereotyping. The possible foci of discussion are obviously many. While the discussion takes place, however, one member of each group, specially prepared in advance, should make notations on the flow of the discussion and the roles played by the participants. Henley's book, cited earlier, is a particularly rich source of observations on the different ways men and women conduct themselves in such interaction, and even having students read her book in advance does not seem to affect their behavior once discussion is underway. The observer can very fruitfully use the scheme identified by Bales (1950) for categorizing behaviors in a discussion setting. The observer can record (a) the sex of the person opening the discussion; (b) the order, by sex, in which the others enter the discussion; (c) the types of verbal inputs contributed by each person (questions, answers, agreements, disagreements, digressions, etc., following the Bales model); (d) interruptions, including the sex of the person interrupting and the person interrupted; and (e) the body postures assumed during the discussion. Henley proposes a number of hypotheses about body posture as a function of sex and as an expression of power relationships.

The key to the entire procedure is the follow-up session, in which the observer reports on what went on in the group(s) during discussion. Before reporting, the observer should make tallies so that data can be presented (a) on the frequencies of each type of behavior for both men and women and (b) as a function of the ratio of women to men in the particular group.

Discussion

Very frequently, despite the content of the discussion, it can be easily demonstrated that the two sexes did perform differently and that these differences are in accord with the more dominant, powerful role of men in our society. It is particularly useful to have observed several groups, which is one advantage in breaking the class up into small groups. By contrasting groups it becomes possible to account for individual differences but also to demonstrate that the general domination of the males is not a function of one unique group. The observer's presentation frequently stimulates more group discussion than the original readings and had a considerable impact on students who previously felt that they were reading about "others" more than about themselves.

As can be anticipated, some students may react with anger at finding they have been "spied upon" and to some extent deceived. This opens the door for a discussion of the ethics of social psychological research, the issue of informed consent, and the circumstances that make the giving of informed consent detrimental to pursuit of a research goal. Again, students who have found the question of ethics in social psychological research rather academic feel quite differently when they find themselves "victimized" by the deceit that is part of so much research in this field.

Suggested Background Readings

Bales R. F. *Interaction process analysis*. Reading, Mass.: Addison-Wesley, 1950.

Bardwick, J. M. *Psychology of women: A study of bio-cultural conflicts*. New York: Harper & Row, 1971.

Guttentag, M., & Bray, H. *Undoing sex stereotypes*. New York: McGraw-Hill, 1976.

Henley, M. M. *Body politics*. Englewood Cliffs, N. J.: Prentice Hall, 1977.

ACTIVITY
65

ATTITUDE CHANGE AND ADVERTISEMENTS
Richard A. Kasschau

Concept

Attitudes can be analyzed in a variety of ways, but one tendency that has long existed is to view an attitude as being composed of three elements—cognitive, emotive, and action components. You can use magazine/newspaper and radio/television advertisements to demonstrate this.

Instructions

Assign your class to gather a number of newspaper/magazine and/or recordings of radio/television advertisements—the more, the better. In analyzing the advertisements that are brought in, first divide the ads into those that appeal to the reader/viewer/listener's intellect, emotions, and physical actions. What ads can be found that appeal to *cognitive* aspects of an attitude? Such ads would emphasize facts about the product, or research-based comparisons of the product with its competitors. The *Crest* ads have for many years emphasized X% fewer cavities when brushing with *Crest*. This is an appeal to our beliefs by supplying facts to convince us of the superiority of the product.

The *emotional* appeals emphasize such factors as beauty or sex or threat. One manufacturer of a rust-preventing additive for the car concludes the appeal by having a garage mechanic say, "You can see me now [meaning, of course, to buy the product], or you can see me later!"—really an emotional appeal based on fear. Products that emphasize the good times available from using the product are also appealing to the viewer's emotions.

Finally, the effect hardest to achieve simply through advertising is an appeal directly to the *action* component, since this means you must act. Appeals that involve getting money back if you purchase and use a product are appealing to the *action* component by enticing you to *try* (behave toward) a product. "Loss-leaders" in a grocery store's ads are attempting to get you into their store and in a buying mood.

Having sensitized your class to the cognitive, emotional and action components of an attitude can lead directly into a detailed discussion of the elements of an ad that influence our attitudes. Four are most commonly identified, and can be capitalized on for a demonstration. They are source, message, channel, and recipient.

Why not propose to your students that they pick an "attitude" or behavior that they would like to alter socially—through advertisement? One possibility would be to try protecting the lawns of your school. Is there a favorite pathway worn in the grass because people don't take the

Adapted from *Teacher's Guide With Tests to Accompany Psychology: Exploring Behavior* by R. A. Kasschau. Copyright 1980 by Prentice-Hall Publishing Company. Reprinted by permission.

moments necessary to walk a few extra steps so as to stay on a paved walkway? Why not try to alter that behavior?

Source knowledgeability might be used by getting the school's gardener to assist in making up signs, with his/her role clearly identified. Trustworthiness could involve having the students themselves make the appeal as one social equal to another in the interest of shared concerns for the beauty of the school. This would also involve similarity of source and target. Finally, what if the power of the administration is implicitly behind the campaign? In each instance it might be possible to try a variety of signs located at different spots around the school to assess which factor causes the greatest shift in attitude as noted by obeying the sign's request to keep off the grass.

And what *message* should be used? Probably only the side of the "argument" encouraging staying off the grass is needed, but can your students think of a slogan that would raise the convenience issue (i.e., the reason paths exist) and plead for compliance: "It's quicker to go straight across here, but the grass will be healthier and so will you if you walk a little further. Please go *that* way and save our grass!" would be one possibility.

The *channel* and the *recipient* are not so easy to vary, but again both should be acknowledged and considered as you mount your campaign.

Discussion

This activity can be used as the basis for discussions of attitudes. How are they formed? How do they operate, that is, how do they affect our behavior? Our perception? How are attitudes changed? It can also be used to discuss the usefulness of advertising. What kinds of appeals seem best suited to changing attitudes?

Suggested Background Readings

Howland, C. I., Janis, I. L., & Kelley, H. H. *Communication and persuasion.* New Haven, Conn.: Yale University Press, 1953.

Kasschau, R. A. *Psychology: Exploring behavior.* Englewood Cliffs, N.J.: Prentice-Hall, 1980.

Middlebrook, P. N. *Social psychology and modern life.* New York: Alfred A. Knopf, 1974. (chap. 4)

ACTIVITY
66

COOPERATION AND COMPETITION
Louis Snellgrove

Concept

Are we aware of the number of times each day that we depend on someone else's cooperation to carry on our daily activities? Are we aware of the number of times a day that we compete with other people? The answers might be surprising! This activity is designed to help students understand how often we depend on someone else cooperating with us and how often we are involve in competing with others.

Instructions

Students should be instructed as follows:

"In both of the following conditions, you should *not* depend upon your memory for a long period of time. As soon as it is practical, make appropriate notes. For example, if you are driving a car and observe an appropriate event, do *not* stop the car just to make notes. Wait until you must stop for some other good reason."

"Over a period of 5 days, make a note of each activity you engage in that involves the cooperation of someone else. Examples might include someone driving a car, stopping at a four-way stop sign, and permitting you to go first even though they arrived first; someone opening a door for you when your arms are full; a friend picking you up for school; and so on. Pay no attention to the amount of time involved in the situations. At the end of each day, count the number of times you were involved in a cooperating situation in which *someone else cooperated with you* in some way. Record this frequency in a table similar to the one below."

"During the same 5-day period make a note of each activity in which you compete with others. Some examples are any type of sports event in which you are a participant; seeing who can be first to get to class or to obtain a date with someone; any type of game involving you and one or more other people, and so on. Again, pay no attention to the length of time involved in any of the activities. At the end of each day, count the number of times you were involved in a competing situation and enter the frequency in the table."

Table for Recording Frequency

	Frequency per day						
Situation	1	2	3	4	5	Total	Mean
Cooperation							
Competition							

Discussion

The discussion should center around questions like these: (1) Did you encounter more situations that involved cooperation or competition? (2)

Was there some particular day on which you found a very high (or low) number of events in either situation? If so, can you account for it? (3) As you counted the situations each day, or while you were taking notes during this activity, did it influence the kind of situation you were in? (4) Did performing this activity make you more aware of how often you are involved in each type of situation? (5) Were you surprised at the number of times you were involved in either situation? (6) If you had this many situations in which you cooperated or competed over a 5-day period, how many would you have in a year? During your lifetime? (7) As you become older, would you expect to have more or less such situations? Why?

In addition to discussing the questions given above, the class may wish to compare results between students in terms of what they considered to be situations involving competition and cooperation (*not* in terms of how much competition and cooperation). The following discussion questions are useful: Did other students' situations remind you of some that you perhaps overlooked? For example, did you include *verbal* competition situations? Did you include as a cooperating activity a situation in which you felt *forced* to do something that you really did not wish to do but did anyway (such as running an errand)? Would this be a cooperating situation?

Students may wish to repeat this activity to obtain a more reliable measure of how many competition and cooperation activities they were involved in.

Suggested Background Readings

Cook, H., & Stingle, S. Cooperative behavior in children. *Psychological Bulletin,* 1974, *81,* 918–933.

Deutsch, M. The effects of cooperation and competition upon group processes. In D. Cartwright & A. F. Zander (Eds.), *Group dynamics: Research and theory.* Evanston, Ill.: Row, Peterson, 1953.

67

EXPERIMENT ON SMILING
Joan W. Walls

Concept

The purposes of this exercise are to explore the expression of emotions, including individual and sex differences in such expression; to demonstrate the power of nonverbal communication; to increase awareness of how self-image is affected by the responses of others; to develop students' skills as experimenters; and to study the influence of experimental variables.

Instructions

Have each of the students in the class participate as an experimenter in collecting data on subjects outside of class. Instruct the student experimenters as follows:

"You are going to be an experimenter and perform an experiment on smiling. Your task is to record people's (subjects') responses to you depending on whether you are smiling or not smiling at them. There are a few rules to follow:

1. Your subject should be a stranger to you.

2. You must gain eye contact with the subject to be sure she or he has seen you. Maintain eye contact for a second or two while you either smile or don't smile at the subject.

3. Decide if you are going to smile or not smile *before* approaching a subject, and then stick to your decision.

4. Whenever possible, pick a subject who is alone. It may affect the results if a subject is with other people.

5. You may wish to record additional data such as the date, the time of day, or the location of the experiment."

"The following chart is an example of how to record responses. Carry such a recording sheet with you and record the responses after each subject responds."

Recording Sheet

Date: _____ Time: _____	*Experimenter smiling*		*Experimenter not smiling*	
Response	Male	Female	Male	Female
Smile				
No smile				
Acknowledgement without smile				
Avoidance				
Other				

Description of response categories:

Smile—subject clearly initiates a smile or responds to your smile.

No smile—subject clearly does not initiate a smile or does not respond to your smile.

Acknowledgement without smile—subject nods head, raises a hand, or shows some other form of greeting without smiling.

Avoidance—subject quickly looks away and avoids a further response.

Other—any other response.

"After completing the experiment, add the total responses for each category. You may then wish to go a step further and determine the percentage of total responses in each category. It is desirable to have at least 4 males and 4 females in each condition (smiling and not smiling), for a total of 16 subjects."

Discussion

It is most effective to total the results for all of the student experimenters in the class or group. The data can be collected and presented to the class later or summarized in class. You may want to use the summary process to demonstrate simple statistical analyses of data. Discussion questions relevant to this experiment include the following:

1. How did it feel not to smile? Was it easy or hard not to smile when a person initiated a smile?

2. How did it feel to smile if your subject did not smile back?

3. What differences did you find between male and female responses? Why?

4. For males and females separately: What difference do you think *your* sex as experimenter made on the results you found?

5. What do you think smiling really means? What "message" is being communicated?

6. What circumstances might have changed your results? Time of day? Season? Area of country? Population setting (city or rural area)?

7. Why do you think some people smile more than others?

The following table of percentages represents the results of a smile experiment I conducted at the University of North Carolina at Chapel Hill in 1966. I used a total of 278 subjects. It might be interesting to compare your results with these.

Some Actual Results

Response	Experimenter smiling			Experimenter not smiling		
	Male ($N = 120$)	Female ($N = 30$)	Total	Male ($N = 44$)	Female ($N = 34$)	Total
Smile	31.7	63.3	38.	5.3	17.6	8.7
No smile	35.8	23.3	33.3	80.8	47.1	72.
Acknowledgement without smile	18.3	3.3	15.3	0	2.9	.8
Avoidance	14.2	10.	13.3	14.2	32.4	18.

Suggested Background Readings

Bayes, M. A. Behavioral cues of interpersonal warmth. *Journal of Consulting and Clinical Psychology*, 1972, *39*, 333–339.

LeFebvre, L. M. Encoding and decoding of ingratiation in modes of smiling and gaze. *British Journal of Social and Clinical Psychology*, 1975, *14*, 33–42.

Rosenblatt, P. C. Behavior in public places. *Journal of Marriage and the Family*, 1974, *36*, 750–755.

ACTIVITY
68

SELF-CONCEPT AND GROUP INTERACTION
R. A. Kasschau, L. W. Fordham, P. A. Stewart, H. G. McCombs, and M. W. Smith

Concept

This activity is designed to demonstrate how our interaction with others influences maintenance of the self-concept. It also provides a good illustration of group dynamics. Students outside of the focal group can learn a great deal through observation of this exercise.

Instructions

Make seven masking-tape labels, each from 3 to 4 inches long, with the following commands written on them:

1. Tell me I'm right.
2. Tell me I'm wrong.
3. Praise me.
4. Ridicule me.
5. Ignore me.
6. Listen to me.
7. Respect me.

Apply the labels to the foreheads of seven members of the class, concealing each label from the person on whose forehead it is placed. It is crucial to the game that each member of the group be able to see and read the other six labels without knowing what is on his or her own forehead. For best results, give students labels that are contradictory to their general nature; for example, "Ignore me" might be assigned to a student who is usually accorded the attention of his or her peers.

Assign a debate topic, phrased as an assertion, to the group. (Such assertions as "Women should be drafted" or "Sixteen-year-old boys are less mature than 16-year-old girls" have proved sufficiently controversial to assure the success of the game.) Instruct members to discuss the topic and reach *unanimous* agreement or disagreement on the assertion. In this exercise the dynamics of the discussion are more important than the actual decision of the group. The group members should not be told so but should be encouraged to continue discussion until the issue is resolved (doubtful) or (more importantly) until they become aware of how their responses to the tape on each member's forehead influence their interactions.

Certain cautions are in order. First, students initially tend to forget about the labels and must be reminded many times. Second, there tends to be a lull in conversation after the person labeled "Ignore me" has made a contribution. Third, occasionally a group may fail to disagree sufficiently to generate enough discussion for the various roles to become obvious to group members. If this occurs, another topic should be given to the group.

Additional members of the class may be involved by having them observe a single participant in the discussion and record his or her reactions, monitor the debate and remind any player who fails to react only in terms of a person's label, or inject comment if there is a lull in the conversation.

Discussion

Can students guess what their labels are? On what cues did they base their guesses? Did they like playing their roles? Why or why not? To what extent do people rely on the real world to support how they view themselves? To what extent are people's self-concepts determined by those around them? What are the implications of answers to the previous question for the typical black person's self-perception? For the typical white person's self-perception?

Suggested Background Readings

Clark, K. B., & Clark, M. P. Racial identification and preference in Negro children. In E. E. Maccoby, T. M. Newcomb, & E. L. Hartley (Eds.), *Readings in social psychology*. New York: Holt, Rinehart, & Winston, 1958.

Shapiro, R. L., Zinner, J., Berkowitz, D. A., & Shapiro, E. R. The impact of group experiences on adolescent development. In M. Sugar (Ed.), *The adolescent in group and family therapy*. New York: Brunner/Mazel, 1975.

69

BODY LANGUAGE IN THE CLASSROOM: HERE'S WHAT YOU CAN DO
Timothy Coyne

Concept

Games and demonstrations can be meaningfully incorporated into a unit on body language in order to strengthen observational and inferential skills which can be translated into real-life situations. The following two exercises force the students to engage in and become aware of nonverbal behavior.

The first exercise is a card game designed to increase the students' awareness of their own body language. The second is a field experience in which students observe and record the behavior of those around them and make inferences based on the concepts of body language they have just learned.

Exercise 1

THE BODY LANGUAGE CARD GAME

Materials Needed

One deck of playing cards per six or seven students.

Instructions

The game is played in three rounds, each round with slightly different rules. The class can be divided into groups of six or seven students. Each player is dealt three cards, two of them face down. The object of the game is for one player to get three of the same card by means of trading with other members of the group. Trades must be to the agreement of both parties. In the first round any kind of communication is permitted. When a winner is declared, a brief discussion follows which serves primarily to clarify the nuances of the game to preclude misunderstandings in the next two rounds.

The second deal is played the same way except that in this round the players must not rely on any verbal communication. In the third round, not only is the verbal communication eliminated, but now the students may only use the neck and head to signal and trade. These restrictions tax the student's ability to transact but, at the same time, emphasize how much we depend on our bodies, as well as our voices, to communicate.

Discussion

The "body language card game" is a consciousness-raising small-group exercise which possesses the advantages of appealing to the students' proclivity toward card playing and of drawing on the students' repertoire of nonverbal behavior in order for them to win.

Adapted from "Body Language in the Classroom: Here's What You Can Do" by Timothy Coyne, *Behavioral and Social Science Teacher,* 1975, *2* (2), 37–41. Copyright 1975 by Behavioral Publications, Inc. Human Sciences Press. Reprinted by permission.

Special credit for many of the ideas presented in this paper must go to the creative influence of Mr. Richard Tyre, curriculum director and assistant principal at Upper Darby High School, Upper Darby, Pennsylvania.

After completion of the play, discussion should focus on what kinds of things the players did to get each other's attention and how transactions were accomplished. Nonverbal communication used to open negotiations, and to show acceptance and rejection of offers, should dominate the discussion.

You may also find that videotaping these games is an excellent way to do an analysis of the body language employed by the players. With slow-motion playback, everyone has an opportunity to thoroughly dissect the behaviors.

Exercise 2	FIELD EXERCISE
Materials Needed	Paper and pencils.
Preparation of Class	Divide class into pairs and send them to the cafeteria (or some other public type of place) for this exercise.
Instructions	A strong closing segment to a unit on body language is this field study exercise, which, in addition to providing empirical knowledge of body language, also helps strengthen the students' abilities at discriminating between observation and inference. The school cafeteria is an excellent place to carry out these observations. Here there is a relative lack of suppression of student behavior compared to other school settings. Hundreds of potential subjects are available who need not know they are being observed.

The field-study team should work as pairs, one observing and reporting and the other recording. Since it is highly unlikely that one team can observe all kinds of behavior simultaneously, it may be useful to have the students classify and localize subjects anatomically, each team focusing on a particular portion of the body.

The students are encouraged to *describe* behavior, not interpret it.

Discussion	When students return to the classroom, have them try to organize this mass of raw information into a human body-language ethogram and tie various behaviors to different communicative loci such as shielding, showing boredom, interest, agreement, etc. The latter task is, of course, quite tentative, and alternative interpretations should always be encouraged.

Two "commandments" of kinesics/proxemics are stressed: (a) that a "kinemorph" may have two or more meanings, often opposite from one another. A kinemorph is a bit of behavior isolated from context. For example, vertical forehead wrinkles might mean Question? or Annoyance!; (b) that a kinemorph is a part of the human gestalt and can only be interpreted with validity if one does contextual interpretations.

Suggested Background Readings	Birdwhistell, R. *Kinesics and context: Essays on body motion communication*. Philadelphia: University of Pennsylvania Press, 1970. Davis, F. The way we speak "body language." *New York Times Magazine*, May 31, 1970, p. 8ff. Hall, E. T. *The silent language*. Greenwich, Conn.: Fawcett, 1959. Hall, E., & Hall, M. *The hidden dimension*. New York: Doubleday, 1966.

ACTIVITY
70

GROUP DYNAMICS: CHOOSING A COLOR
James M. Johnson

Concept

This activity provides an excellent example of the manner in which hidden agenda may operate to hinder or help the overt actions of a group. A good, logical cover-up exercise for "power vacuums created by the lack of specific directions," the activity is designed for multiples of 7–10 students.

Instructions

First introduce students to the concept of role playing and to the eight roles listed below. Fashion your own characterizations, as there are no easily located standard descriptions of these roles. Next, ask groups of 7–10 students to arrange themselves in a circle. With no further instructions, place in the center of each circle a large envelope with these instructions printed on the front: "Enclosed you will find three envelopes that contain directions for this group session. Open Envelope I at once. Adhere to the timelines and open Envelopes II and III as instructed."

Envelope I should contain the following instructions on a separate piece of paper: "Time allowed: 15 minutes. Task: The group is to choose a color. Each member is to take one white envelope and follow the individual instructions within it. DO NOT LET ANYONE ELSE SEE YOUR INSTRUCTIONS." Each of the 7–10 individual instruction envelopes should contain one card indicating the participant's role and the position he or she is to take. In two instances, only special knowledge (which implies a role) is given. The cards should read as follows:

Card 1. Role: Information-seeking. Position: Support blue.

Card 2. Role: Tension relieving. Position: Introduce the idea of a different color—orange.

Card 3. Role: Clarifying. Position: Support red.

Card 4. Role: Gate-keeping. Position: Against red.

Card 5. Role: Initiating. Position: Support green.

Cards 6 and 7: You have the special knowledge that the group is going to be asked to select a chairperson later on. You are to conduct yourself in such a manner that they will select you as chairperson.

Card 8. Role: Following. Position: Against red.

Card 9. Role: Information-giving. Position: Against blue.

Card 10. Role: Harmonizing. Position: Against green.

If there are fewer than 10 participants per group, eliminate as many of the *last* three roles as necessary; they are expendable. Seven roles are the minimum needed.

Envelope II, to be opened after 15 minutes, should contain the

---

Adapted from *Instructional Strategies and Curriculum Units for Secondary Behavioral Sciences* edited by James M. Johnson, State University of New York College at Plattsburgh, 1973. Reprinted by permission.

following directions: "Time allowed: 5 minutes. Task: You are to choose a group chairperson."

Envelope III, to be opened 5 minutes later, should contain the following directions: "Time allowed: 10 minutes. Task: You are to evaluate the first phase of this group session in a discussion led by the newly elected chairperson."

Discussion

Focus the discussion on questions surrounding the role interactions. What behavior was effective in promoting the roles and positions assigned to individuals? What behavior was harmful?

Suggested Background Readings

Borgatta, E. F., & Crowther, B. *A workbook for the study of social interaction.* Chicago: Rand McNally, 1965.

Marlowe, L. *Social psychology.* Boston: Holbrook Press, 1971. (chaps. 10, 12)

Middlebrook, P. N. *Social psychology and modern life.* New York: Alfred A. Knopf, 1974. (chaps. 10, 11)

CHAPTER VII
PERSONALITY

The seven activities described in this chapter are all designed for classroom use. Activities 71 and 72 illustrate the generalities frequently found in personality descriptions and how easy it is to assume the validity of those descriptions. Activity 73 covers cognitive styles such as field dependence–independence and global versus detailed perception. Suggestibility and susceptibility to set are dealt with in Activity 74. Activity 75 is a role-playing exercise that familiarizes students with defense mechanisms. Factors affecting level of aspiration in a perceptual-motor task are the subject of Activity 76, and impression formation is covered in Activity 77.

71

PERSONALITY TESTS
Nancy Felipe Russo

Concept

This exercise is based on an article by Bertram Forer (1949) and shows the fallacy of using personal agreement as a validation method. It effectively demonstrates how easy it is to agree with vague statements.

Instructions

You must construct a "personality test" and "personality sketch." First design the "personality test." The following format is optional but is easy and often actually used:

Personal Evaluation Inventory

(Name or identification code of student)

Instructions: Check the adjectives that apply to you as you feel you actually are, not as how you'd like to be. Work quickly, giving your first impressions.

_____ nervous	_____ humorous
_____ likeable	_____ insecure
_____ musical	_____ shy
_____ intelligent	_____ critical

Make the adjective list cover the page—see a thesaurus for positive and negative adjectives. Hand out this "test" to the class, telling them that you will score it and give them a confidential personality sketch for their own use. Collect the test as if for scoring. Before the next class print up a personality sketch with the statements below, putting each student's name on one and making it look "official." At the next class tell students they are each receiving the summary of the personality type that best fits them.

Summary for Personality Type A

You have a great need for other people to like and admire you.

You have a tendency to be critical of yourself.

You have a great deal of unused capacity that you have not turned to your advantage.

While you have some personality weaknesses, you are generally able to compensate for them.

Your adjustment to the opposite sex has presented problems to you.

More disciplined and self-controlled outside, you tend to be worrisome and insecure inside.

At times you have serious doubts as to whether you have made the right decision or done the right thing.

You prefer a certain amount of change and variety and become dissatisfied when hemmed in by restrictions and limitations.

You pride yourself on being an independent thinker and do not accept other's statements without satisfactory proof.

You have found it unwise to be too frank in revealing yourself to others.

Before discussing the personality sketches, ask the class to rate them: "On the back of your sketch rate on a scale from 0 (poor) to 5 (perfect) how effective the scale was in revealing your personality. Now turn the paper over and check each statement as either true or false about yourself or put a question mark if you cannot tell." Most students should agree with most of the statements. Collect and tabulate their answers (the lesson in data summary is a bonus), and then tell the real story.

Discussion

This activity provides many topics for discussion. For example, what would you say to therapists who say they are good diagnosticians because their clients agree with their observations? What would you say to graphologists? To astrologers? You can also discuss quantitative methods of validation. The ethics of deception can be raised and explored. This activity can also be used to discuss measures of personality.

Suggested Background Readings

Ellis, A. The validity of personality questionnaires. *Psychological Bulletin,* 1943, *43,* 385–440.

Forer, B. The fallacy of personal validation: A classroom demonstration of gullibility. *Journal of Abnormal and Social Psychology,* 1949, *44,* 118–123.

Goldfried, M. R., & Kent, R. N. Traditional versus behavioral personality assessment: A comparison of methodological and theoretical assumptions. *Psychological Bulletin,* 1972, *77,* 409–420.

Houston, J. P., Bee, H., Hatfield, E., & Rimm, D. C. *Invitation to psychology.* New York: Academic Press, 1979. (chaps. 14, 15)

Morris, C. G. *Psychology: An introduction* (3rd ed.). Englewood Cliffs, N.J.: Prentice-Hall, 1979. (chap. 13)

ACTIVITY
72

IMPRESSIONABILITY
Barry Singer

Concept

This exercise resulted from attempts to find a vehicle for permitting students to consider dispassionately their own impressionability. Many students are impressed by descriptions in magazines or books of personality traits associated with their astrological signs. This activity is designed to give students an experiential demonstration of their own impressionability with respect to generalized personality descriptions based on astrological characteristics.

Instructions

Take a fairly lengthy, complex astrological description of personality traits associated with some particular sign out of a standard work of astrology, or make up such a description yourself. Type 12 versions of this description, changing only the dates and names corresponding to the 12 different astrological signs.

In class, spread the students out and otherwise simulate test conditions. Ask each student what his or her sign is and present him or her with a description labeled accordingly. Tell the class you are doing an experiment to test the accuracy of astrological descriptions. Also present the students with a questionnaire that asks them to rate how well the description fits them personally and how well it fits their best friend who is *not* of their sign.

Discussion

When the ratings are tabulated, the following results dependably occur: First, if, for instance, everyone actually reads a Virgo description labeled differently for each different sign, typically about half of the non-Virgos in the class will rate the description as accurate or as even more accurate than the Virgos rate it. Second, most students in the class will rate the descriptions as fitting their best friends of different signs less well than themselves. Thus, the non-Virgos will attest that the descriptions fit their best friends less well than they fit themselves, when the descriptions ought to fit each equally well or equally poorly; or their best friends may even be Virgos, who supposedly should match the descriptions.

Thus, students can be shown quantitatively how easily they can be misled by general descriptions and how likely they are to be subjective when they think such descriptions refer to themselves rather than others. However, instructors using this gimmick must debrief their students subsequent to the exercise, fully informing them of the nature of the deception in accordance with APA's *Ethical Principles in the Conduct of Research with Human Participants* (see Appendix D). Instructors may also want to discuss with the class the ethics of the deception practiced in this experiment. Is it the only method available to convince students of their own impressionability?

Suggested Background Readings

Braun, J., & Linder, D. E. *Psychology today: An introduction* (4th ed.). New York: Random House, 1979. (chap. 26)

Houston, J. P., Bee, H., Hatfield, E., & Rimm, D. C. *Invitation to psychology*. New York: Academic Press, 1979. (chap. 19)

Weiner, B. et al. *Discovering psychology*. New York: St. Martin's Press, 1977. (chaps. 18, 19)

ACTIVITY
73

COGNITIVE STYLES
Mary Margaret Moffett

Concept

Traditionally, psychologists have investigated personality in terms of general character types or specific personality traits. Character types are consistent groupings of personality traits; an example is the hero—selfless, courageous, strong, honest, clever. Personality traits describe particular, more limited consistencies in an individual's behavior or style of functioning. They are often conceptualized on a continuum from one extreme to the other—for example, honest/dishonest, reliable/unreliable, kind/unkind. Recent research has shifted from such "moralistic" and judgmental character attributes to cognitive styles—that is, consistencies in our ways of processing information—which are less value laden. Some illustrative cognitive styles are field-dependence/field-independence and detail-perception/global-perception. The first dimension describes the extent to which an individual initially either perceives an object independent of its context or perceives the total gestalt. The second dimension describes the extent to which an individual either analyzes all the little details before responding or gets a global "good enough" perception and responds. With cognitive styles there are advantages and disadvantages in being at any point on a given continuum. For example, there are situations in which functioning is more efficient if one is highly attentive to detail, such as in electronic repair, and there are situations in which attention to the global context is more useful, such as in interior design. In still other situations both styles may be equally successful.

The activity below is designed to introduce students to the concept of cognitive styles, to illustrate individual differences in cognitive styles, and to give students an idea of the kinds of cognitive tasks used to assess cognitive styles.

Materials Needed

You will need the following materials for the activity.

1. A handout—enough for the whole class—containing four hidden shapes. To create the handout, reproduce the shapes on page 179 on a single ditto master, without the gray shading.

2. Four display shapes. Make these by reproducing each of the gray-shaded shapes on a sheet of paper, in outline, and enlarging to twice their present size.

3. A handout—enough for the whole class—on which you have reproduced the four gray-shaded shapes in place in the camouflage.

4. A handout—enough for the whole class—on which you have reproduced three items that test detail-perception/global-perception. You can find two items in Kagan, Rosman, Day, Albert, and Phillips (1964, p. 22) and a third in Messer (1977, p. 1027), or you can create your own. The items consist of one specimen figure and six similar figures, one of

which is identical to the specimen and five of which differ from the specimen, each in some small detail.

Preparation of Class

Tell students you are going to give them a few tasks from two tests used in personality assessment. One test assesses field-dependence/field-independence; the other assesses detail-perception/global-perception. Tell students that on these tests, unlike on intelligence tests, there are about as many advantages to low or middle scores as there are to high scores. Stress that their scores will not be reliable or valid because you will only be using a few items from each test. Tell them also that their participation is not likely to cause them any embarrassment and that they will not have to reveal their scores. Those who wish to decline to participate may do so freely and quietly, without penalty.

Instructions

Pass out Handout 1. Tell students that you are going to display a shape; they are to find it and trace it in the camouflage on the handout and *then look at you when they are done.* Direct their attention to the first camouflaged shape, hold up the first display shape (be sure everyone can see it) until about half the class has found it, traced it, and looked up, and then say "Stop." Go on to the other shapes, following the same procedure. Do not allow students to go back to a shape once you have stopped holding it up.

Pass out Handout 4. Instruct students to find in each item the figure that matches the specimen. Give them as much time as they need to complete the items.

To score the field-dependent/field-independent items, pass out Handout 3. Students get a point for each shape they are able to find. (Note that there is more than one correct "hiding place" for most of the shapes.) Someone who had just started to trace the shape when you said "Stop" should get $1/2$ point. To score the detail-perception/global-perception items, tell students the correct answers.

Discussion

Research has found some modest correlations between cognitive styles and certain interests, abilities, and personality traits. The findings below are based on correlations that are statistically significant but account for only 10–20% of the variance at most; that is, the relationships exist but they are weak. Thus, for example, although field-independent people tend to be males, many females are field-independent and many males are field-dependent. Discuss these limitations of the findings with students.

Field-independent people (those who score high) tend to be males, to take an active approach to the environment, to use isolation and intellectualization as defenses, to major in math, engineering, and natural sciences, and to have higher self-esteem. Field-dependent people (those who score low) tend to be females, to be more responsive to social cues, to have a better memory for social events in incidental learning, to use repression and denial as defenses, and to be better at psychology.

People with detail perception (those who score high) tend to be interested in science, to get along better in school, to work slowly on multiple-choice tests, to consider more alternatives in various situations, and to be more accurate when fine discriminations are required. People with global perception (those who score low) tend to be restless, to be more easily distracted, to be arty, to be interested in literature, to work quickly on multiple-choice tests, to choose the first alternative that looks reasonable, and to be more productive and accurate when speed is required.

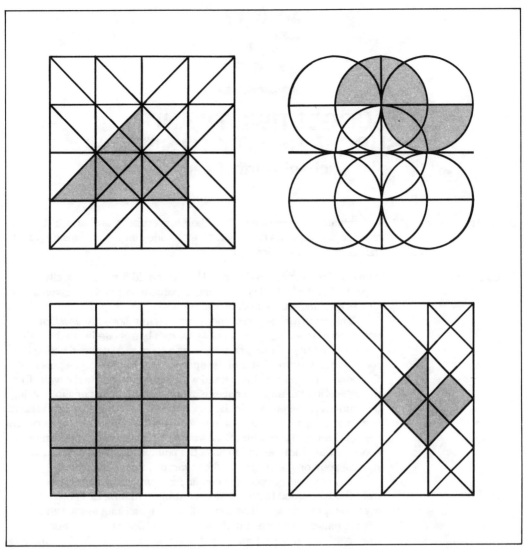

Four Camouflaged Shapes

If students are willing to mark their sex on their papers, you can shuffle and redistribute the papers and then do some statistical calculations—means, modes, medians, standard deviations, and t tests—on sex differences (see Appendix A).

Suggested Background Readings

Jones, N. F., Meyer, M., & Eiduson, B. An introductory lecture on personality assessment. *Journal of Personality Assessment,* 1972, *36,* 479–492. (Reprints available from N. F. Jones, School of Professional Psychology, 2300 South Gaylord, Denver, CO 80208.)

Kagan, J., Rosman, B. L., Day, D., Albert, J., & Phillips, W. Information processing in the child: Significance of analytic and reflective attitudes. *Psychological Monographs,* 1964, *78* (1, Whole No. 578.)

Messer, S. B. Reflection–impulsivity: A review. *Psychological Bulletin,* 1976, *83,* 1026–1052.

Witkin, H. A., & Goodenough, D. R. Field dependence and interpersonal behavior. *Psychological Bulletin,* 1977, *84,* 661–689.

ACTIVITY
74

SUGGESTIBILITY AND SUSCEPTIBILITY TO SET
Michael Wertheimer

Concept

Individuals differ considerably in their suggestibility and susceptibility to set. The two activities described here provide quantified measures of these two characteristics.

Instructions

The two demonstrations described below should first be generally explained to students. Those willing to participate should be given a code number for anonymity in data collection.

The setup for the first demonstration is as follows: To a wall at a point about 5 feet high affix a pulley with its barrel parallel to the wall. (The pulley can be fashioned by nailing a spool to a stick and wiring the stick to a wall fixture that is at the appropriate height—e.g., a pencil sharpener.) Have the subject stand with his or her back to the wall. To the subject's collar attach a paper clip and, tied to the paper clip, a string that runs over the pulley. To the other end of the string tie a light weight (e.g., a small spool) with a pointer (e.g., a toothpick glued to the spool). On the wall behind the pointer affix a yardstick. Have each subject stand far enough away from the wall to have the pointer register at a common starting point on the yardstick—for example, the 12-inch mark.

To test subjects, you will need an assistant with a stopwatch or a watch with a second hand. Have each subject, in turn, close his or her eyes and stand straight. Then, signalling your assistant to start timing, begin a patter to the effect that the subject is falling forward. For example: "You aren't standing up straight any more. You're beginning to lean forward a little. I can see that you are beginning to fall forward. You are falling forward. You are leaning so far forward that you will fall in a moment." Continue the patter for 30 seconds, or less if the subject actually falls forward (in which case you should take care that the subject does not get hurt). Your assistant should watch the pointer while you are talking and record (using the subject's code number) the maximum deviation from the starting point. If a subject actually falls forward, the entry should be the difference between 36″ and the starting point, plus—12″ in our example. The assistant should also record the length of time from the beginning of the trial until the subject loses balance. If the subject does not lose balance, the entry should be 30+ seconds. When all subjects have been tested, record scores on the two measures (distance and time) on the chalkboard, and examine them for variability.

For the second demonstration, cut 11 pieces of cardboard about 4 inches × 12 inches. On successive pieces, draw bold straight lines of the following lengths: 1″, 2″, 3″, 4″, 5″, 6″, 6″, 6″, 6″, 7″, 8″. Have students write their code number on a piece of paper and number from 1 to 11. Tell them that you are going to display, in succession, 11 lines and that you want them to estimate how long each line is, to the nearest inch. When you have displayed all the lines, have students total their estimates for the last three 6-inch lines and subtract from this total their estimate for the first 6-inch line. This figure is their score. Record the scores (anonymously) on the chalkboard, and have students examine these scores for variability also.

Discussion

The class might investigate whether there is any correlation between scores on the two demonstrations; code numbers can be used to match individuals' scores, and a correlation coefficient can be computed to determine if a significant relationship exists between how suggestible someone is and how susceptible they are to set (see Appendix A). Have the students discuss the adequacy of the tests as measures of the characteristics in question. What other ways might be used to measure suggestibility or to measure susceptibility to set? What personality characteristics do students assign to someone described as "highly suggestible"? What characteristics do they assign to someone who is not easily influenced?

Suggested Background Readings

Dash, A. S. A study of the expectancy bias and the suggestion bias of teachers. *Indian Journal of Psychology*, 1973, *48*, 11–14.
Evans, F. Suggestibility in the normal waking state. *Psychological Bulletin*, 1967, *67*, 114–129.

ACTIVITY
75

DEFENSE MECHANISMS
Jack J. Greider

Concept

This activity is designed to increase student familiarity with the ways in which defense mechanisms are used. In addition to being a good teaching tool, the activity allows for the expression of a considerable amount of creativity on the part of the students. Defense mechanisms covered include regression, rationalization, repression, projection, fantasy, compensation, identification, and reaction formation.

Instructions

Ask for eight student volunteers for a role-playing exercise. I usually choose four males and four females, since I have found mixed pairs to work best in this activity. Have these eight students leave the room and go with them to explain what they are to do. First group them in male–female pairs and assign two of the defense mechanisms to each pair. Instruct each pair of students to make up two skits, one for each of the mechanisms. I usually allow them about 15 minutes to prepare their skits. While they are working, go back into the room, list the defense mechanisms on the chalkboard, and discuss each one briefly with the class. Then call the role players back into the room to put on their skits. Have each pair perform one of their two skits, and after going through the pairs have each pair do their second skit. The job of the class is to guess which mechanism each skit represents.

Discussion

In discussion you can point out the place of defense mechanisms in personality theory. You should comment on the role of defense mechanisms in normal functioning. When are these mechanisms helpful? When are they harmful? Conduct an anonymous survey of your students asking them to indicate whether or not they have used any of the defense mechanisms during the past year. Do they use some defense mechanisms more than others? If so, which ones?

Suggested Background Readings

Clum, G. A., & Clum, J. Mood variability and defense mechanism preference. *Psychological Reports,* 1973, *32,* 910.

Houston, J. P., Bee, H., Hatfield, E., & Rimm, D. C. *Invitation to psychology.* New York: Academic Press, 1979. (chap. 11)

Viney, L. L., & Manton, M. Defense mechanism preferences and the expression of anxiety. *Social Behavior and Personality,* 1974, *2,* 50–55.

Weiner, B. et al. *Discovering psychology.* New York: St. Martin's Press, 1977. (chap. 15)

ACTIVITY
76

LEVEL OF ASPIRATION
P. S. Fernald and L. D. Fernald, Jr.

Concept

Research has shown that our "reach" often exceeds our grasp. Several factors that influence "reach" or aspiration level are highlighted in the following activity.

Instructions

Ask for four volunteers and have them leave the room. Inform the remaining students that you wish to test three hypotheses: (1) Group standards influence level of aspiration. (2) Level of aspiration remains close to actual performance, with a tendency to be above rather than below it. (3) Success leads to an increase in level of aspiration, and failure leads to a decrease.

Write the hypotheses on the chalkboard along with the following table, and describe its use in testing the hypotheses (see below):

Volunteer	Standard	First Estimate	Score	Second Estimate
1	15			
2	15			
3	35			
4	35			

Bring the volunteers into the room one at a time. Do not allow them to see the chalkboard. Have them stand facing a table on which you have placed two coffee cans 3 feet apart, one can containing 60 marbles, the other empty. Explain to the volunteers that they are going to take a test of manual dexterity. The task is to transfer as many marbles as possible from the full can to the empty can in 30 seconds. They can transfer only one marble at a time, using only one hand. Tell the first two volunteers, "Most high school students place about 15 marbles in the empty can during a 30-second interval." For the second two volunteers, substitute 35 for 15. Be sure to emphasize the score of "most high school students"; if the standard is mentioned only casually, it may be ignored. Next, ask the volunteers to estimate the number of marbles they expect to transfer. Then have them perform the task. When 30 seconds are up, count the number of marbles transferred, inform the volunteers, and tell them they will have a second trial. Again ask for an estimate of expected performance, and then have them repeat the task. (The score on the second trial is of no consequence for the demonstration, but it may give the volunteers some satisfaction in terms of improved performance.)

Hypothesis 1 can be tested by comparing the initial estimates of the first two volunteers with those of the second two volunteers. Typically, the estimates offer strong support for this hypothesis. It is important to mention, however, that the effect is great because the volunteers did not have prior experience with the task. Hypothesis 2 can be tested by comparing second estimates with initial scores. Typically, second estimates are very close to scores; in the majority of cases they are higher. With regard to Hypothesis 3, comparison of the first and second estimates of the first two volunteers typically confirms the hypothesized effect of success, and a similar comparison for the last two volunteers typically supports the hypothesis about failure (providing that the estimates were too high to achieve).

Discussion

Discuss the results obtained in terms of support for your three hypotheses. What happens to people when their level of aspiration is too high? Too low? How do you think the results of this activity might be applied to performance in school? What factors tend to affect level of aspiration?

Suggested Background Readings

Birch, D. & Veroff, J. *Motivation: A study of action.* Belmont, Calif.: Brooks/Cole, 1968.

Frank, J. D. Recent studies of the level of aspiration. *Psychological Bulletin,* 1941, *38,* 218–226.

Ghabrial, T. M. Some characteristics of level of aspiration of university students. *Psychologia,* 1974, *17,* 16–19.

PERSON PERCEPTION
Marcia E. Lasswell, Floyd L. Ruch, David S. Gorfein, and Neil Warren

Concept

Students may be only dimly aware that they form impressions every time they encounter a new person. They may think they are unaffected by such factors as the person's warmth or physical attractiveness. The objective of this activity is to demonstrate the power that certain traits have on person perception.

In a pioneering study in 1946, Solomon Asch investigated how variation of single personality traits affected the overall impression given by an individual. When Asch described a person to his subjects as warm, they formed positive impressions of that person; when he described a person as cold, they formed negative impressions. Given the descriptors "polite" or "blunt," however, subjects formed more neutral impressions. Asch concluded that certain traits have significantly more influence on person perception than others do. He called the more influential descriptors central traits, the less influential ones peripheral traits.

In more recent research, Robert Gifford (1975) found that the personality descriptors most influential in person perception are those that are evaluative, stable, and familiar. Most descriptors are evaluative—that is, they imply a judgment (good/bad, beautiful/ugly). Stable descriptors refer to traits that people possess over time and situations, such as artistic, dominating, and intelligent. Familiar descriptors are the more common, better-known terms—for example, shy (vs. reticent), talkative (vs. loquacious).

Instructions

The following materials will be needed for the activity.

1. A handout—enough for half of the class—that lists the following adjectives: intelligent, skillful, industrious, warm, determined, practical, cautious.

2. A handout—enough for half of the class—that lists the following adjectives: intelligent, skillful, industrious, cold, determined, practical, cautious.

3. A handout—enough for the whole class—that contains the Adjective Checklist provided on the next page.

Tell students that they are going to participate in an experiment on person perception. It will not require them to reveal any personal information, nor is it likely to cause them any embarrassment. Those who wish to decline to participate may do so freely and quietly, without penalty.

Before class, shuffle Handouts 1 and 2 together. Put the adjectives on Handout 3 on the chalkboard, listing the favorable adjectives in one

From *Psychology and Life,* Brief 7th Edition, Instructor's Notebook by Marcia E. Lasswell, Floyd L. Ruch, David S. Gorfein, and Neil Warren. Copyright © 1967 by Scott, Foresman and Company. Reprinted by permission.

Adjective Checklist

Listed below are adjectives often used to describe people. Check those that best describe the hypothetical new student.

_____ generous	_____ ungenerous
_____ wise	_____ shrewd
_____ happy	_____ unhappy
_____ good-natured	_____ irritable
_____ humorous	_____ humorless
_____ sociable	_____ unsociable
_____ popular	_____ unpopular
_____ reliable	_____ unreliable
_____ important	_____ insignificant
_____ humane	_____ ruthless
_____ good-looking	_____ unattractive
_____ persistent	_____ unstable
_____ serious	_____ frivolous
_____ restrained	_____ talkative
_____ altruistic	_____ self-centered
_____ imaginative	_____ hardheaded
_____ strong	_____ weak
_____ honest	_____ dishonest

vertical column and the unfavorable adjectives in a second vertical column. Next to each vertical column, on the horizontal axis, put the headings W and C (for warm condition and cold condition). When class begins, distribute Handouts 1 and 2. Say that the adjectives describe a hypothetical new student, and ask the students to construct a mental picture of the new student—his or her friends, hobbies, interests, relationship with parents, etc. Allow students about 5 minutes, then distribute Handout 3, repeating aloud the instructions that appear on it. When students have completed the checklist, call out each adjective, asking for a show of hands from students in the warm condition who checked it and then from students in the cold condition who checked it. Record the numbers in the appropriate columns.

The data that you have collected may be analyzed by means of a *t* test. In constructing scores for the two groups, you could use the number of positive attributes given by the students in the warm condition versus those in the cold condition.

Discussion

In all likelihood, far more students in the warm condition will have chosen certain favorable adjectives than will have students in the cold condition, and far more students in the cold condition will have chosen certain unfavorable adjectives than will have students in the warm condition. Compare Asch's results: Most of his "warm" subjects chose the adjectives generous, wise, happy, good-natured, humorous, sociable, popular, humane, altruistic, and imaginative; most of his "cold" subjects chose the corresponding unfavorable adjectives. Reliable, important, good-looking, persistent, serious, restrained, strong, and honest—and the corresponding unfavorable adjectives—did not seem to be correlated with warmth or coldness. See Wishner (1960) for more information.

You might discuss with students how first impressions, based on very little information, may have strong effects on subsequent behaviors. For example, Kelley (1950) described a guest lecturer to some students as rather warm, to others as rather cold. The "warm" students not only rated the lecturer more positively, but 56% participated with him in class discussion, as compared with 32% of the "cold" students. If students agree that their first impressions of a person can affect their behavior, ask them how their behavior might affect the behavior of the person. Bring out the possibility that one may behave coolly toward a person whom one perceives as cold and that the person may reciprocate, justifying the original (and possibly false) first impression. You might also discuss what factors your students think affect their first impressions. Possibilities are appearance (dress, physical attractiveness), comportment, tone of voice, smile, and so forth.

Suggested Background Readings

Asch, S. E. Forming impressions of personality. *Journal of Abnormal and Social Psychology,* 1946, *41,* 258–290.

Gifford, R. K. Information properties of descriptive words. *Journal of Personality and Social Psychology,* 1975, *31,* 727–734.

Kelley, H. H. The warm–cold variable in first impressions of persons. *Journal of Personality,* 1950, *18,* 431–439.

Wishner, J. Reanalysis of "Impressions of personality." *Psychological Review,* 1960, *67,* 96–112.

CHAPTER VIII
MISCELLANEOUS

As the title implies, this chapter is a collection of activities that do not fit readily into one of the other chapter headings but that range the gamut of the psychological enterprise. Activity 78 involves observation of animal behavior in a natural habitat. Activity 79 is an analysis of crisis and conflict resolution. Data on sleep and dreaming are collected and analyzed in Activity 80. Activity 81 demonstrates the ease with which people attribute "mental illness" to other people based on observation of their behavior. Activity 82 relates creativity to artistic ability. Activities 83 and 84 are studies of reaction time; the latter activity uses a chain reaction procedure. Activity 85 demonstrates neural transmission using students as neurons. The next two activities are studies of human emotion: Activity 86 attempts to label the dimensions of emotion, and Activity 87 examines facial expressions in emotion, based on the work of Paul Ekman. Finally, Activity 88 uses ethograms in the observation and recording of animal behavior.

78

ANIMAL BEHAVIOR IN THE NATURAL HABITAT
Marty Klein

Concept

Systematic observation, naturalistic observation, and field study are all labels for the same kind of activity—a systematic set of observations noted and recorded from animals in their natural habitat. Although naturalistic studies sacrifice the control over variables that one can achieve in the laboratory, they nevertheless are extremely useful in providing evidence that can only be gathered on behavior in the field. While these studies are valuable in their own right, they also serve to generate behavioral questions that frequently can be tested in the experimental laboratory.

Instructions

The assignment is to *systematically* observe the behavior of a species of animal—a particular individual or group—over a period of time. (Suggestions include squirrels, birds, raccoons, cattle, chickens, or pigeons). As part of the assignment, the student should review the literature on the previously used methods and earlier findings for this species. This project is normally fairly long-term (2–3 weeks at least) and culminates in a written report. However, individual elements of the long-term project may be selected for short-term study if desired. Observation periods should be systematically planned to cover as much of the day as possible over the course of the project. However, in many cases, daily observation at the same time will yield interesting results on relatively few behavior classes. Students should have a notebook, a wristwatch, and, if possible, a pair of binoculars.

The following factors should be considered for systematic study:

Description of the habitat. This includes a detailed description of all pertinent variables and features of the habitat such as territorial boundaries, feeding area, nest site, rest area, range, path habits, and so forth. A detailed map showing these features and including important items such as buildings, trees, and bushes is a good way to summarize this information.

Time and weather factors. How do different weather conditions affect the daily behavior patterns? How do the patterns vary with time, both within a day and over the longer course of the project?

Systematic observation of specific behavior classes. The major classes to consider are resting, contacting, eliminating, drinking, feeding, care of body surfaces, predator defenses, fighting, sexual behavior, nesting, and care of young.

Accurate description of the behaviors within these classes should be a major goal of the project. Patterns of transition from one behavior class to another should also be observed (e.g., after feeding, pigeons first drink and then feed their young).

Daily activity pattern. A detailed daily activity pattern for the individual (or groups) under study should be constructed. The span of this description, of course, will depend on the timing and duration of the observation periods.

Interactions with other individuals or species. Usually, many species of animals share the same territory (e.g., birds, squirrels, raccoons, insects). How do these animals interact? Why is it possible for them to share a territory? Such interactions might include any symbiotic or parasitic relationships.

Discussion

As a follow-up to the written reports, ask the students to share what they have learned about the *procedures* of field study. If they were to write a manual for field study, what points would they want to be sure to include? Ask the students to share with the class one or two facts that were unknown to them prior to their field studies. Have students design, based on their observations in the field, a hypothetical laboratory experiment that would test a hypothesis generated from their field studies. What results would they predict?

Suggested Background Readings

Denny, M. R., & Ratner, S. *Comparative psychology* (2nd ed.). Homewood, Ill.: Dorsey Press, 1970.

Eibl-Eibesfeldt, I., & Kramer, S. Ethology, the comparative study of animal behavior. *Quarterly Review of Biology,* 1958, *33,* 181–211.

Mussen, P., Rosenzweig, M. R. et al. *Psychology: An introduction* (2nd ed.). Lexington, Mass.: D. C. Heath, 1977. (chaps. 23, 24)

79

ROMEO, JULIET, AND CONFLICT RESOLUTION
Robert A. Goodale

Concept

Up to the age of 14 the number of young persons who commit suicide is only about 1 in 200,000, although many more attempt it. By age 19 the number of deaths due to suicide has increased tenfold. Investigation of successful suicides and suicide attempts shows a pattern of helplessness and hopelessness among participants and feelings of isolation, alienation, and failure at integration into the larger society.

A famous story of teenage suicide is that of Romeo and Juliet. Juliet and Romeo fall madly in love and secretly marry even though their respective families are engaged in a longstanding feud marked by hatred, bitterness, and death. At the same time, Juliet's parents plan her marriage to an older man, and later Romeo is banned to another land for slaying Juliet's cousin. Shakespeare works the dynamics of love and hate, parents and children, duty and impulse, and life and death into a heroic crisis that sends Juliet to the family clergyman for help in her most desperate hour. Faced with being pledged by her parents to marry a man she does not love, and having already defied her parents by secretly marrying the now-banned Romeo only the day before, Juliet concocts a bizarre plan with Friar Laurence to preserve her pure love for Romeo and protect herself from compromise. Before the play ends, Shakespeare skillfully interweaves additional contrasts between church and state and the individual versus society, and any resolution of the conflict dooms some member of the cast to moral compromise.

Modern psychology would characterize Juliet's plight as one of conflict resolution and crisis. Quite consciously Romeo and Juliet make several decisions that corrupt the trust they enjoy from several relationships, and any major change or disclosure at the point at which Juliet seeks out the friar will result in rejection, humiliation, family scandal, and perhaps even the loss of each other. From the perspective of psychologist Morton Deutsch, Romeo and Juliet are engaged in competitive struggle with the people around them. Communication among all of the conflicting parties becomes impoverished and unreliable, solution of the problem takes on a win–lose rigidity, and the differences among parties are emphasized instead of their commonalities. The antagonistic forces at work expand and escalate until only a destructive outcome for any or all parties is imminent. Under Shakespeare's direction all of the parties do lose, of course, and though the conflicting dynamics eventually are made clear to all, the resolution for all is something none of them would have chosen.

The purpose of the present exercise is to draw attention to the dynamics of conflict and crisis and to consider methods of arriving at productive solutions rather than destructive ones. In Deutsch's (1973) view, productive solution finding is akin to creative problem solving—the task is to get as many interested parties as possible involved in looking for mutually rewarding trade-offs rather than Pyrrhic victories. According to Deutsch, productive process requires (a) open communication, (b) mutual recognition and respect for the concerns of all parties involved, and (c) a trusting, friendly attitude that emphasizes common interests and minimizes differences among the parties. Substituting productive process for the competitive process that Shakespeare gave Romeo and Juliet, the class will consider alternative solutions for the star-crossed couple other than the one they chose—love through death.

Preparation of Class

Depending on how much you prefer that students get their information directly, either assign or summarize for them the story of Romeo and Juliet. Films of the play are also available. With the students, go over the critical events and key elements that shape the crisis: the reigning social mores that decree that Juliet's parents will choose her bridegroom, the decision by the pair to keep their love a secret from their feuding parents, Romeo's decision to kill Tybalt in order to avenge the death of Mercutio, and so forth. Pick up the story at the point where Juliet goes to Friar Laurence with the news that Romeo has been banished for killing Tybalt and that she herself will be publically pledged to marry Paris, her parents' choice, on the following day. At this point Juliet is in a state of panic because she must resolve her conflict before morning.

Instructions

Tell the class that this time when Juliet and the friar meet, they must work together to reach a realistic, productive resolution utilizing the three principles of productive process identified by Deutsch, rather than choosing the destructive process that Shakespeare gave them, which would have resulted in a variety of negative consequences for the lovers and their families even if the scheme had succeeded.

Have the class consider, for example, the benefits that could arise if Juliet and the friar went to all of the principal parties and revealed the entire story before morning (open communication). Have several students role-play the principal parties and express their perceptions of the problem (recognition and respect for the views and concerns of all). Consider whether Juliet, when imploring the friar for help, had a realistic understanding of how each of the parties would feel about her marriage to Romeo or if she was largely responding to what she imagined they would do if they knew (trust vs. mistrust).

The point is to explore alternative solutions for productive outcomes. Individuals in crisis are severely constrained in their thinking, and part of the service that good friends and therapists provide at such times is a discussion of alternatives, an examination of what is real and what is imagined, and a nonjudgmental reminder of their strengths in the past and of how apparent setback can often be a stimulus for growth. Recognize that in actual practice a person in crisis rejects all solutions as costing too much, since, if they did not, he or she would have picked one of them earlier and warded off the crisis. Discuss what it was in Romeo and Juliet that led them to box themselves in as badly as they did before the crisis came to a head.

Discussion

1. Explore with your students the series of events that seem to lead people to presume that suicide is the most reasonable solution to a tough crisis.

2. How memorable would Shakespeare's classic be if he had led Romeo and Juliet into productive process right from the start? What does it mean that so many people over the years have identified with Romeo and Juliet and have seen them as victims of parental insensitivity?

3. If one party is searching for a productive solution and no one else involved seems to care, what should the one party do?

4. If the class is comfortable exploring such topics, examine present conflicts students have with their parents such as not being allowed to have a car, having to babysit younger brothers and sisters, rigid homework schedules, or any other conflicts students feel free to bring up. To what extent have students applied Deutsch's three steps to productive resolution to each conflict? To what extent have they characterized the problem as a personal defeat rather than an opportunity for self-growth? Examine how the same situations result in a problem for some students but not for others.

5. Evaluate the homily "You catch more flies with honey than vinegar."

Suggested Background Readings

Deutsch, M. *The resolution of conflict: Constructive and destructive processes.* New Haven, Conn.: Yale University Press, 1973.

Goffman, E. On cooling the mark out: Some aspects of adaptation to failure. In W. G. Bennis, D. E. Berlew, E. H. Schein, & F. I. Steele (Eds.), *Interpersonal dynamics: Essays and readings on human interaction* (3rd ed.). Homewood, Ill.: Dorsey Press, 1973.

Nass, S. *Crisis intervention.* Dubuque, Iowa: Kendall/Hunt, 1977.

ACTIVITY
80

TO SLEEP, PERCHANCE TO DREAM
Ludy T. Benjamin, Jr.

Concept

There are probably more myths and misunderstandings about sleep and dreaming than about any other aspect of human behavior except sex. For most people, sleep and dreaming will occupy one third of their lives, yet few individuals are aware of even the most rudimentary information about this activity. For example, consider the following facts: Apparently everyone dreams; that is, there are no nondreamers, only nonrecallers. In an 8-hour night of sleep most people will have from four to five dreams, usually on quite unrelated topics. The great majority of dreams are in color. Sleep learning apparently does not occur. Dreams are not always filled with easily interpretable psychological meanings, as popular literature would have one believe.

The study of sleep and dreaming is still in its infancy. Most of what we know about this area is the result of research occurring in the last 25 years and is principally due to the development of electrophysiological techniques (particularly the electroencephalograph, or EEG) and the discovery, in 1953, of rapid eye movements (REMs) during sleep.

The purposes of this exercise are (a) to help students focus attention on their own sleep and dreaming patterns, (b) to generate data for class discussion, (c) to introduce students to the concept of data collection in sleep and dreaming, (d) to illustrate appropriate statistical measures for summarizing the data, and (e) to aid students in understanding the interpretation of data in general and these data in particular.

Preparation of Class

Pass out the "Sleep and Dreaming Record" to each student, providing multiple copies—one for each day that records will be kept (14 consecutive nights provides a good sample). Tell the students why the data are being collected and indicate that participation is voluntary. Explain that they can conceal their identity by marking their records with a number (six or seven digits in length) that they make up on their own. This procedure allows them to identify their statistics in reference to others in class when the summary data are provided later. Note that it takes only about 5 minutes each day to complete the record.

Instructions

Ask all students to begin their records on the same day and to keep their record sheets at home. Request that during the time the records are being kept, discussion among students regarding their sleep and dreaming patterns be minimal to avoid unintentional influences on the data. Give explicit instructions on record keeping. (It is a good idea to have one "practice run" to insure that everyone understands the record-keeping system before continuing for 14 days.) The record provided is only a sample. Feel free to modify it as appropriate.

When the time period is completed and students have turned in all of their records, the tedious part begins for the teacher—the summarization of the data, for which a calculator is most helpful. Each student's records should be summarized separately, and data should be analyzed for the group as a whole. A summary sheet for the students should then be prepared, which lists everyone who participated (by number) and provides the group analyses. For example, Student #107654 can examine that column number of the summary sheet to find a mean sleep time of 7.3 hours (over 14 days), with a range of 5.6–9.7 hours. The student can then compare these figures with those of other students and with those for the class as a whole, based on the group data.

Sleep and Dreaming Record

Student Number _____   Date _____

1. Total sleep time (in hours) _____. On the time line below, block out your sleep periods, including naps.

| 6:00 | 10:00 | 2:00 | 6:00 | 10:00 | 2:00 | 6:00 |
| p.m. | p.m. | a.m. | a.m. | a.m. | p.m. | p.m. |

2. Total number of awakenings during major sleep period. _____ (Do not count the final morning awakening.)

3. On the scale below, rate the quality of your night's sleep (in your opinion). Circle one of the numbers from plus four to minus four.

---

bad   −4   −3   −2   −1   0   +1   +2   +3   +4   good

4. In your judgment, how many separate dreams can you recall at least a fragment of? _____

5. It is possible that you will recall some of your dreams better than others. Using percentages, estimate the amount of each dream recalled.

Dream 1 _____   Dream 2 _____   Dream 3 _____   Dream 4 _____

6. How many of these dreams could you relate to presleep experiences of the dream day? _____

7. Did you appear as a character in the dreams you recall? In how many? _____

8. How many of your dreams were in color? _____

9. Were there stimuli in your dreams of a nonvisual nature? Check the following if appropriate.

sound _____   taste _____   touch _____   smell _____

Discussion

The data students generate will add considerable personal interest to the topic of sleep and dreaming. Further, the statistical treatments will help them understand how data are summarized and analyzed to make them more meaningful. It might be useful to save the summary statistics from classes for comparison with those of future classes.

Optional

Although it is not necessary, teachers may wish to provide some statistical measures of relationship between some of the variables for which they have collected data by using the technique of correlation. For example, is there a relationship between the number of hours people sleep and the number of dreams they recall? Or is there a relationship between the subjective sleep quality rating and the number of awakenings one experiences during the night? A number of correlational analyses can be computed to answer these and other questions. To compute these values, a calculator is needed. Some calculators have a built-in correlation function; otherwise, the computational formula in Appendix A should be used. It is important to remember that correlation is a measure of the degree to which two variables are related and does not necessarily specify the *nature* of the relationship. That is, one *cannot* assume that if two variables are shown by correlation to be related, that the relationship is one of cause and effect.

Suggested Background Readings

Dement, W. C. *Some must watch while some must sleep.* San Francisco: Freeman, 1974.

Webb, W. B. *Sleep: The gentle tyrant.* Englewood Cliffs, N.J.: Prentice-Hall, 1975.

ACTIVITY
81

MENTAL ILLNESS
James M. Gardner

Concept

We often make judgments about the behavior of other people, determining whether particular acts were or were not appropriate. Occasionally we may even decide, based on our observations, that someone is "mentally ill." This exercise offers a classroom opportunity to study such attributions.

Instructions

Ask for six volunteers to play roles in a skit. Take them out of the room and have them choose a role from six 3 × 5 inch cards bearing the following descriptions:

1. You are an escaped convict, previously convicted of murder.
2. You are a successful business executive whose spouse just announced the existence of a love affair, whose child is in the hospital, and whose car broke down this morning.
3. You are married with two children and unemployed; you desperately need a job and are on your way to an interview.
4. You are on your way to a sale.
5. You are lonely, have few friends, became bored watching TV, and are going somewhere just to have something to do.
6. You are waiting at the bus stop for the bus. Your role is to try to engage each of the waiting passengers in conversation so that the class can observe how they act. Some questions that you might ask are: Do you have the proper time? Does the bus usually run late?

While the actors study their roles, return to the room and instruct the other students to observe closely the behavior of each actor. Bring in the actor who drew the sixth role—the catalyst. Then bring in the other actors one by one, and let them interact with the catalyst for about 1 minute each.

When the skit is over, have the actors return to their seats. On the chalkboard, set up a matrix with the names of the actors in a vertical column on the left; list them in any order, except put the catalyst's name last. Tell the class that the six actors were playing roles, that you are going to list those roles across the top of the matrix, and that you are going to poll the class to determine how many believe each actor could have been playing each role. Also tell them that you are going to include a role that no one played. Then list the roles one at a time, polling students on each one before you list the next. List the roles in the same order as they appear above, but insert "a mentally ill person" between the third and fourth roles.

Adapted from the "Mental Illness Game" by James M. Gardner, *Teaching of Psychology,* 1976, *3*(3), 141–142. Copyright 1976 by Division Two of the American Psychological Association. Reprinted by permission.

When the voting is completed, examine the data. First, determine which actors appeared to play several roles and which were identified with only one role. Next, determine which roles were clearly identified and which appeared to be played by many actors. Then ask the actors to state which role they played. It will become apparent that no one was assigned the role of "a mentally ill person." Now check how many believed each of the six actors to be playing that role. Compare the total number here to totals for other roles. Usually the total for "a mentally ill person" is one of the highest.

Discussion

This outcome can lead to a discussion of how easy it is for people to be labeled mentally ill when there is no psychological problem present. Ask the students to verbalize what behaviors they observed in the actors that they felt were indicative of mental illness. Is there any agreement on those behaviors? Were those behaviors exhibited by actors who were not thought to be mentally ill? You can add a number of topics to the discussion such as witch hunts and the legal definition of insanity. You can also discuss the concept of mental illness. Does the use of the term *illness* promote a medical model? What other terms are used and how are they different?

Suggested Background Readings

Gardner, J. M. *Community psychology: The left hand of the magician.* New York: Plenum, 1980.

Sahakian, W. S. (Ed.). *Psychopathology today.* Itasca, Ill.: F. E. Peacock, 1970.

Szasz, T. S. The myth of mental illness. *American Psychologist,* 1960, *15,* 113–118.

Szasz, T. S. *The manufacture of madness.* New York: Delta, 1970.

A GENERAL MODEL FOR DEVELOPING CLASSROOM CREATIVITY EXERCISES
Russell E. Walls

As a psychologist and artist teaching an interdisciplinary course on creativity for the past three years, I have been working on a series of experiential exercises designed to develop empathy with the creative process. One general model that I use to generate exercises is readily available to the motivated teacher.

The major source material is the extensive literature on creativity. The easiest access to this literature for the newcomer is the *Journal of Creative Behavior*. It provides an excellent cross-section of articles on every major aspect of research related to creativity and also publishes an exhaustive list of books, dissertations, theses, and films on creativity on a regular basis. The model in question involves fairly direct adaptation of actual experiments to the classroom setting. To illustrate the process I will summarize a 1976 study by Getzels and Csikszentmihalyi (Getzels, 1977) and then discuss how I adapt the study to my own class.

Concept

Graduate art students from the University of Chicago were brought, one at a time, into a room with two tables. On one table was a wide assortment of objects. The second table was left empty to provide a drawing surface. Each student was asked to choose objects from the first table to use as a basis for making a drawing. Students were videotaped as they chose their objects and made their drawings.

Later analysis produced some very interesting findings. Essentially, two types of artists were revealed. One type handled only two or three objects, chose conventional objects to draw (books, wine glass, etc.), and knew from the start what they planned to draw. The second type handled many objects and used all of their senses in interacting with them—squeezing, smelling, tasting, and tossing them into the air. Also, they chose more unusual objects and did not decide what their drawings were to be until about 75% of the way through the drawings (the average amount of time taken by the two types to complete their drawings was about the same). The final phase of the study was a 7-year follow-up to see which students actually manifested the most creativity in their field (as measured by such things as having a painting bought by a museum, for example). The general finding was that artists of the second type ended up making more original contributions to art.

Instructions

I adapt this study to my creativity class in the following manner. I set up a large table loaded with a vast assortment of objects, both commonplace and unusual. I then bring in the entire class at the same time (18–20 students) and ask them to choose as many or as few objects as they desire to use as a basis for a drawing. They then sit somewhere in the room at a place of their choice (on the floor, at a table, etc.) and are given 15–20 minutes for their drawing. I then call time and ask them to repeat the procedure, but with a change in the instructions. This time I tell them to handle at least 15 objects and to use as many of their senses as possible in exploring each object. I demonstrate by picking up an object, tossing it in the air, smelling it, tasting it, rubbing it, using it to make a noise, and so forth. I also tell them to wait until they feel they are somewhere from one half to three quarters of the way through before deciding what they are drawing. Again, I allow 15–20 minutes for completion. The final phase involves tacking up all the drawings on the wall and having everyone vote on which ones they like best (this can be done the second day if your class periods are only an hour long).

Discussion

After the results are in (thus far 75% usually prefer the second drawings), I discuss the original study by Getzel and Csikszentmihalyi and have an open-ended discussion on what the study teaches the class about creativity and how they can apply the results to their own attempts to become more creative. I typically tie this in with a general discussion on the personality characteristics of creative people (lists of which can be found in a number of introductory psychology texts or in Dellas & Gaier, 1970) and why it is that such characteristics tend to enhance creativity. The resulting discussions are rich indeed!

I hope that anyone who has the interest can apply this general model to their own reading of the literature on creativity. With just a little ingenuity the number of exercises you can generate is virtually unlimited. You might want to warm up with an article made to order for this purpose by Michael Andrews (1977). Another idea is to have each of your students read several articles and generate exercises for the rest of the class (small groups may also be suitable for this purpose).

Suggested Background Readings

Andrews, M. F. Pine cone: Sensory awareness module. *Journal of Creative Behavior* 1977, 229–232.

Dellos, M., & Gaier, E. L. Identification of creativity: The individual. *Psychological Bulletin,* 1970, *73,* 55–73.

Getzels, J. W. *The creative vision: A longitudinal study of problem finding in art.* New York: Wiley, 1977.

Note: Back issues of the Journal of Creative Behavior *are readily available from Journal of Creative Behavior, State University College at Buffalo, 1300 Elmwood Avenue, Buffalo, NY 14222.*

83

REACTION TIME

Concept

Reaction time was one of the earliest topics to attract psychological experimenters, perhaps because of its susceptibility to measurement and what it tells us about the human organism. Simply expressed, reaction time is the speed with which the brain processes information—that is, the time interval between input and output. For instructional purposes, it can easily be measured in a series of experiments that will involve the whole class. A suggested procedure follows.

Instructions

Have students form experimenter–subject pairs. Each pair will need a yardstick and pencil and paper for recording data. To measure simple reaction time (single stimulus, single response), the yardstick is placed vertically and flat against a wall. Its 36-inch end is aligned with a mark on the wall slightly above eye level. The experimenter stands to the side, pinning the yardstick against the wall with his or her thumb at the 34-inch mark. The subject stands directly in front of the yardstick with the palm and fingers of his or her favored hand flat against the wall and the thumb stationed perpendicularly about one fourth of an inch away from the yardstick at the 2-inch mark. The experimenter instructs the subject to stop the yardstick's fall with his or her thumb when the experimenter releases it. The subject is given two practice trials, and the experimenter then records the subject's performance on four performance trials. On each trial the experimenter forewarns the subject that the trial will begin with the question "Ready?" but the experimenter varies the interval from warning to release randomly between 1 and 4 seconds. Reaction is first recorded as the distance the yardstick falls from the 2-inch mark to the mark at which the subject's thumb stops it. Distance can then be converted to time by using a curve constructed from the following table:

Conversion Table

Distance (inches)	Time (seconds)
1.9	.10
4.3	.15
7.7	.20
12.0	.25
17.3	.30
23.5	.35
30.7	.40

Discriminative reaction time (two or more stimuli, response to only one) can be measured by the same basic procedure as above, with the modification that the experimenter instructs the subject to stop the fall of the yardstick if the experimenter releases it with an upward vertical motion of the thumb but not if the experimenter's thumb moves vertically downward on release.

To measure choice reaction time (two or more stimuli, different response to each), the experimenter is positioned as before and the subject again stands directly in front of the yardstick, but this time the subject places both hands flat against the wall, one on each side of the yardstick, and stations both thumbs above the 2-inch mark. The experimenter instructs the subject to stop the fall of the yardstick with the right thumb if the experimenter's release motion is vertically upward and to stop it with the left thumb if the release motion is vertically downward. Again the experimenter gives the subject two practice trials followed by four performance trials, forewarning the subject with a "Ready?" and varying the waiting interval on each trial.

An incorrect response by the subject (e.g., responding when he or she shouldn't under the discriminative condition or using the wrong thumb under the choice condition) necessitates starting the four trials over again.

Discussion

Each experimental condition may be repeated once or twice more in four-trial blocks, provided a random order of conditions is followed. The subject's mean reaction time on each block of trials can then be calculated (by averaging the four trials), and the values can be compared. Comparisons can be made across subjects as well, and a mean reaction time can be calculated for all subjects under each experimental condition.

Suggested Background Readings

Andreas, B. G. *Experimental psychology* (2nd ed.). New York: Wiley, 1972. (chap. 10)

Postman, L., & Egan, J. P. *Experimental psychology: An introduction.* New York: Harper & Row, 1949. (chap. 12)

Underwood, B. J. *Experimental psychology* (2nd ed.). New York: Appleton-Century-Crofts, 1966. (chap. 7)

ACTIVITY
84

CHAIN REACTION TIME
Michael Wertheimer

Concept

The experiments described here permit the measurement of simple and choice reaction times using the entire class at once. The procedures come from Edwin G. Boring, who used them in his introductory psychology class at Harvard University.

Instructions

The only equipment needed for the experiments is a stopwatch. The first procedure deals with simple reaction time. A single stimulus is presented, calling for a single response; the simple reaction time is the interval between the presentation and the response.

Have all students in the class line up in single file facing the same direction. The right hand of each student should be raised about 1 inch above the right shoulder of the next student. The hand of the student at the head of the line should be positioned as though it were over the right shoulder of a next person in line. Tell students that as soon as they are tapped on the right shoulder, they are to tap the next student in line on the right shoulder. Begin the experiment by tapping the first student's shoulder and activating the stopwatch. Let the stopwatch run until the right hand of the last student starts its downward movement. Record the time on the chalkboard under the heading "simple reaction time." Repeat the exercise four times in order to get a reasonably stable reaction time for the whole chain. Record these times in the same column as the first. Then calculate a mean simple reaction time for the whole class and a mean simple reaction time for the individual student. (In this case, the mean reaction time for the individual student is computed by dividing the class mean by the number of students—see Appendix A for computation of mean.)

Have students hold their right hands over the right shoulders of those in front of them and their left hands over these persons' left shoulders. Tell students that if they are tapped on the left shoulder they should tap the left shoulder of the next person. Initiate the experiment with a tap on either the right or left shoulder of the first student, as you please. (Students should not be able to see what is happening behind them.) Time the performance as before, and then have students repeat the exercise four times. Randomly vary the shoulder that you tap on each of the four performances. Record times on the chalkboard under "choice reaction time." Calculate means for the class and the individual student, and compare them to the values obtained in the first experiment. The mean reaction times on the second experiment should be longer than those on the first.

Discussion

The latter observation can lead into a discussion of some issues that psychologists were dealing with at the turn of the century, such as how much time the choice process takes, for, in effect, the difference between the individual student means on the two experiments is the amount of time it took to make a decision. Have students think about other situations in which choice reactions are called for. What effect does the complexity of the situation have? What other factors besides complexity affect reaction time?

Suggested Background Readings

Andreas, B. G. *Experimental psychology* (2nd ed.). New York: Wiley, 1972. (chap. 10)

Postman, L., & Egan J. P. *Experimental psychology: An introduction.* New York: Harper & Row, 1949. (chap. 12)

Underwood, B. J. *Experimental psychology* (2nd ed.). New York: Appleton-Century-Crofts, 1966. (chap. 7)

ACTIVITY
85

CONDUCTION OF A
NEURONAL IMPULSE
Richard A. Kasschau

Concept

How afferent (sensory) neurons connect to other afferent and associative neurons largely determines how much information is preserved or lost as a message is relayed from receptor to cortex. The following activity can be used to demonstrate preservation or loss of information.

Instructions

You will need to arrange your classroom so that there are distinct "columns" of seats—meaning seats arranged in columns from front to back. Instruct each student that when he or she is tapped on the shoulder, he or she should tap the shoulder of the student sitting in front of him or her. Speed of "neuron-to-neuron communication" can be improved by presenting the activity as a race.

With this simple arrangement, ask each student at the back to tap the shoulder of the student sitting in front of him or her. Students at the front should be instructed to say something or raise their hands when they are tapped on the shoulder.

Now arrange the students so that all students to the *left* side of the room (as *they* view it!) will tap the shoulder of a student one row forward and one to the *right* of where they are sitting. Students sitting on the *right* will tap students one row forward and one to the *left* of them. This means that a triangular communication system has been established, but don't tell your students yet. Messages starting anywhere across the back row will collapse toward the middle column, all messages tending to arrive at the student seated at the center of the front row.

In order to ensure that the messages are collapsing correctly, instruct individual students on the back row to "fire" by tapping the person one in front and to their left or right as appropriate. As students are tapped, ask them to tap the correct person in front of them and then hold their own hands in the air so that the class can examine the path of the message after it reaches the front.

A simpler set of instructions can be utilized by asking all students to tap forward and to the right (*or* left) as a first choice, or forward if no one sits further to their right. Now all messages will collapse toward the right (or left) front seat, and more students are involved in the total activity, especially those in the front corners of your room who otherwise simply observe what is going on.

You can also use this triangular system to show how these all-or-none cells relay information about the severity of the stimulation by changing the rules so that each neuron will respond as many times and as often as it is stimulated. Again, ask a few "neurons" to fire on the back

Adapted from *Teacher's Guide With Tests to Accompany Psychology: Exploring Behavior* by R. A. Kasschau. Copyright 1980 by Prentice-Hall Publishing Company. Reprinted by permission.

row, one at a time. Since each neuron from back to front is stimulated only once, each will fire only once. Now ask the student sitting at the center rear and those on both rear corners to fire simultaneously. Now the front neuron will respond three times. Finally, ask all members of the back row to fire simultaneously. The front neuron will respond as many times as there are students along the back row. Failure to do so shows loss of information in the "system"—a likely event.

A final possibility: Communication along nerves is, of course, a combined electrical and chemical process—electrical within the individual neurons and chemical between them. Relaying a message at the synapse is the slowest part of the communication process within a nerve. To demonstrate this, instead of tapping as a means to stimulate, have each student hold a paper cup in each hand. The one in front is loaded with water and held forward; the other cup (empty!) is held over the shoulder in the other hand by each student. Every "neuron" communicates by pouring only when his or her empty cup has had something poured into it. This can be used to show convincingly how much slower the communication is at the synapse than within the individual neurons. Caution: Make sure each student is pouring a small amount of water relative to the size of his or her cup. Otherwise, as messages "collapse," cups *will* overflow! Obviously, students on the back row will be the source of the water, and the students along the front row will need a place to pour liquid as it reaches them.

Discussion

After the initial activity of linear, forward shoulder-tapping has been tried several times, ask the students on the front row what they "know" when they are tapped on the shoulder. Of course, what they know is that the student or "neuron" at the back of the room in their row was active moments earlier. They know from where the message came.

In the triangular communication network, try several different students at the back so that the class begins to see the many different roots by which messages can get to the center front. At this point ask the student at center front to shut his or her eyes and then designate (by pointing) someone along the back to "fire." Ask the student at front to identify who "fired." What will be shown, of course, is that when the messages of neurons collapse onto progressively fewer neurons, information is lost irretrievably and the accuracy of the message being relayed is less.

There are many other possibilities with this arrangement. You could show the effects of inhibition or facilitation by having some neurons that only fire if stimulated twice. Other "neurons" might stimulate two or three neurons if they themselves are stimulated.

Suggested Background Readings

Kasschau, R. A. *Psychology: Exploring behavior.* Englewood Cliffs, N.J.: Prentice-Hall, 1980.

Krech, D., Crutchfield, R. S., Livson, N., & Krech, H. *Psychology: A basic course.* New York: Alfred A. Knopf, 1976. (chap. 12)

Thompson, R. F. *Physiological psychology.* San Francisco: W. H. Freeman, 1971. (Unit 4)

86

HUMAN EMOTIONS
Richard A. Kasschau

Concept

Emotion can be defined as a conscious experience including a state of (physiological) arousal and a mediating interpretation. As such it is assumed to emphasize two factors: (1) some degree of arousal, and (2) an attempt by the experiencing organism to label the experience. Nonetheless, emotion is still a very complex phenomenon to study.

Indeed, the two most widespread research strategies have been (1) attempts to label the dimensions of emotion, or (2) theoretical attempts to integrate physiological and cognitive factors—from the James-Lange theory of 1884 to the most modern attempts such as those of Schachter and Singer (1962) or Solomon and Corbit (1974). See also Ekman and Friesen (1971).

Instructions

A couple of days before using this demonstration, assign your students to bring in newspaper and magazine photos showing peoples' faces. Make sure there is a variety of emotions expressed, perhaps by asking each student to bring in 5–10 such photographs. Also prepare a large poster board labeled as in the figure on the next page. The squares in the figure should be labeled with numbers. Along one axis, number seven positions stretching from *pleasant* to *unpleasant;* along the other, seven positions from *acceptance* to *rejection.* Finally, also prepare one additional strip of poster board material labeled *sleep–tension* (or *sleep–arousal*) in lettering similar to that used on the poster. The extra strip of posterboard should also have seven numbered positions and be large enough to cover the labels of either of the other dimensions.

Ask your students to sort the pictures that have been brought in first along a 7-position pleasant–unpleasant dimension, placing each picture in one of seven positions. On the back of the picture itself note the rating it received from each student. Next repeat this process on a 7-point acceptance–rejection scale. Finally, repeat the process once more on a scale of arousal—a sleep–tension (arousal) scale.

Now introduce the poster board containing the figure. On *this* figure students should have no trouble finding pictures that can fit into each square from most pleasant and accepting to most unpleasant and rejecting—using their prior average ratings of the position of each picture on each individual scale. Thus, a picture rated 1 (very accepting) and 1 (very pleasant) would be positioned in the lower left corner.

Repeat the same process, but now have your students place each picture on the 7-point sleep–tension (or arousal) scale. Then, using the extra strip label to create a table using either of the previous dimensions

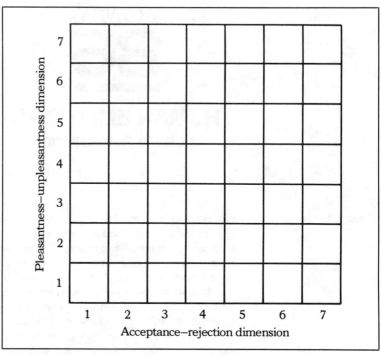

Grid for Classroom Poster

paired with the 7-position sleep–tension (or arousal) scale, position each picture on its appropriate square.

Discussion

What your students should quickly come to realize is that at the sleep end of the arousal scale it makes no sense to distinguish between a pleasant or unpleasant face as expressing emotion, or between an accepting or rejecting face as expressing an emotion when asleep. In short, what should develop across the square pattern of 49 possible positions is that when sleep–tension is one dimension, the pattern of the photographed emotions on the table is triangular. It reaches its greatest array of pleasantness–unpleasantness at the aroused end of the activity scale, and collapses toward some midpoint (neither pleasant nor unpleasant) as level of arousal declines. In essence, (if you find these results!) your students have just demonstrated the impact of level of arousal on the diversity and intensity of emotions that can be experienced. As level of arousal increases, so does the diversity and intensity of emotions experienced.

And to make another point, when the photographs are arrayed on the pleasant–unpleasant and the acceptance–rejection scales simultaneously, is there evidence that these two scales measure the same thing? That is, do the ratings tend to covary, so that a rating of 7 (rejection) tends to be accompanied by a rating of 7 (unpleasant)? If so, then the pattern of photographs on the poster board should tend to be elliptical, with the largest number of photographs arrayed on the dimension stretching from 1,1 to 7,7.

Suggested Background Readings

Arnold, M. B. (Ed.). *The nature of emotion.* Baltimore: Penguin Books, 1969.

Ekman, P., & Friesen, W. V. Constants across cultures in the face and emotion. *Journal of Personality and Social Psychology, 1971, 17,* 124–129.

Schachter, S., & Singer, J. E. Cognitive, social and physiological determinants of emotional state. *Psychological Review,* 1962, *69,* 379–399.

Solomon, R. L., & Corbit, J. D. An opponent-process theory of motivation: I. Temporal dynamics of affect. *Psychological Review,* 1974, *81,* 119–145.

ACTIVITY
87

FLASHING FACES
Linda Winchell

Concept

One phase of the study of emotions of interest to students and teachers alike is the expression of emotions. Whenever psychologists have studied emotional expression, some have maintained that the expression of emotions is learned and is therefore unique to each culture. Others agree with Charles Darwin, who maintained that because facial expressions are biologically based, one can find universality in expression.

Whichever position is true, it is generally agreed that the face provides the most signals for expression of emotions. The forehead, eyebrows, eyelids, cheeks, nose, lips, and chin all serve to give clues to the feelings one is experiencing. There appear to be "rules" individuals use to "read" faces, but seldom can they verbalize those rules. These have not been learned in a systematic way; instead, they are picked up by chance from one's family.

The purpose of this demonstration is to help students evaluate how well they are able to identify what emotion is being expressed in a facial expression. If time allows, students could try to list the "rules" they used to determine what emotion was being expressed.

Materials Needed

Teachers should obtain a copy of Ekman and Friesen's *Unmasking the Face*. On pages 175–201, Ekman has compiled a set of practice faces that express one or more of the following six emotions: surprise, fear, disgust, anger, happiness, and sadness. Cut out the pictures (anywhere from 20 to 40 of the pictures) and paste them on index cards, as suggested by the author. Be certain to write the correct number on the back of the index cards so that it will be possible to look up the correct answers listed on pages 130–134. Judgment sheets (see next page) are to be duplicated and distributed to the students.

Instructions

One of the "judgment sheets" should be given to each student. At this time it might be helpful to define the terms *contempt* and *disgust* on the judgment sheets, as many students have difficulty with the differences in these terms. Shuffle the cards and show them one at a time to the class. Ask your students to make a quick judgment in each case as to which emotion listed on the judgment sheet is expressed in the face.

When you are finished with all the cards, refer to page 130 of *Unmasking the Face* and slowly read the correct answer for each of the faces. Students are to circle each judgment they have correct. Count totals and record that number on the judgment sheet. Count the number of each of the emotions labeled correctly by the whole class and record that number in the blank next to the emotion.

Adapted from *Unmasking the Face* by P. Ekman and W. Friesen. Copyright 1975 by Prentice-Hall Publishing Company. Reprinted by permission.

ACTIVITIES HANDBOOK

Judgment Sheet

Total correct

Anger	____	Happiness	____
Contempt	____	Sadness	____
Disgust	____	Surprise	____
Fear	____	Neutral	____

1.	11.	21.	31.
2.	12.	22.	32.
3.	13.	23.	33.
4.	14.	24.	34.
5.	15.	25.	35.
6.	16.	26.	36.
7.	17.	27.	37.
8.	18.	28.	38.
9.	19.	29.	39.
10.	20.	30.	40.

Total correct _____

Name _____ Period _____

Discussion

1. Make a distribution chart showing the total number of correct judgments for each card. Discuss how well or poorly the students were able to identify emotions being expressed. What do these results say about their abilities to "read" faces? Were some of the expressions easier than the others? Photos were shuffled and arranged randomly to provide a variety of the eight labels; did placement make some emotions easier to read? Ask each student which emotion he or she identified correctly most often. Make a distribution chart and then note trends with possible explanations.

2. Ask students which emotion they correctly identified least often; note trends with possible explanations.

3. If there is time, students can analyze the pictures displaying certain emotions to see if they can list the "rules" they used to "read" the faces.

4. Those showing more adeptness at "reading" faces may wish to try Set C, which is a group of 10 faces which reflect a blend of two emotions.

5. The teacher may wish to describe the cross-cultural research Ekman has done to support his thesis of universality of interpretation.

Suggested Background Readings

Darwin, C. *Expression of emotions in man and animals.* Chicago: University of Chicago Press, 1965.

Ekman, P. Face muscles talk every language. *Psychology Today,* April 1975, pp. 33–39.

Ekman, P., & Friesen, W. *Unmasking the face.* Englewood Cliffs, N.J.: Prentice Hall, 1975.

Ekman, P. *Darwin and facial expressions.* New York: Academic Press, 1973.

Izard, C. *The face of emotion.* New York: Appleton-Century-Crofts, 1971.

Vine, I. Communication by facial-visual signals. In *Social behavior in birds and mammals.* New York: Academic Press, 1969.

ACTIVITY
88

ETHOGRAMS
Marty Klein

Concept

An ethogram is an accumulation of systematic observational data. This simple technique is one of the most difficult to reliably execute. An ethologist must initially invent categories of behavior to score and then employ a sampling technique to decide if the criterion for any of the categories has been satisfied. The difficulty lies both in the formation of categories that adequately assess the relevant behavioral variables and in the solidification of criteria for scoring these categories. High reliability between two *independent* observers strengthens the credibility of observational data, but such reliability is developed only after substantial experience on the part of the observers.

Instructions

For this activity, you will need data sheets for your students, wristwatches, and an active animal in a cage (e.g., a gerbil, hamster, pigeon). Before class, place the caged animal in an area open to observation. It would be best to have the animal hungry and thirsty and then to place food and water in the cage just prior to observation. It would also be good to have some objects in the cage for the animal to interact with (e.g., a running wheel).

Devise a classification system for about 10 behaviors, some easily observable and some more subtle. The students should be given a list of these behaviors with descriptions of them, as in the following example.

Response #	Name	Description
R_1	wall orientation	orientation response in which animal's head and body are directed toward one of the four walls
R_2	walking	animal walks in any direction
R_3	eating	animal eats
R_4	drinking	animal drinks
R_5	grooming	animal licks its body
R_6	standing or sitting still	animal remains motionless

A data sheet, as diagrammed on the next page, should also be handed out at this time. The one illustrated here handles up to 10 responses for twenty 30-second intervals, or a total of 10 minutes.

Interval recording is used to collect the data. Each 30 seconds, the observer is to check off any and all behaviors that occurred during the previous 30-second interval (going across one line on the data sheet). The next interval is scored on the following line, and so forth. The decision in all cases is binary—either the behavior occurred one or more times in the previous interval or it did not.

Data Sheet

	R₁	R₂	R₃	R₄	R₅	R₆	R₇	R₈	R₉	R₁₀
A										
B										
C										
D										
E										
F										
T										

The ethogram may be displayed in a number of ways. Two useful ways are a histogram, or bar chart, and a cumulative graph. In the histogram, each response class is listed on the x-axis, and the number of times that response was observed is recorded on the y-axis:

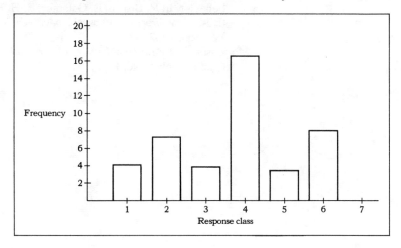

A more useful presentation is the cumulative graph, which shows the cumulative number of occurrences of each behavior over time:

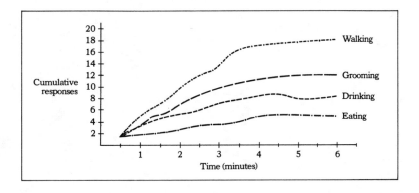

Have the observers pair up and compare their observations. Below is a simple way to calculate interobserver accuracy:

$$\text{Interobserver reliability} = \frac{\text{No. of agreements}}{\text{No. of agreements} + \text{No. of disagreements}}$$

Discussion

How does this sampling procedure (interval sampling) overestimate (proportionately) or underestimate behavior rates? Note that the behavioral classes can be as global or microscopic as desired; for example, the categories may have all been devoted to eating, with R_1 = approach food, R_2 = sniffing, R_3 = touch food, R_4 = swallowing, and so forth. What are the limitations on extending the analysis in these ways? Compare the potential usefulness of the cumulative graph with that of the histogram. How might these be employed in an experiment in which an independent variable is manipulated after obtaining baseline measures? Note that this technique is very similar to procedures used in human behavior modification programs, which often have the subject collect his or her own baseline and treatment data.

Suggested Background Readings

Denny, M. R., & Ratner, S. *Comparative psychology* (2nd ed.). Homewood, Ill. Dorsey Press, 1970.

Hess, E. H. Ethology: An approach toward the complete analysis of behavior. In R. Brown, E. Galanter, E. H. Hess, & G. Mandler (Eds.) *New directions in psychology*. New York: Holt, Rinehart & Winston, 1962.

Mortenson, F. J. *Animal behavior: Theory and research*. Monterey, Calif.: Brooks/Cole, 1975.

APPENDIXES

A

BASIC STATISTICAL METHODS
Charles M. Stoup

This appendix is designed to provide a basic understanding of a few of the statistical techniques commonly used to analyze data from psychological experiments. While it is not intended as a complete introduction to statistical analysis, the techniques it presents should enable you to analyze and interpret the data from most of the activities described in this handbook. Any techniques not described here may be found in most introductory statistics texts, several of which are listed at the end of this appendix.

Measurement

For information about a subject or group of subjects to be useful as data, it must be reducible to numerical form. This process of assigning numbers to observations is called *measurement*. Measurement is of concern to psychologists because the ways in which numbers are assigned to observations vary a great deal depending on the variable being observed. Thus, the psychologist (indeed, all behavioral scientists) must consider the *level of measurement* that corresponds to a particular dependent variable—where level of measurement indicates the degree of correspondence between the numbers assigned to the observations and the actual characteristics of the subjects being observed. That is, the level of measurement describes the *nature* of the information produced by the operations that define the dependent variable. Four broad classes or levels of measurement may be identified: nominal-, ordinal-, interval-, and ratio-level measurements.

Nominal-level measurement. A nominal variable is one that assigns labels to observations such that each observation receives one label or another but never more than one. That is, nominal-level measurement allows us only to state whether one observation is the *same as* or *different from* another observation with respect to the characteristic being measured. For example, individuals may be classified according to their eye color, with the colors being coded as brown = 1, blue = 2, green = 3, and other = 4. Similarly, the football jerseys worn by the players on a team are marked with conspicuous numbers, which serve

only to identify different players. Both of these examples constitute nominal-level measurement, since in each case only one label may be assigned to the different units of observation (i.e., subjects), and the labels serve only to distinguish equivalent or different observations without allowing any statements concerning the magnitude of the characteristic being measured. Thus, it makes no sense to say that an individual with eye color coded as "3" has more of any characteristic than an individual with eye color coded as "1"—the measurement only specifies that the individuals differ with respect to this characteristic.

Ordinal-level measurement. An ordinal variable has all the characteristics of a nominal variable and, in addition, assigns labels to observations in such a way that the observations can meaningfully be placed in rank order. If we observe a group of individuals and classify each of them as being short = 1, medium = 2, or tall = 3, we have performed ordinal-level measurement on the height variable, since the three categories can be rank ordered with respect to the "amount" of height observed. Another example of ordinal-level measurement is the classification system used to denote a person's "rank" in college. Individuals are classified as freshmen = 1, sophomores = 2, juniors = 3, or seniors = 4, with the class designation signifying the amount of progress made by the student toward a college degree.

Ordinal-level measurement is quite common in psychology, since it is often impossible to make absolute quantitative measurements of psychological attributes. The major drawback of ordinal-level measurement is that the differences between adjacent classes in the rank ordering are not necessarily equal. This deficiency limits the kinds of statistical analyses possible with ordinal-level data.

Interval-level measurement. An interval-level variable meets the requirements of ordinal-level measurement and also has equal distances between adjacent measurement classes. Interval-level measurement implies the use of a *unit* of measurement: Each measurement category is the same distance from the categories above and below it.

The most commonly cited example of interval-level measurement is the Fahrenheit temperature scale. The scale is clearly both nominal and ordinal and, in addition, has equal intervals between adjacent classes. Thus, the temperature difference between $40°F$ and $50°F$ is the same as the difference between $60°F$ and $70°F$. This fact allows us to apply more powerful and sophisticated statistical techniques to data resulting from interval-level measurement than to ordinal- or nominal-level data. The only limitation of interval-level measurement is that the scales resulting from it do not possess an absolute zero point that signifies the complete absence of the attribute being measured. While the Fahrenheit temperature scale has a point labeled $0°$, that point is arbitrarily defined and does not indicate the complete absence of temperature. This limitation prevents us from meaningfully using interval-level data to form *ratios* of measurements. That is, it would *not* be valid for us to say that a temperature of $100°F$ is twice as "hot" as a temperature of $50°F$, since both temperatures are referenced to a completely arbitrary zero point.

Ratio-level measurement. This level of measurement is said to be the highest level of measurement, since ratio-level scales have all the characteristics of the other measurement levels and also possess a zero point that represents the absolute absence of the variable being measured. Ratio-level measurement is common in the physical sciences, as represented by measurements of length, mass, voltage, velocity, and pressure. One of the more commonly used ratio-level scales in psychology is the measurement of time, as in the measurement of reaction time or the time required to complete a task. In ratio-level measurement it is meaningful to compare the magnitude of measurements in ratio form: 6 inches is twice as long as 3 inches, and 2 hours is twice as long a time as 1 hour.

When analyzing the data from a psychological experiment or demonstration, a good place to begin is with a determination of the level of measurement that corresponds to your dependent variable. As we shall see, the level of the dependent variable used can have an important impact on the types of statistical analyses that are appropriate for use with the data from a particular experiment.

Computational Notation

To make effective use of the formulae for the various statistical techniques presented in this appendix, it is necessary that the reader have a basic understanding of the notation used in them. Two basic concepts must be understood in order to use most statistical formulae: subscripting of variables and summation notation.

Subscripting of variables. Subscripting enables us to refer to a set of numbers (e.g., data) without actually writing all of them down every

time we need them in a computation. This is accomplished by first choosing an arbitrary letter (usually X or Y) to stand for the variable that we have measured and then adding a subscript (usually i or j) to the variable symbol. This gives us a subscripted variable, X_i (read X sub i), where X indicates the value of a variable, and i indicates which particular observation we are referring to. We can refer to any observation in a set by allowing the subscript i to take on any value from 1 to n, where n is the number of observations in the set. For example, if we were to randomly select 3 students from a psychology class, we could let the numbers 1, 2, and 3 represent the students; in this case $n = 3$. Now if we let X stand for the ages of the students, we might obtain the following data: $X_1 = 18, X_2 = 17, X_3 = 18$. Since we can represent these observations by the subscripted variable X_i, with i varying from 1 to 3, we have a convenient shorthand for representing this set of data. In general, if we have a group of n observations, we may denote them by the symbols $X_1, X_2, \ldots, X_n$, with X_i denoting the ith observation.

Summation notation. In many of the statistical procedures presented below, it is necessary to add up a set of scores as a part of the necessary computations. Summation notation provides us with a convenient shorthand way of representing this "adding-up" process. In summation notation, the symbol Σ (the Greek capital letter sigma) stands for the process of summation (adding up). For example,

$$\sum_{i=1}^{n} X_i$$

instructs us to add up all the values of X_i as i varies from 1 to n. That is,

$$\sum_{i=1}^{n} X_i = X_1 + X_2 + X_3 + \cdots + X_n.$$

Summation notation provides us with an increase in precision and economy, thus increasing the readability of our computational formulae.

As an example of the use of summation notation, consider the three psychology students described above and their corresponding ages, $X_1 = 18, X_2 = 17, X_3 = 18$. To compute the average age of these students, it is necessary to find the sum of their respective ages. We could write this sum as

$$X_1 + X_2 + X_3 = 17 + 18 + 18 = 53,$$

or, using summation notation, as

$$\sum_{i=1}^{n} X_i = 53.$$

If we consider a set of scores with 20 observations (i.e., $n = 20$), the economy of summation notation becomes quite obvious.

Measures of Central Tendency

It is often necessary (or at least convenient) to be able to characterize an entire set of scores or measurements by just a few statistics. One category of such descriptive statistics is called *measures of central tendency;* these measures produce single numbers that can be thought of as the "typical" or "most likely" observation. We will be concerned with the three most common measures of central tendency: the *mode,* the *median,* and the *arithmetic mean.*

Mode. The mode is the simplest measure of central tendency to obtain, since it requires no actual computations to be performed on the data. The mode is defined as the most frequently occurring value of the variable. That is, for a given set of scores, the mode is that score value that occurs more often than any other score. For example, if the scores for 10 individuals on a 10-point quiz were 2, 4, 5, 6, 6, 7, 7, 7, 9, 9, the mode for this set of scores would be 7, since 7 occurs more often than any other value.

The mode is easy to "compute," but its usefulness is limited by the fact that its value is unaffected by the distribution of any scores other than the modal value. Consider the following set of scores: 1, 1, 2, 2, 3, 3, 4, 7, 7, 7. Here, as in the previous example, the modal value is 7. Note that the values of the mode for these two sets of scores do not in any way reflect the radically different shapes of the two distributions. This clearly shows that the mode uses very little of the information present in a distribution. Thus the mode is generally not the preferred measure of central tendency when it is possible to compute one of the other measures.

Because of its simplicity, the mode can be determined for data at any level of measurement. However, if the data represent nominal-level measurement, the mode is the *only* appropriate measure of central tendency.

Median. The median is defined as that value on the measurement scale above which half of the observations fall and below which half of the observations fall. To find the median of a set of scores, it is necessary to rank order the scores from smallest to largest and then find the middle value—the one with an equal number of scores above and below it. If there are an even number of scores in the set, the median is the average of the middle *pair* of observations.

Since the median is obtained by rank ordering the observations, it cannot be computed unless the data can be meaningfully placed in an order. Thus, computation of the median requires that the observations be at the ordinal, interval, or ratio level of measurement. By definition, the median cannot be computed for nominal-level data. The median makes use of more of the information in the data than does the mode, since the median is based on the rank order of the observations. The median does not, however, reflect the actual *value*

of every observation in the set. This characteristic makes the median useful with very asymmetric distributions, which are commonly found in measures such as annual income or in tasks involving speeded responses (such as reaction times). However, if one wishes the measure of central tendency to reflect the value of each observation, the median is not the measure to use.

Mean. The arithmetic mean is the most widely used measure of central tendency, largely because of its logical appeal and the precise way in which it is defined. Symbolically, the mean is defined as

$$\bar{X} = \frac{\sum_{i=1}^{n} X_i}{n},$$

where n is the number of observations, X_i represents the variable that was measured, and $\bar{X}$ (pronounced X-bar) is the conventional symbol used for the mean. To find the mean, simply add up the values of the measured variable and then divide this sum by the number of observations. For the data from the first example given earlier, the mean, $\bar{X}$, would be

$$\bar{X} = \frac{2 + 4 + 5 + 6 + 6 + 7 + 7 + 7 + 9 + 9}{10}$$

$$= \frac{62}{10} = 6.2.$$

By definition, every value in the set of observations contributes to the value of the mean. Because of this, the mean is sensitive to the presence of a few very high or very low values in the set of scores. This characteristic limits the usefulness of the mean for describing the central tendency of very asymmetric distributions; in such cases the median is the measure of choice.

The appropriate use of the mean requires that the data represent either interval- or ratio-level measurement, since the actual values of the observations are used in its computation. The mean cannot be meaningfully computed on nominal- or ordinal-level measurements.

Describing the Variability of Data

The measure of central tendency obtained from a set of data provides us with an estimate of the "most typical" value in the set. While this measure provides useful information about the characteristics of the data, it does not give us a complete description of all of the attributes of the data that we might consider important. In addition to a measure of central tendency, it is often necessary for us to be able to describe the *variability* of a set of data, where by variability we mean the extent to which the scores in a set of data differ among themselves.

The most common measures of variability are the *standard deviation* and the related statistic, the *variance.* The variance and the standard deviation are computed using the same steps, with the standard deviation defined as the square root of the variance. Computation of these two statistics is as follows:

$$\text{variance} = S^2 = \frac{\displaystyle\sum_{i=1}^{n} X_i^2 - \left(\frac{\displaystyle\sum_{i=1}^{n} X_i}{n}\right)^2}{n-1},$$

where

$$\sum_{i=1}^{n} X_i^2 = X_1^2 + X_2^2 + X_3^2 + \cdots + X_n^2,$$

$$\left(\sum_{i=1}^{n} X_i\right)^2 = (X_1 + X_2 + X_3 + \cdots + X_n)^2,$$

and n = number of observations;

standard deviation = $S = \sqrt{S^2}$.

As a computational example, consider the data we used earlier to illustrate the computation of the mean. For our computations, we require the following sums:

$$\sum_{i=1}^{n} X_i$$
$$= 2 + 4 + 5 + 6 + 6 + 7 + 7 + 7 + 9 + 9$$
$$= 62$$

$$\sum_{i=1}^{n} X_i^2 = 2^2 + 4^2 + \cdots + 9^2 = 426$$

$$n = 10.$$

Thus,

$$S^2 = \frac{426 - \dfrac{(62)^2}{10}}{9}$$

$$= \frac{426 - \dfrac{3844}{10}}{9} = \frac{426 - 384.4}{9}$$

$$= \frac{41.6}{9}$$

$$= 4.62$$

and the standard deviation is given by

$$S = \sqrt{S^2}$$
$$= \sqrt{4.62}$$
$$= 2.15.$$

(Note: The formula given here for computing the variance and standard deviation is not the formula commonly used to *define* these two statistics. The definitional formula for the variance is

$$S^2 = \frac{\displaystyle\sum_{i=1}^{n} (X_i - \bar{X})^2}{n-1}.$$

The formula given earlier is a more convenient computational form of this definitional formula.)

Both the variance and standard deviation provide us with useful information concerning the variability (dispersion) of a set of observations. The variance, however, is not particularly useful as a *descriptive* statistic of variability, since it is expressed in terms of squared units of measurement (i.e., if one were measuring height in terms of inches, the variance would be expressed in inches²). (As we shall see later in this appendix, this drawback does not prevent the variance from being extremely important in the derivation of other statistics.) The standard deviation does not share this limitation, since it is expressed in terms of the original units of measurement and thus can be interpreted directly as a measure of the variability exhibited by a set of data.

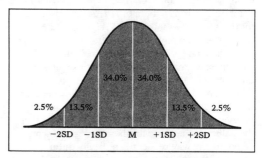

Normal Distribution

The standard deviation is particularly useful in relation to variables that produce what are called *normal distributions*. When graphed, normally distributed variables produce the familiar symmetric, bell-shaped curves often obtained when large numbers of observations are made on a single variable. The measurement of many of the physical characteristics of humans produce normal (or approximately normal) distributions; height, weight, and hat size are just a few examples. In addition, many other variables, such as scores on standardized aptitude tests (e.g., the Scholastic Aptitude Test—SAT), are scaled so as to produce normal distributions. Knowing that a variable is normally distributed enables us to make some fairly precise statements concerning the distribution of the values of that variable. For a normally distributed variable, 68.3% of the observations fall within the interval ranging from 1 standard deviation below the mean to 1 standard deviation above the mean (i.e., ±1 standard deviation unit around the mean). Similarly, 95.4% of the observations fall within ±2 standard deviation units around the mean. Finally, 99.7% of the observations fall within ±3 standard deviation units around the mean. These values hold for any normally distributed variable and provide us with a great deal of information about the characteristics of that variable. For example, the SAT scores are scaled to have a mean of 500 and a standard deviation of 100. (These values have changed somewhat in recent years but will suffice for the sake of illustration.) This means that 68.3% of all persons taking the SAT obtain scores between 400 and 600 (± 1 standard deviation unit), and 95.4% obtain scores between 300 and 700 (± 2 standard deviation units). Knowing the mean and standard deviation of any normally distributed variable enables us to make these kinds of statements concerning the actual distribution of the scores.

Correlation

Up to this point we have been concerned with descriptive statistics of groups of data, such as the mean and standard deviation. All of these statistics involve only one variable or dimension and are concerned with summarizing large amounts of data. However, we often are interested in determining whether there is a *relationship* between two variables—that is, whether two variables tend to "go together" in any manner. The statistic developed for this purpose is called the *coefficient of correlation,* and it is commonly used in psychological research.

Suppose we consider the (somewhat trivial) question of determining whether there is a relationship between people's heights and weights. To answer this question we could measure a group of students on both variables and obtain a distribution of heights (call this variable X) and a distribution of weights (variable Y). We can get a rough idea of the relationship between these two variables by constructing what is called a scatter diagram. To make a scatter diagram, one constructs a graph with variable X on the abscissa (horizontal axis) and variable Y on the ordinate (vertical axis). Since each person measured yields two scores, we take a person's score on variable X and first draw an imaginary line up from that point on the abscissa and then draw another imaginary line across from the point on the ordinate corresponding to that person's score on variable Y. Where these two lines cross we draw a point, and this point represents *one person's* scores on both variables. If we followed these steps for all of the students measured, we would obtain a complete scatter diagram.

Inspection of scatter diagrams can provide us with some approximate information regarding both the direction and the strength of the relationship. A direct or *positive* relationship is shown by a scatter diagram that points upward to the right. (This assumes that the graph follows the convention of having the zero point of each variable at the origin, with increasing values of X to the right on the abscissa and increasing values of Y upward on the ordinate.) If the points fall into no discernible pattern, that is, if they form a more or less circular shape, there is probably no relationship present. If the pattern points upward to the left, a *negative* relationship is shown. The strength of the relationship is shown by how closely the pattern

approximates a straight line. If the points fall on a straight line pointing upward to the right, then a perfect positive relationship is present. A straight line pointing upward to the left signifies a perfect negative relationship.

Looking at scatter diagrams provides only an approximate estimate of the direction and strength of a relationship, but the coefficient of correlation gives an exact answer. A convenient computational formula for the correlation coefficient is as follows:

$$r_{xy} = \frac{\Sigma X_i Y_i - \dfrac{(\Sigma X_i)(\Sigma Y_i)}{n}}{\sqrt{\left(\Sigma X_i^2 - \dfrac{(\Sigma X_i)^2}{n}\right) \cdot \left(\Sigma Y_i^2 - \dfrac{(\Sigma Y_i)^2}{n}\right)}},$$

where all summations are over $i = 1$ to n; $\Sigma X_i Y_i = (X_1 \cdot Y_1) + (X_2 \cdot Y_2) + \cdots + (X_n \cdot Y_n)$; all other summations are as described in previous sections; and r_{xy} is the conventional symbol for the correlation coefficient.

As an example of the computation of the correlation coefficient, consider the following hypothetical scores obtained by 10 students on an English test (X) and a math test (Y), each with 10 points possible.

Student	X	Y
1	4	6
2	7	9
3	9	8
4	4	4
5	3	2
6	6	7
7	7	7
8	5	6
9	8	10
10	4	4

The necessary sums are $\Sigma X_i = 57$, $\Sigma X_i^2 = 361$, $\Sigma Y_i = 63$, $\Sigma Y_i^2 = 451$, and $\Sigma X_i Y_i = 398$. Using these values in the formula, we obtain

$$r_{xy} = \frac{398 - \dfrac{(57)(63)}{10}}{\sqrt{\left(361 - \dfrac{(57)^2}{10}\right)\left(451 - \dfrac{(63)^2}{10}\right)}}$$

$$= \frac{398 - 359.1}{\sqrt{(361 - 324.9)(451 - 396.9)}}$$

$$= \frac{38.9}{\sqrt{(36.1)(54.1)}}$$

$$= \frac{38.9}{\sqrt{1953.01}} = \frac{38.9}{44.2}$$

$$= +.88.$$

Thus, the value of the correlation coefficient for the hypothetical test data is +.88, which indicates a strong positive relationship between the scores on the two tests.

The value obtained for the correlation coefficient provides information concerning both the direction and the relative strength of the relationship between the two variables. The direction of the relationship is indicated by the sign (+ or −) attached to the correlation coefficient. A positive relationship (positive value of r_{xy}) signifies that as the values of one variable increase, the values of the other variable tend to increase as well. A negative relationship (negative value of r_{xy}) can be interpreted to mean that as the values of one variable increase, the values of the other variable tend to decrease; that is, the relationship between the two variables is an inverse one. The relative strength of the relationship between the two variables is indicated by the absolute value of the correlation coefficient. That is, the fact that one correlation coefficient is positive and one is negative *does not* mean that the positive correlation signifies a stronger relationship. A correlation of −.65 implies a stronger relationship than one of +.40, since the absolute value (ignoring the sign) of −.65 is greater than that of +.45.

Several other characteristics of the correlation coefficient should be mentioned. First, the values of the correlation coefficient can only range from −1.0 to +1.0 (that is, $-1.0 \leqslant r_{xy} \leqslant +1.0$). Any computed values of r_{xy} that fall outside of this range indicate that a computational error has occurred. Second, a value for r_{xy} of +.60 does not indicate twice as strong a relationship as an r_{xy} of +.30. Correlation coefficients cannot be used to form meaningful ratios of the strength of relationships. Finally, obtaining a large value of the correlation coefficient does not imply that the two variables are causally related, that is, that the change in the values of one variable *caused* the values of the other variable to change. A nonzero correlation implies only that there is a relationship between the two variables, not that the change in the value of one variable caused a change in the other variable.

Tests on Means

A common problem in psychological research is deciding whether the means from two groups in an experiment are sufficiently different in value to warrant the conclusion that the experimental treatment given to one of the groups produced a "significant" effect. In such situations, we are concerned with testing the hypothesis (termed the *null hypothesis*, H_0) that the difference between the two means is zero:

$$H_0: \mu_1 - \mu_2 = 0.$$

Note that this is just another way of saying that the two means μ_1 and μ_2 (μ is the lower-case Greek letter mu) are equal. We wish to test this null hypothesis against the *alternative hypothesis*, H_1:

$$H_1: \mu_1 - \mu_2 \neq 0.$$

Hypotheses of this form are tested by using what is called a *t test on the means*. These *t* tests have two basic forms: the *independent samples* test and the *dependent samples* test.

Independent samples test. The independent samples *t* test is used whenever the

subjects in the two groups (experimental group vs. control group; Treatment 1 vs. Treatment 2, etc.) are assigned completely at random and the observations made on the subjects in the two groups are independent of each other. The formula for the independent samples *t* test is

$$t = \frac{\bar{X}_1 - \bar{X}_2}{\sqrt{S_p^2 \left(\dfrac{1}{n_1} + \dfrac{1}{n_2} \right)}}$$

$$S_p^2 = \frac{(n_1 - 1)S_1^2 + (n_2 - 1)S_2^2}{n_1 + n_2 - 2}$$

where $\bar{X}_1$ = mean of the first group, $\bar{X}_2$ = mean of the second group, and $n_1 + n_2 - 2$ is called the degrees of freedom (*df*) associated with this particular test. Computation of the independent samples *t* test requires that we know the mean and variance for Group 1 and the mean and variance for Group 2.

To complete the test, the obtained value of *t* is compared to a value of the *t* distribution for the appropriate degrees of freedom obtained from a table of *t* values. An abbreviated list of the *t* values corresponding to the .05 level of significance is presented in Table 1. Assuming that H_0 is true, we

Table 1
Critical Values of Student's t *Distribution for Level of Significance* (α) *of .05 for Two-Tailed Test*

df	t_c
1	12.706
2	4.303
3	3.182
4	2.776
5	2.571
6	2.447
7	2.365
8	2.306
9	2.262
10	2.228
11	2.201
12	2.179
13	2.160
14	2.145
15	2.131
16	2.120
17	2.110
18	2.101
19	2.093
20	2.086
22	2.074
24	2.064
26	2.056
28	2.048
30	2.042
40	2.021
60	2.000
120	1.980
∞	1.960

would expect to obtain a computed value of t equal to (or greater than) the value listed in Table 1 for the correct degrees of freedom only 5% of the time by random or chance variation alone. Thus, if we obtain a value of t greater than the corresponding value from the table, we can feel safe in rejecting H_0 and concluding that the means of the two groups are significantly different at the .05 level of significance; we are inferring that something other than chance factors produced that large a difference.

As an example, consider the following situation. An experimenter wishes to compare the effectiveness of two methods of teaching vocabulary words in a foreign language. A total of 20 students are randomly divided into two equal groups, with each group taught according to one of the methods for a 2-week period. At the end of this 2-week learning period, the students in both groups are given a standardized vocabulary test that yields the following results:

$$\overline{X}_1 = 70 \qquad \overline{X}_2 = 60$$
$$S_1^2 = 80 \qquad S_1^2 = 75$$
$$n_1 = 10 \qquad n_2 = 10.$$

The computation of t is as follows:

$$S_p^2 = \frac{(10 - 1)80 + (10 - 1)75}{10 + 10 - 2}$$

$$= \frac{(9)80 + (9)75}{18}$$

$$= 77.5$$

$$t = \frac{70 - 60}{\sqrt{77.5\left(\dfrac{1}{10} + \dfrac{1}{10}\right)}}$$

$$= \frac{10}{\sqrt{15.5}}$$

$$= \frac{10}{3.937}$$

$$= 2.54.$$

This value of t is then compared to the value obtained from the table for $df = 10 + 10 - 2 = 18$, which yields a table value of 2.101. Since our obtained t value of 2.54 is *greater* than the value of 2.101 obtained from the table, we reject $H_0: \mu_1 - \mu_2 = 0$ and conclude that the alternative hypothesis, $H_1: \mu_1 - \mu_2 = 0$, is supported by the data. That is, we would conclude that Method 1 of teaching foreign language vocabulary is more effective than Method 2.

Dependent samples test. The dependent samples test is used when some degree of dependency exists between the two groups; subjects are *not* assigned to the two groups in a completely random manner. For example, in the independent samples experiment described above, the teacher could have given the 20 students a test of their ability in the foreign language prior to the

beginning of the experiment and then grouped the students into pairs according to their scores on the test; the two students scoring highest would be Pair 1, the next two students Pair 2, and so forth. Then the teacher could have randomly selected one member of Pair 1 to receive the first teaching method and continued this procedure until one member from each pair had been selected for Method 1 and the other member of each pair for Method 2. This procedure would tend to reduce the variability between the groups, since each member of the Method 1 group would have a counterpart in the Method 2 group who scored similarly on the initial test.

A very common way of introducing a dependency between the two groups is to have each subject in the experiment serve in both treatment conditions. This is called a *repeated-measures* design, and the data from a study conducted in this manner could be analyzed using the dependent sample t test. (Note: To avoid sequence effects in the repeated-measures design, half of the subjects should receive Treatment 1 followed by Treatment 2, with the other half of the subjects receiving the treatments in the reverse order.)

The data from a dependent samples test may be analyzed by using the *direct-differences method*. In this method, a difference score, d_i is obtained for each *pair* of observations:

$$d_1 = X_1 - X_2 \text{ for Pair 1}$$
$$d_2 = X_1 - X_2 \text{ for Pair 2} \ldots$$
$$d_n = X_1 - X_2 \text{ for Pair } n$$

The value of t is then obtained by

$$t_{n-1} = \frac{\overline{d}}{S_d/\sqrt{n}},$$

where $\overline{d}$ is the mean of the difference scores,

$$\overline{d} = \frac{\displaystyle\sum_{i=1}^{n} d_i}{n},$$

S_d is the standard deviation of the difference score,

$$S_d = \sqrt{\frac{\Sigma d_i{}^2 - \dfrac{(\Sigma d_i)^2}{n}}{n - 1}},$$

n = number of *pairs* of observations, and $df = n - 1$.

The value of t obtained by the direct-differences method is then compared to the values of t from Table 1 in the same manner as in the independent samples case described above, except that the degrees of freedom for this test are given by $n - 1$ (one fewer than the number of pairs). The logic of the test and the hypotheses tested are basically the same as those described above.

As an example, consider the following data obtained in a repeated-measures experiment that used 8 subjects:

Subject	1	2	3	4	5	6	7	8
Condition A	12	31	17	17	8	14	25	4
Condition B	8	17	12	19	5	6	20	3
d_i	4	14	5	−2	3	8	5	1

The necessary sums are

$$\sum_{i=1}^{n} d_i = 38$$

and

$$\sum_{i=1}^{n} d_i{}^2 = 340.$$

The mean difference score is

$$\overline{d} = \frac{\Sigma d_i}{n} = \frac{38}{8} = 4.75.$$

The standard deviation of the difference scores, S_d, is

$$S_d = \sqrt{\frac{340 - \dfrac{38^2}{8}}{8 - 1}}$$

$$= \sqrt{\frac{340 - 180.5}{7}}$$

$$= 4.77.$$

The value of t is given by

$$t = \frac{4.75}{4.77/\sqrt{8}}$$

$$= \frac{4.75}{1.68}$$

$$= 2.81,$$

with $df = 8 - 1 = 7$.

To test the hypothesis that the means of the two conditions are the same, $H_0 : \mu_1 - \mu_2 = 0$, we compare our obtained t value to the value of t from Table 1 when $df = 7$. Since our obtained value of 2.81 is greater than the table value of 2.365, we reject the null hypothesis and conclude that there is a significant difference between the means of the two conditions at the .05 level of significance. Had our computed value been less than the value from the table, we would have been forced to conclude that the present data provided no evidence that there was a difference in effectiveness between our two treatment conditions.

Analysis of Frequency Data
A common procedure in psychological experimentation involves making observations that permit nominal measurement of each observational unit (person, animal, etc.) with respect to two variables. For example, students can

be classified both with respect to sex (male or female) and academic major. For data of this type, the *frequencies* of the various combinations of levels of the two variables may be tabulated in a *contingency table*. With data of this form, we are generally concerned with testing the null hypothesis which states that the two classification variables are *independent*, against the alternative hypothesis that they are not independent.

We will consider only the simplest kind of test of independence: the chi-square (X^2) test of independence for a 2×2 contingency table. (More general procedures for tests of independence for larger contingency tables can be found in any of the suggested readings listed at the end of this appendix.) To compute the X^2 test of independence, we represent the cell and marginal frequencies with the following notation:

A	B	A + B
C	D	C + D
A + C	B + D	N

Chi-square is then calculated as follows:

$$X^2 = \frac{N(AD - BC)^2}{(A + B)(C + D)(A + C)(B + D)}.$$

As an example of the computation of the X^2 test of independence, consider the following hypothetical data from 100 patients in a psychiatric institution:

	Treatment method		
Evaluation	Therapy A	Therapy B	
Improvement	20	40	60
No improvement	25	15	40
	45	55	100

We want to test whether there is an association between treatment method and subsequent evaluation. Computation of X^2 is as follows:

$$X^2 = \frac{100(20 \cdot 15 - 40 \cdot 25)^2}{(60 \cdot 40 \cdot 45 \cdot 55)}$$

$$= 8.25.$$

This value of X^2 is then compared to a tabled value of X^2 for the appropriate degrees of freedom and level of significance. For a 2×2 contingency table, the degrees of freedom are always equal to 1. Thus, the tabled value of X^2 for $df = 1$ at the .05 level of significance is 3.84. Since our obtained value of X^2, 8.25, exceeds the tabled value of 3.84, we reject the hypothesis that the two classification variables are independent and conclude that an association does exist between the treatment method used and subsequent psychological evaluation. If our obtained value had been less than 3.84, we would have been led to conclude that no evidence existed in the present data which would lead us to conclude that an association existed between the two variables.

A caution concerning the X^2 test of independence is in order: The test given above should not be used for cases in which the cell frequencies are small (less than 10). A test of independence is still possible in such cases, but the computational procedure is somewhat different. The appropriate formula may be found in the references listed at the end of this appendix.

Suggested Readings

Coladarci, A., & Coladarci, T. *Elementary descriptive statistics: For those who think they can't*. Belmont; Calif.: Wadsworth, 1980.
Provides a straightforward, clear introduction to descriptive statistics. This book would be especially useful as a review and extension of the material presented in Sections 1–5 of this appendix.

Ferguson, G. A. *Statistical analysis in psychology and education* (5th ed.). New York: McGraw-Hill, 1981.
Provides a comprehensive treatment of statistical analysis including analysis of variance techniques appropriate for experiments employing more than two treatment conditions.

Weinberg, S. L., & Goldberg, K. P. *Basic statistics for education and the behavioral sciences*. Boston: Houghton Mifflin, 1979.
Provides a clear, thorough introduction to statistical analysis.

B

A BIBLIOGRAPHY ON DO-IT-YOURSELF LABORATORY AND CLASSROOM APPARATUS

Animal Apparatus

A. Activity

Christiano, J. M. Setting up a high school psychology laboratory. *Behavioral and Social Science Teacher,* 1975, *2*(2), 34–37. A general description of the problems and advantages of setting up a high school psychology laboratory. Describes how a lab may be started from scratch and how equipment may be built. Discusses the need for well-trained student lab assistants.

Pfister, H. P., Mudge, R. R., & Harcombe, A. O. A multipurpose activity platform utilized in the open-field setting. *Behavior Research Methods and Instrumentation,* 1978, *10*(1), 21–22. Describes an automated multipurpose activity platform (MAP) that can be used to measure activity in the horizontal plane. The MPA has no built-in data storage facility and needs to be interfaced with a recording system. The system has been used successfully in measuring open-field activity of rats.

Stong, C. L. An apparatus for simulating high altitudes and testing their effects on small animals. *Scientific American,* 1965, *213*(3), 239–254. A complete review of the procedure and results on testing the physiological effects of high altitudes on white rats, with a detailed description of the experimental apparatus involved (diagrams).

B. Feeding

Bostwick, A. D., & Porter, J. J. An efficient, inexpensive food hopper for monitoring feeding habits of rats. *Behavior Research Methods and Instrumentation,* 1977, *9*(5), 471–472. Describes a food hopper designed for the constant monitoring of home-cage free-feeding patterns of rats. The apparatus is inexpensive and is designed to attach to standard rat housing cages.

Stong, C. L. An amateur asks: Does a hummingbird find its way to nectar through its sense of smell? *Scientific American,* 1960, *202*(2), 157–166. A brief introduction to the olfactory sense phenomenon in birds, incorporated in a discussion of instinct vs. learned behavior. Gives a complete description of an experiment used to test the sense of smell in wild hummingbirds, including method, procedure, and results.

C. Learning

Abplanalp, P. Stabilized construction of a Hebb-Williams maze. *Behavior Research Methods and Instrumentation,* 1972, *4*(3), 174. Describes a method of constructing a Hebb-Williams maze which enables the internal walls to be conveniently moved about to construct different pathways from startbox to goal. The arrangement is cheaper and less cumbersome than building a separate maze for each problem.

Abramson, C. I., Collier, D. M., & Marcucella, H. An aversive conditioning unit for ants. *Behavior Research Methods and Instrumentation,* 1977, *9*(6), 505–507. Describes an apparatus for studying aversive conditioning in ants. The aversive stimulus is mechanically produced vibration, and responses are recorded automatically by an infrared photocell system. Preliminary data on the acquisition and extinction of escape responses in three ants are presented.

Etscorn, F. A home tank aquatic shuttlebox. *Behavior Research Methods and Instrumentation,* 1974, *6*(1), 77. Annotation not available.

Hay, D. A., & Crossley, S. A. The design of mazes to study *Drosophila* behavior. *Behavior Genetics,* 1977, *7*(5), 389–402. Although mazes have been widely used in studying phototaxis, geotaxis, and more recently, learning in *Drosophila,* there is no uniformity in maze design, and little is known about the effects such apparatus differences may have on behavior. The new maze design described here is based on T-junctions molded individually in acrylic and provides an inexpensive and standardized means of building mazes to any desired specification. The need for uniformity in maze design is demonstrated with an experiment on 3 variables at the start of a maze that affect the subsequent response of 4 strains of *D. melanogaster* in different ways. Some applications for future *Drosophila* research using mazes are considered (25 references included).

Londo, N. A runway for the cockroach. *Behavior Research Methods and Instrumentation,* 1970, *2* (3), 118−119. Describes a runway and training procedure that minimizes handling. Acquisition and extinction trials are presented to illustrate the technique.

Millar, R. D., & Malott, R. W. An inexpensive discrimination apparatus for classroom use with pigeons. *Psychological Record,* 1968, *18* (3), 369−372. Presents an apparatus for classroom use with pigeons which is similar in function to the Wisconsin General Test apparatus.

Plant, L. The gerbil jar: A basic home experience in operant conditioning. *Teaching of Psychology,* 1980, *7,* 109. Describes a home-made operant chamber for use with gerbils and includes several appropriate conditioning tasks.

Potts, A., & Bitterman, M. E. A runway for the fish. *Behavior Research Methods and Instrumentation,* 1968, *1* (1), 26−27. Describes a runway and a training procedure. Acquisition and extinction curves for 12 goldfish trained in space trials are plotted in terms of 3 measures.

Stong, C. L. A simple analogue computer that simulates Pavlov's dogs. *Scientific American,* 1963, *208* (6), 159−166. An introduction to Pavlov's research on classical conditioning, with an explanation of his original experiment. Includes a description of the function of the analogue laboratory and instructions for implementing a collection of basic experiments in classical conditioning (graphs and illustrative diagrams included).

Stong, C. L. How to study learning in the sow bug and photographing live crustaceans. *Scientific American,* 1967, *216* (5), 142−148. Detailed description of two experiments. The first involves maze learning in the sow bug, an invertebrate that must avoid direct light in order to prevent evaporation of its body fluids. The second describes procedures for recording the anatomical details of live crustaceans by high-speed photomicrography.

Stong, C. L. The color vision of pigeons is tested in a Skinner box. *Scientific American,* 1970, *223* (4), 124−129. A guide to constructing a Skinner box in which pigeons can learn to reward themselves for pecking at light of a predetermined color. Gives a detailed description of the apparatus and circuitry, with illustrations. Also describes simple experiments and their results.

Stong, C. L. The voiceprints of birdsongs and cockroaches in a maze. *Scientific American,* 1974, *230* (2), 110−115. A two-part article. Part 1 describes how a young scientist tape-records birdsongs and reproduces them on an electrocardiograph. Part 2 discusses the effects of temperature change on the retention of learning in cockroaches. Detailed directions for building apparatus for both experiments are given.

Stong, C. L. How to build and work with a Skinner box for the training of small animals. *Scientific American,* 1975, *233* (5), 128−134. A class activity. Describes in detail how to build a Skinner box (or where to buy a kit for building one). Explains how to train and care for the animals and how to analyze and graph data from simple experiments.

Wise, L. M., & Pope, M. S. An inexpensive discriminative Y-maze. *Psychological Record,* 1969, *19* (1), 93−94. Describes a Y-shaped maze designed to minimize the handling of subjects and to increase operating efficiency. Construction is simple and inexpensive.

Zych, K. A., Raymond, B., McHale, M. W., & Allen, H. A new runway for goldfish. *Psychological Record,* 1972, *22* (1), 121−123. Describes the development of a betta tank with a built-in runway. The apparatus permits housing goldfish in the same water that circulates in the runway. Subjects need not be removed from the runway for the duration of study.

D. Observation

Stong, C. L. How to collect and preserve the delicate webs of spiders. *Scientific American,* 1963, *208* (2), 159−166. A description of the webs that different spiders spin and where to look for them. Includes illustrations and directions for spraying the webs with lacquer and mounting them.

Stong, C. L. The joys of culturing spiders and

investigating their webs. *Scientific American,* 1972, *227*(6), 108–111. A class activity in which students catch spiders, build boxes to house them, observe patterns of web-building, and conduct simple experiments. A detailed how-to guide to the study of spider behavior.

Stong, C. L. The pleasures and problems of raising snails in the home. *Scientific American,* 1975, *232*(2), 104–107. A do-it-yourself guide to raising snails and experimenting with their behavior. Tells where to obtain the snails, how to build them a home, and what to feed them. Gives a detailed diagram of snail anatomy and suggestions for observing snail behavior.

E. Taste Studies

Marks, H. E. A simple, inexpensive apparatus to measure taste preference behavior in mice. *Journal of Biological Psychology,* 1977, *19*(2), 20–21. Describes a preference testing apparatus consisting of a plastic cage, 2 plastic pipes, 2 small specimen bottles, and 2 rubber stoppers. Only 1 animal out of 80 failed to adapt to the preference cages within the 6 days allotted for adaptation.

General Apparatus

A. Graphic Recorder

Stong, C. L. An inexpensive machine to record observational data automatically. *Scientific American,* 1966, *215*(1), 114–118. A detailed description of how to build a simple graphic recorder for use in recording observational data, including an explanation of how each component functions (illustrative diagrams).

B. Observation Windows

Burton, R. V. An inexpensive and portable means for one-way observation. *Child Development,* 1971, *42*(3), 959–962. Annotation not available.

Horowitz, H. Observation room windows. *American Psychologist,* 1969, *24*(3), 304–308. Presents general criteria for observation-room windows. Various glazing materials available for proper lighting and the typical transmission and reflection characteristics of each, acoustical factors relating to sound control, and general design considerations are discussed.

Lott, D. F., & Woll, R. J. A device permitting one-way vision without a mirror image. *Perceptual and Motor Skills,* 1966, *23*(2), 533–534. Describes a device that makes it possible for the experimenter to observe subjects while subjects see neither the experimenter nor reflections of themselves. The basic optical principles and several suggested applications are presented.

Passman, R. H. The smoked plastic screen: An alternative to the one-way mirror. *Journal of Experimental Child Psychology,* 1974, *17*(2), 374–376. Describes a double-thickness, smoked-plastic screen as an alternative to the one-way mirror. Relative to the glass mirror, the use of the plastic screen provides a safe, nondistracting, durable, lightweight, and inexpensive method for unobserved viewing without an appreciable loss in light transmission.

C. Slide Transparencies

Bushell, D., Jr. A rapid method for making inexpensive slide projector transparencies. *Journal of the Experimental Analysis of Behavior,* 1968, *11*(23), 172. Methods and materials are described. In contrast to R. D. Petre's method, this method "eliminates the need to handle 3 sheets of material and special coloring materials for each slide."

D. Stimulus Control

Cox, V. C., & Smith, R. G. A concentric bi-polar electrode for use in small animals. *Perceptual and Motor Skills,* 1967, *24*(1), 205–206. A description is provided of a rigid bipolar concentric electrode suitable for recording and stimulation with small animals. Details concerning construction materials and fabrication technique are also provided.

Human Apparatus

A. Auditory Perception

Huggins, A. W. Accurate delays for auditory feedback experiments. *Quarterly Journal of Experimental Psychology,* 1967, *19*(1), 78–80. Describes a way of modifying a tape recorder for producing accurately controllable delays for experiments with delayed auditory feedback. Any value of delay from 80 msec to 1.2 sec can be obtained to the nearest msec, and the range can be extended by some minor changes. The delay is continuously monitored on a digital electronic timer.

B. Biofeedback

Heisel, D. M. *The biofeedback guide: Affiliating with excellence.* New York: Gordon & Breach, 1977. 269 pp.

Describes a variety of devices and techniques that can be used to experience biofeedback. Biofeedback hardware, such as alpha brain wave monitors, and biofeedback software strategies for individuals and groups are discussed.

C. Learning

Goldstein, S. R. A simple variable-interval, variable-ratio generation for student use. *Teaching of Psychology Newsletter,* May 1973, p. 14. Describes an easily constructed Roulette-like device which signals the delivery of random events appropriate to any variable schedule desired.

Munro, D. An inexpensive automatic material reward dispenser for use with children. *Bulletin of the British Psychological Society,* 1970, *23* (80), 194. Describes the mechanism and operation of an inexpensive device that can deliver small rewards such as sweets and peanuts in material-reward experiments.

D. Visual Perception

Benjamin, L. T., Jr. Perceptual demonstrations—Or, what to do with an equipment budget of $75. *Teaching of Psychology,* 1976, *3* (1), 37–39. A collection of ideas for equipment and visual materials to be used in a course in perception, including displacement goggles, visual cliff, Pulfrich apparatus, distorted room and trapezoidal window, Muller-Lyer apparatus, and overhead transparencies and slides. Also includes additional references that can be used to further experimentation and/or class demonstration.

Cowan, T. M. Creating illusions of movement by an overhead projector. *Teaching of Psychology,* 1974, *1* (2), 80–82. Describes various ways in which an overhead projector can be used with simple constructions to produce different visual effects for a classroom demonstration. Includes eight different types of visual effects: the phi phenomenon, Michotte's perceptual causality, the Fujii and Johnson illusions, the cycloid illusion, and three complex constructions. Also included are illustrative figures for utilizing the visual effects.

Fried, R. A simple additive color mixer for exploration of the color solid. *Bulletin of the Psychonomic Society,* 1975, *5* (4), 325–326. Describes a simple additive color mixer requiring only 3 degrees of mechanical translation and permitting manipulation of hue, saturation, and intensity of 3 primary light sources.

Jankowicz, A. Z., & Heffernan, D. An inexpensive unit for demonstrations of the phi and autokinetic phenomena. *Perceptual and Motor Skills,* 1977, *45* (1), 69–70. Describes a small apparatus for demonstrating the phi phenomenon and the autokinetic effect. Circuit diagrams for construction of the device are included.

Larson, J. H. The Pulfrich illusion—A twist for the simple pendulum. *Journal of College Science Teaching,* 1979, *9,* 89–90. Describes simple instructions for a laboratory activity—the Pulfrich illusion. Includes a basic explanation of the Pulfrich illusion plus some other possible hypotheses developed by students.

Mansueto, C. S., & Adevia, G. Development and evaluation of a portable rod and frame test. *Journal of Psychosomatic Research,* 1967, *11* (2), 207–211. Describes a miniaturized rod and frame apparatus developed and tested on 50 subjects. Although ranks on the two tests correlated highly ($P =$ .91), there was a systematic difference between the mean scores on the two tests. The miniaturized test seemed to be consistently easier for the subjects—there was a mean difference of approximately 1.6 degrees, significant at the .01 level, between the two tests. After the apparatus was altered, this difference disappeared. Ranks of scores on the test were shown to approximate those of error scores obtained on Witkin's standard rod-and-frame test ($P = .97$).

Morris, J. B. The rod-and-frame box: A portable version of the rod-and-frame test. *Perceptual and Motor Skills,* 1967, *25* (1), 152. Annotation not available.

Oltman, P. K. A portable rod-and-frame apparatus. *Perceptual and Motor Skills,* 1968, *26* (2), 503–506. Subjects were 83 female and 80 male college students. Scores on the portable apparatus test correlated .89 with scores obtained on Witkin's original rod-and-frame test.

Parrott, G. L. Techniques of teaching perception and social processes. *High School Behavioral Science,* 1976, *3* (2), 80–82. Details classroom and home experiments with M. Sherrifs' autokinetic phenomenon which use easily available equipment. Ways of building a tachistoscope with a slide projector and a folding camera are presented, along with a schematic design.

Rodgers, W. A., Mayhew, J. E., & Frisby, J. P. A simple apparatus for measuring visual illusions of orientation. *Perception,*

1975, *4*(4), 475–476. Describes a small, economical, and portable device that can be used to study both simultaneous and successive orientation illusions in a systematic fashion (e.g., allowing psychophysical functions to be plotted relating size of illusion to orientation of an inducing figure). The device is suitable for teaching as well as research, and its all-purpose nature allows students to carry out projects of their own design.

Rouse, R. O., & Tarpy, R. M. A simple tachistoscope for student labs. *Behavior Research Methods and Instrumentation,* 1969, *1* (4), 156–157. Describes an inexpensive tachistoscope that utilizes a camera shutter to control exposure duration and a potentiometer to vary light intensity. Stimuli can be drawn or typed on 3 × 5 inch index cards.

Stong, C. L. Moiré patterns provide both recreation and some analogues for solving problems. *Scientific American,* 1964, *211*(5), 134–142. Includes (a) numerous instructions for creating different types of moiré patterns, (b) some of the visual effects produced, (c) an address for ordering kits containing more precise patterns for more interesting experiments, and (d) some illustrative examples of moiré patterns.

Stong, C. L. Generating visual illusions with two kinds of apparatus. *Scientific American,* 1971, *224*(3), 110–114. Two simple illustrations of optical illusions. Directions are also given for building two instruments with which students can investigate time-related phenomena in the sense of vision that account for illusions such as motion pictures and television.

Walker, J. L. Visual illusions that can be achieved by putting a dark filter over one eye. *Scientific American,* 1978, *238*(3), 142–143; 146; 148–153. Includes instructions for setting up a demonstration of the Pulfrich illusion and suggestions for variations of the illusion. Discusses how visual adaptation plays a major role in the illusion and describes other experiments dealing with visual latency (diagrams and graphs).

APPENDIX
C

BIBLIOGRAPHY OF ADDITIONAL ACTIVITIES, IDEAS, AND DEMONSTRATIONS

(Entries are grouped according to chapter topics)

I Methodology

Beck Middle School. *Of mice and men: Interdisciplinary unit* (revised). Unpublished paper, Beck Middle School, 1975. 72 pp. (Available from Richard D. Levy, Beck Middle School, Cropwell Road, Cherry Hill, NJ 08003.) A complete unit in which students observe the physical appearance and behavior of mice. Students also record, graph, and analyze data, carry out a group project, and read the novel *Flowers for Algernon.*

Bunker, B. B. et al. *Helping students do research: How to do a survey in a behavioral science course* (ERIC Document Reproduction Service No. ED 128 280), 1976. 27 pp. (Available from ERIC Document Reproduction Service, P.O. Box 190, Arlington, VA 22210.) A description of a 3-week project in a high school behavioral science class. Presents a detailed design adaptable to other classrooms and daily lists of objectives. Sample data and questionnaire included.

Epstein, R. *Developing a psychology research center as part of a high school psychology program: Report of a demonstration project.* Riverdale, N.J.: Economy Press, 1975. 7 pp. (Available from Psychology Research Center, Indian Hills High School, Oakland, NJ 07436.) A pamphlet covering the following aspects of developing a student research center: purpose of the center, necessary equipment, student-designed experiments, and student volunteers. Also includes samples of student experiments.

Horwitz, S. P., & Hunter, W. J. There's something fishy about this scale. *CEDR Quarterly,* Summer 1978, pp. 12–13. A class activity on how to make a "fisherman's ruler" that illustrates some important properties of the ordinal scale. Demonstrates that ordinal numbers cannot be added together meaningfully and that measures from an ordinal scale should not be used to compute average scores.

Newhouse, C. Territoriality in the red-winged blackbird. *American Biology Teacher,* 1977, *39* (3), 168–170. A study done by the author on territoriality in red-winged blackbirds and on the educational potential of having a class undertake a similar study. Suggests some variations. Requires no specialized equipment, little preparation, and no skills other than observational techniques.

Parrott, G. L. Introducing statistical correlations. *High School Behavioral Science,* 1975, *3* (1), 27–29. A discussion of two ways to introduce statistical correlations to students while keeping their interest levels high.

Shayer, M., & Wharry, D. Piaget in the classroom. Part I: Testing a whole class at the same time. *School Science Review,* 1974, *55* (192), 447–458. A method of testing a class that is designed to reveal the level of thinking of the individual student in the context of the science instruction that he or she is receiving.

II Sensory Processes and Perception

Bergeron, R. N. "A roasted caterpillar, anyone?" An experiment in social psychology. *Social Education,* 1972, *36,* 677–678. An experiment in which students learn concepts of behavior modification while examining cultural attitudes toward food. Students were given the chance to taste roasted caterpillars. After a lecture and discussion more students were willing to try them than when no introduction to caterpillars-as-gourmet-food was given.

Larson, J. H. The Pulfrich illusion—A twist for the simple pendulum. *Journal of College Science Teaching,* 1979, *9,* 89–90. Describes simple instructions for a laboratory activity—the Pulfrich illusion. Includes a basic explanation of the Pulfrich illusion, plus some other possible hypotheses developed by students.

Parrott, G. L. Techniques of teaching perception and social processes. *High School Behavioral Science,* 1976, *3* (2), 80–82. An examination of the autokinetic phenomenon, a social judgment aspect of perception, in a class activity for high school students. Demonstrates the design of an inexpensive device for tachistoscope presentation of visual material. Presents class and individual projects.

Polt, J. M. Experiments in animal behavior. *American Biology Teacher,* 1971, *33,* 472–479. Experiments for the secondary class that can be done without extensive space or elaborate equipment. Experiments include mealworm orientation and learning, sensory processes in crickets, and imprinting and learning in chicks.

Stong, C. L. Generating visual illusions with two kinds of apparatus. *Scientific American,* 1971, *224* (3), 110–114. Two simple illustrations of optical illusions. Directions are also given for the building of two instruments with which students can investigate time-related phenomena in the sense of vision that account for illusions such as motion pictures and television.

Vannan, D. A. Perceiving perception. *Science Activities,* 1973, *10* (1), 26–27. An activity designed to stimulate student interest in optical illusions. By preparing posters of a number of optical illusions and mounting them on the classroom wall, students will be motivated to seek an explanation for these phenomena.

Walker, J. Illusions in the snow: More fun with random dots on the television screen. *Scientific American,* 1980, *242* (5), 176–184. Describes a set of perceptual demonstrations of depth, stroboscopic motion, stereopsis, and other visual phenomena.

Walker, J. L. Visual illusions that can be achieved by putting a dark filter over one eye. *Scientific American,* 1978, *238* (3), 142–143; 146; 148–153. Includes instructions for setting up a demonstration of the Pulfrich illusion and suggestions for variations of the illusion. Discusses how visual adaptation plays a major role in the illusion and describes other experiments dealing with visual latency (diagrams and graphs).

III Learning and Conditioning

Hunt, K., & Shields, R. Using gerbils in the undergraduate operant laboratory. *Teaching of Psychology,* 1978, *5* (4), 210–211. A brief discussion of the advantages of using gerbils versus the conventional white rat to study basic operant conditioning principles. Includes such topics as maintenance, cost, size, and behavior during conditioning.

Polt, J. M. Experiments in animal behavior. *American Biology Teacher,* 1971, *33,* 472–479. Experiments for the secondary class that can be done without extensive space or elaborate equipment. Experiments include

mealworm orientation and learning, sensory processes in crickets, and imprinting and learning in chicks.

Stong, C. L. How to study learning in the sow bug and photographing live crustaceans. *Scientific American,* 1967, *216* (5), 142–148. Detailed descriptions of two experiments. The first involves maze learning in the sow bug, an invertebrate that must avoid direct light in order to prevent evaporation of its body fluids. The second describes procedure for recording the anatomical details of live crustaceans by high-speed photomicography.

Stong, C. L. The color vision of pigeons is tested in a Skinner box. *Scientific American,* 1970, *223* (4), 124–129. A guide to constructing a Skinner box in which pigeons can learn to reward themselves for pecking at light of a predetermined color. Gives a detailed description of the apparatus and circuitry, with illustrations. Also describes simple experiments and their results.

Stong, C. L. The voiceprints of birdsongs and cockroaches in a maze. *Scientific American,* 1974, *230* (2), 110–115. A two-part article. Part 1 describes how a young scientist tape-records birdsongs and reproduces them on an electrocardiograph. Part 2 discusses the effects of temperature change on the retention of learning in cockroaches. Detailed directions for building apparatus for both experiments are given.

Stong, C. L. How to build and work with a Skinner box for the training of small animals. *Scientific American,* 1975, *233* (5), 128–131; 134. A class activity. Describes in detail how to build a Skinner box (or where to buy a kit for building one). Explains how to train and care for the animals and how to analyze and graph data from simple experiments.

IV Memory and Cognition

Shayer, M., & Wharry, D. Piaget in the classroom. Part I: Testing a whole class at the same time. *School Science Review,* 1974, *55* (192), 447–458. A method of testing a class that is designed to reveal the level of thinking of the individual student in the context of the science instruction that he or she is receiving.

V Developmental Psychology

Croom, B. J. Aging education for the high school student. *Social Education,* May 1978, pp. 406–408. A 2- to 3-week activity unit in which students participate with aging adults in their community. Students formulate testable hypotheses and are encouraged to apply the process of inquiry. Lists 27 activities designed to increase student awareness of the process and problems of aging.

DeOrio, R. Junior high school students and young children. *Young Children,* 1974, *29,* 214–216.

A child development unit in which 9th graders observe and work with children in a lab in their own school.

Dillon, K., & Goodman, S. Think old: Twenty-five classroom exercises for courses in aging. *Teaching of Psychology,* 1980, *7,* 96–99. An annotated bibliography of 25 articles describing classroom activities on the biology, psychology, and sociology of aging.

Richardson, J. L., & Garfield, N. *Child development guide.* New York: Girl Scouts of the U.S.A., 1973. 163 pp. (Available from the publisher, 830 Third Avenue, New York, NY 10022.) A guide to encourage Girl Scouts to observe and work with children, draw conclusions based on their experiences, and create their own projects. Divided into four units: infancy, childhood years, helping children learn, and children and love. Includes a section of suggested "how-to" activities.

Thomas, G. R. Parent–child relationships in literature. *Periodically,* December 28, 1973, pp. 3–4. A short teaching unit using literature to explore the parent–child relationship in a high school psychology class. Includes sample questions, a list of suggested books, and a discussion of *Sons and Lovers.*

VI Social Psychology

Bergeron, R. N. "A roasted caterpillar, anyone?" An experiment in social psychology. *Social Education,* 1972, *36,* 677–678. An experiment in which students learn concepts of behavior modification while examining cultural attitudes toward food. Students were given the chance to taste roasted caterpillars. After a lecture and discussion more students were willing to try them than when no introduction to caterpillars-as-gourmet-food was given.

Bunker, B. B. et al. *Helping students do research: How to do a survey in a behavioral science course* (ERIC Document Reproduction Service No. ED 128 280), 1976. 27 pp. (Available from ERIC Document Reproduction Service, P.O. Box 190, Arlington, VA 22210.) A description of a 3-week project in a high school behavioral science class. Presents a detailed design adaptable to other classrooms and daily lists of objectives. Sample data and questionnaire included.

Clark, L. Jack and Jill fight back: Classroom activities. *Media and Methods,* 1975, *12* (2), 23–27. Eleven activities designed to increase students' awareness of sex role stereotyping. Students examine advertisements, assign genders to objects, listen to popular records, and answer thought-provoking questionnaires.

Epstein, R. Teaching thought control to secondary school students. *The Social Studies,* 1975, *66,* 158–160. Report of a successful technique for teaching average and above average students about the nature of thought control (brainwashing). Utilizes literature, films, and lectures on forms of totalitarianism and an in-class experiment involving the perception of the differences between tap water and spring water.

Extension Gaming Service. *Games about sexism, sex role stereotyping, and related women's issues.* (Available from University of Michigan, Extension Service, 412 Maynard St., Ann Arbor, MI 48109). A list of games including costs and where they may be obtained. No activities described. The list is divided into two groups of games—those that address feminist issues and those on broader social issues.

Gould, E., Jeter, H. P., & Cook, A. High school students as social scientists. *Professional Psychology,* 1972, *3,* 251–258. An application of the learning-by-doing approach for the high school experimental psychology class.

Hoverland, H. A. Gaming in the classroom. *People Watching,* 1972, *1* (2), 86–90. A class activity called the "Common Target Game" in which students must individually develop one of two strategies to arrive at the same goal. Traces the use of this game in classrooms in the United States and France.

Jakubiec, D. J. Group processes in the teaching of high school psychology. *Behavioral and Social Science Teacher,* 1975, *2* (2), 41–44. Two classroom exercises, "Pick a Leader" and "Twenty Minutes to Live," designed to be used by several small groups within the class. Emphasis on personal development and illustrating psychological concepts of group processes.

Parrott, G. L. Research on a shoestring. *Behavioral and Social Science Teacher,* 1973–74, *1* (1), 67–68. Two simple data-gathering experiments on status that high school students can do without any specialized equipment.

Parrott, G. L. Research in field settings as a resource for the behavioral and social science teacher. *Behavioral and Social Science Teacher,* 1974, *1* (2), 132–134. Two examples of creative behavioral research conducted without special instruments or equipment. Describes social psychology studies in field settings with subjects who unknowingly participate. The first topic is inhibition of horn-honking responses, and the second deals with racial and sexual factors in helping the deaf.

Travis, R. L. The language of the body. *Media and Methods,* 1977, *14* (1), 106–110. A unit for teaching about body language. Includes suggested readings, class activities, and ideas for topics to be covered. Also includes a list of print and audiovisual resources.

VII Personality

Canfield, J., & Wells, H. C. *100 ways to enhance self-concept in the classroom: A handbook for teachers and parents.* Englewood Cliffs, N.J.: Prentice-Hall, 1976. 253 pp. $11.95 cloth, $5.95 paper. A handbook of 100 practical and easily applicable ways to enhance the self-concept of children at home or in the school. Techniques drawn from gestalt therapy, psychosynthesis, guided fantasy, sensory awareness, transactional analysis, and expressive art and movement.

Forer, B. The fallacy of personal validation: A classroom demonstration of gullibility. *Journal of Abnormal and Social Psychology,* 1949, *44,* 118–123. Students given personality sketches (supposedly based on the DIB) rated the effectiveness of the correctness of the entire sketch and finally the truth of the 13 statements in the sketch. Most considered the test highly accurate.

Gardner, J. M. The myth of mental illness game: Sick is just a four letter word. *Teaching of Psychology,* 1976, *3* (3), 141–142. A class exercise that illustrates the "myth of mental illness" to the students. Participants give synonyms for and define mental illness, play the Mental Illness Game, and meet with ex-patients of institutions.

Hawley, R. C., & Hawley, I. L. *A handbook of personal growth activities for classroom use.* Amherst, Mass.: Education Research Associates, 1972. 120 pp. (Available from the publisher, Box 767, Amherst, MA 01002.) Ninety-four personal growth activities for elementary and high school students. Each is designed for 20–30 students and to increase the awareness of the individual. They involve creative thinking, problem solving, critical thinking, cooperation, communication, and awareness.

Kellog, R. L. The Psychological Defense Game comes to you complete with definitions. *Simulation/Gaming/News,* 1976, *3* (1), 12–16. A game designed to make individuals aware of how psychological defenses are used in their own and others' behavior. Provides definitions of 10 common defense mechanisms that students will become familiar with in the course of the game.

Matiya, J. C. Do others perceive us as we perceive ourselves? A classroom exercise. *High School Behavioral Science,* 1977, *4* (2), 84–86. An exercise that focuses on similarities and differences that may exist between one's self-concept and the perceptions of others. Includes four steps: self-description, description of the self by others, analysis of the self-data, and follow-up discussion.

VIII Miscellaneous

Barsky, P. D. Individual research projects in high school psychology. *Behavioral and Social Science Teacher,* 1975, *2* (2), 44–47. A review of the problems and the benefits of individual research projects in the high school. Gives a brief description of nine projects successfully completed by students in the author's classes.

Bridner, E. L., Jr. Psycho-history in the classroom: Application of Tomkins' theory of commitment to reform. *Social Studies Journal,* 1978, *7* (1), 29–34. An explanation of how the Silvan Tomkins theory of psycho-history can be adapted for use in high school social studies classrooms. Examples of the theory's usage in psychology are presented.

DeLong, J., & Gennaro, E. D. Experiments in cricket behavior. *American Biology Teacher,* 1975, *37,* 300–302. Four experiments in cricket behavior that do not require elaborate equipment: aggression and hierarchy, territoriality, courtship and mating, and color preference.

George, R. C. Six ways to heighten pupil participation. *High School Behavioral Science,* 1977, *4* (2), 79–83. Six affective techniques utilized in a 10-week psychology mini-course at the high school level. Activities include converting the classroom into an art gallery, an exercise in establishing categories, and a "need to achieve" game.

Johnson, M., & Wertheimer, M. (Eds.). *Psychology teacher's resource book: First course* (3rd ed). Washington, D.C.: American Psychological Association, 1979. 274 pp. (Available from the American Psychological Association, 1200 Seventeenth Street, N.W., Washington, D.C. 20036.) An aid for anyone who teaches introductory psychology. Includes reviews of introductory texts, books of readings, and lab manuals; lists of high-interest supplementary readings, audiovisuals, and reference materials; sources of lab instruments and supplies; and addresses of national organizations and publishers concerned with the teaching of psychology.

McCormack, A. J. ESP—Believe it or not. *Science Activities,* Dec.–Jan. 1974, pp. 15–18. A description of several well-documented cases of extrasensory perception. Discusses ways in which ESP experiments can be conducted in the classroom.

McCutcheon, L. E. The Remote Associates Test as a teaching device. *Behavioral and Social Science Teacher,* 1974, *1* (2), 135–138. A class activity in which students administer the Remote Associates Test in a unit on psychological testing. Intended to promote greater student involvement in the introductory high school psychology class. Results are analyzed as a classroom model for the teacher.

National Institute of Mental Health. *Guide to mental health education materials: A directory for mental health educators* (DHEW Publication No. ADM 74-35). Washington, D.C.: U.S. Government Printing Office, 1975. 56 pp. A list of pamphlets, leaflets, reports, periodicals, bibliographies, work kits, play scripts, discussion guides, films, radio programs, and posters.

Newhouse, C. Territoriality in the red-winged blackbird. *American Biology Teacher,* 1977, *39* (3), 168–170. A study done by the author on territoriality in red-winged blackbirds and on the educational potential of having a class undertake a similar study. Suggests some variations. Requires no specialized equipment, little preparation, and no skills other than observational techniques.

Pfeiffer, J. W., & Jones, J. E. *A handbook of structured experiences for human relations training* (Vol. 1). San Diego, Calif.: University Associates, 1974. 116 pp. (Available from the publisher, P.O. Box 80637, San Diego, CA 92138.) A book of group exercises in which a leader directs activity and collects data for processing by the participants. Arranged in order according to the skill and expertise required of the leader. Questionnaires, worksheets, guides, and charts are included.

Schrank, J. *Teaching human beings: 101 subversive activities for the classroom.* Boston: Beacon Press, 1972. 192 pp. Activities designed to help students grow and learn. Presents a wide variety of multimedia methods to stimulate students to think about themselves and society.

Stong, C. L. How to collect and preserve the delicate webs of spiders. *Scientific American,* 1963, *208* (2), 159–166. A description of the webs that different spiders spin and where to look for them. Includes illustrations and directions for spraying the webs with lacquer and mounting them.

Stong, C. L. An amateur's experiment in animal behavior and a study of the salty rain of Venezuela. *Scientific American,* 1966, *215* (9), 135–138. Two different experiments are described in detail. The first is on the behavior of chicks—do they have an innate preference for color as they do for form? The second is on the content of marine salts in rain water in Venezuela.

Stong, C. L. The joys of culturing spiders and investigating their webs. *Scientific American,* 1972, *227* (6), 108–111. A class activity in which students catch spiders, build boxes to house them, observe patterns of web-building, and conduct simple experiments. A detailed how-to guide to the study of spider behavior.

Stong, C. L. The pleasures and problems of raising snails in the home. *Scientific American,* 1975, *232* (2), 104–107. A do-it-yourself guide to raising snails and experimenting with their behavior. Tells where to obtain the snails, how to build them a home, and what to feed them. Gives a detailed diagram of snail anatomy and suggestions for observing snail behavior.

D

A SELECTED BIBLIOGRAPHY OF ETHICAL PRINCIPLES AND GUIDELINES FOR THE TEACHING OF PSYCHOLOGY

The following guidelines were developed by various governing bodies of the American Psychological Association to assist high school psychology teachers and college instructors in safeguarding the rights and welfare of students and of animal and human subjects. All guidelines have been approved by the Council of Representatives and are official policy of the Association.

Ethical Guidelines for High School Psychology Teachers. This document, intended for high school psychology teachers, deals with a wide range of ethical issues a teacher may encounter in the classroom. Topics covered include, among others, debriefing students at the end of classroom demonstrations, confidentiality of information gathered, events that lead to the discontinuation of a demonstration, consequences of certain types of classroom experiments, and dealing with value-laden areas of human behavior. Request copies from the Clearinghouse on Precollege Psychology, Educational Affairs Office, American Psychological Association, 1200 Seventeenth St., N.W., Washington, D.C. 20036. (free)

Ethical Principles in the Conduct of Research with Human Participants. The principles in this document make explicit an investigator's ethical responsibilities toward participants over the course of research—from the initial decision to pursue a study to the steps necessary to protect the confidentiality of research data. Specific cases and examples are used when discussing various principles. Although primarily intended for use in research, many of the principles apply equally to demonstrations and activities employed in the teaching of psychology. Copies may be obtained from the Order Department, American Psychological Association, 1200 Seventeenth St., N.W., Washington, D.C. 20036. ($4.50)

Guidelines for the Use of Animals in School Science Behavior Projects. These guidelines are intended for secondary-school psychology classroom science projects that involve experiments with live animals. The guidelines stress that live animals should only be used in this type of setting under the close supervision of a qualified individual. They also stress humane care and treatment during all aspects of the project. For a copy of these guidelines write to Clearinghouse on Precollege Psychology, Educational Affairs Office, American Psychological Association, 1200 Seventeenth St., N.W., Washington, D.C. 20036. (free)

Guidelines for the Use of Human Participants in Research or Demonstrations Conducted by High School Students. These guidelines are intended for the high school psychology classroom, where demonstrations, activities, or research projects involve the use of human participants. Specific guidelines include, among others, explanations of proper supervision, participant's rights to refuse to participate, possible undesirable consequences of some experiments, and anonymity of information gathered. For a copy of these guidelines write to the Clearinghouse on Precollege Psychology, Educational Affairs Office, American Psychological Association, 1200 Seventeenth St., N.W., Washington, D.C. 20036. (free)

Principles for the Care and Use of Animals. These principles were developed to guide individuals in their use of animals in research, teaching, and practical applications. All research conducted by members of the American Psychological Association or published in its journals must conform to these principles. The guidelines state that they should be conspicuously posted in every laboratory, teaching facility, and applied setting where animals are used. These guidelines are intended for use primarily by college students, college faculty, and independent researchers. For a copy of these guidelines write to Scientific Affairs, American Psychological Association, 1200 Seventeenth St., N.W., Washington, D.C. 20036. (free)

CONTRIBUTORS

John K. Bare
Department of Psychology
Carleton College
Northfield, MN 55057

Ludy T. Benjamin, Jr.
Department of Psychology
Texas A&M University
College Station, TX 77843

Peggy Brick
Dwight Morrow High School
Englewood, NJ 07631

Ray Brumbaugh
Bowman Gray School of
    Medicine
Psychiatry Department/Marital
    Health
Winston-Salem, NC 27103

Samuel Cameron
Department of Psychology
Beaver College
Glenside, PA 19038

Jack Christiano
McQuaid Jesuit High School
Rochester, NY 14602

Deborah L. Coates
Catholic University
Boys Town Center
Washington, D.C. 20064

David L. Cole
Department of Psychology
Occidental College
Los Angeles, CA 90041

Timothy Coyne
address unavailable

William B. Cushman
Department of Psychology
University of Maryland
College Park, MD 20742

Charlotte Doyle
Department of Psychology
Sarah Lawrence College
Bronxville, NY 10708

John J. Duda
Department of Psychology
State University College of New
    York
Geneseo, NY 14454

T. L. Engle
1025 Northlawn Dr.
Fort Wayne, IN 46802

Bernadette Fantino
address unavailable

Clifford L. Fawl
Department of Psychology
Nebraska Wesleyan University
Lincoln, NE 68504

L. D. Fernald, Jr.
10 Denton Rd.
Wellesley, MA 02181

P. S. Fernald
Department of Psychology
University of New Hampshire
Durham, NH 03824

L. W. Fordham
address unavailable

James M. Gardner
Department of Psychology
University of Witwatersrand
2001 Johannesburg, South Africa

Robert A. Goodale
Department of Psychology
Boston State College
Boston, MA 02115

Joel Goodman
Center for Humanistic Education
University of Massachusetts
Amherst, MA 01003

David S. Gorfein
Department of Psychology
Adelphi University
Garden City, NY 11530

Jack J. Greider
Wichita High School North
1437 Rochester
Wichita, KS 67203

B. R. Hergenhahn
Department of Psychology
Hamline University
St. Paul, MN 55104

David Holmer
East High School
Bremerton, WA 98310

William J. Hunter
Education Department
Mount Saint Vincent University
Halifax, Nova Scotia, Canada
    B3M 2J6

James Jenkins
Department of Psychology
Elliott Hall
University of Minnesota
Minneapolis, MN 55455

James M. Johnson
Department of Psychology
State University of New York
Plattsburgh, NY 12901

Richard A. Kasschau
Department of Psychology
University of Houston
Houston, TX 77004

Patricia Keith-Spiegel
Department of Psychology
California State University
Northridge, CA 91324

Marty Klein
Department of Psychology
Nebraska Wesleyan University
Lincoln, NE 68504

Marcia E. Lasswell
Graduate Department of
   Psychology
University of Southern California
University Park
Los Angeles, CA 90007

Allan L. LaVoie
Department of Psychology
Davis and Elkins College
Elkins, WV 26241

Bernard Mausner
Department of Psychology
Beaver College
Glenside, PA 19038

H. G. McCombs
Department of Psychology
Wayne State University
Detroit, MI 48202

Wilbert J. McKeachie
Department of Psychology
University of Michigan
Ann Arbor, MI 48109

Mary Margaret Moffett
23 Pine Rock Road
East Falmouth, MA 02536

J. Russell Nazzaro
Department of Psychology
University of North Florida
Jacksonville, FL 32216

James Newton
address unavailable

Barbara F. Nodine
Department of Psychology
Beaver College
Glenside, PA 19038

Freda G. Rebelsky
Department of Psychology
Boston University
Boston, MA 02215

Floyd L. Ruch
Psychological Services, Inc.
Los Angeles, CA 90010

Nancy Felipe Russo
Women's Program
American Psychological
   Association
1200 Seventeenth St., N.W.
Washington, DC 20036

W. E. Scoville
Department of Psychology
University of Wisconsin
Oshkosh, WI 54901

Barry Singer
Department of Psychology
California State University
Long Beach, CA 90840

M. W. Smith
address unavailable

Louis Snellgrove
Department of Psychology
Lambuth College
Jackson, TN 38301

David J. Stang
4122 Edmunds St., N.W.
Washington, DC 20007

P. A. Stewart
420 S. Marion Parkway #1802
Denver, CO 80209

Carolyn Stierhem
Atlantic City High School
Atlantic City, NJ 08401

Edward Stork
address unavailable

Charles M. Stoup
Department of Psychology
Texas A&M University
College Station, TX 77843

Peter M. Vietze
National Institute of Child
   Health and Human
   Development
National Institutes of Health
Bethesda, MD 20205

Joan W. Walls
Department of Psychology
Appalachian State University
Boone, NC 28608

Russell E. Walls
Department of Psychology
Appalachian State University
Boone, NC 28608

Neil Warren
Professor Emeritus
University of Southern California
Los Angeles, CA 90007

David Watson
Department of Psychology
University of Hawaii
Honolulu, HI 96822

Michael Wertheimer
Department of Psychology
University of Colorado
Boulder, CO 80309

Linda Winchell
Pike High School
Indianapolis, IN 46206

Paul J. Woods
Department of Psychology
Hollins College
Roanoke, VA 24020

Philip G. Zimbardo
Department of Psychology
Stanford University
Stanford, CA 94305